Suicide in Twentieth-Century Japan

Japan's suicide phenomenon has fascinated both the media and academics, although many questions and paradoxes embedded in the debate on suicide have remained unaddressed in the existing literature, including the assumption that Japan is a 'Suicide Nation.' This tendency causes common misconceptions about the suicide phenomenon and its features.

Aiming to redress the situation, this book explores how the idea of suicide in Japan was shaped, reinterpreted, and reinvented from the 1900s to the 1980s. Providing a timely contribution to the underexplored history of suicide, it also adds to the current heated debates on the contemporary way we organize our thoughts on life and death, health and wealth, on the value of the individual, and on gender. The book explores the genealogy and development of modern suicide in Japan by examining the ways in which beliefs about the nation's character, historical views of suicide, and the cultural legitimation of voluntary death acted to influence even the scientific conceptualization of suicide in Japan. It thus unveils the way in which the language on suicide was transformed throughout the century according to the fluctuating relationship between suicide and the discourse on national identity, and pathological and cultural narratives. In doing so, it proposes a new path to understanding the norms and mechanisms of the process of the conceptualization of suicide itself.

Filling a critical gap in three particular fields of historical study – the history of suicide, the history of death, and the cultural history of twentieth-century Japan – the book will be of great interest to students and scholars of Japanese Studies and Japanese History.

Francesca Di Marco is an independent researcher and cultural historian, specializing in the history of modern Japan.

Routledge Studies in the Modern History of Asia

1 **The Police in Occupation Japan**
Control, corruption and resistance to reform
Christopher Aldous

2 **Chinese Workers**
A new history
Jackie Sheehan

3 **The Aftermath of Partition in South Asia**
Tai Yong Tan and Gyanesh Kudaisya

4 **The Australia–Japan Political Alignment**
1952 to the present
Alan Rix

5 **Japan and Singapore in the World Economy**
Japan's economic advance into Singapore, 1870–1965
Shimizu Hiroshi and Hirakawa Hitoshi

6 **The Triads as Business**
Yiu Kong Chu

7 **Contemporary Taiwanese Cultural Nationalism**
A-chin Hsiau

8 **Religion and Nationalism in India**
The case of the Punjab
Harnik Deol

9 **Japanese Industrialisation**
Historical and cultural perspectives
Ian Inkster

10 **War and Nationalism in China**
1925–1945
Hans J. van de Ven

11 **Hong Kong in Transition**
One country, two systems
Edited by Robert Ash, Peter Ferdinand, Brian Hook and Robin Porter

12 **Japan's Postwar Economic Recovery and Anglo-Japanese Relations, 1948–1962**
Noriko Yokoi

13 **Japanese Army Stragglers and Memories of the War in Japan, 1950–1975**
Beatrice Trefalt

14 **Ending the Vietnam War**
The Vietnamese communists' perspective
Ang Cheng Guan

15 **The Development of the Japanese Nursing Profession**
Adopting and adapting Western influences
Aya Takahashi

16 **Women's Suffrage in Asia**
Gender nationalism and democracy
Louise Edwards and Mina Roces

17 **The Anglo-Japanese Alliance, 1902–1922**
Phillips Payson O'Brien

18 **The United States and Cambodia, 1870–1969**
From curiosity to confrontation
Kenton Clymer

19 **Capitalist Restructuring and the Pacific Rim**
Ravi Arvind Palat

20 **The United States and Cambodia, 1969–2000**
A troubled relationship
Kenton Clymer

21 **British Business in Post-Colonial Malaysia, 1957–70**
'Neo-colonialism' or 'disengagement'?
Nicholas J. White

22 **The Rise and Decline of Thai Absolutism**
Kullada Kesboonchoo Mead

23 **Russian Views of Japan, 1792–1913**
An anthology of travel writing
David N. Wells

24 **The Internment of Western Civilians under the Japanese, 1941–1945**
A patchwork of internment
Bernice Archer

25 **The British Empire and Tibet**
1900–1922
Wendy Palace

26 **Nationalism in Southeast Asia**
If the people are with us
Nicholas Tarling

27 **Women, Work and the Japanese Economic Miracle**
The case of the cotton textile industry, 1945–1975
Helen Macnaughtan

28 **A Colonial Economy in Crisis**
Burma's rice cultivators and the world depression of the 1930s
Ian Brown

29 **A Vietnamese Royal Exile in Japan**
Prince Cuong De (1882–1951)
Tran My-Van

30 **Corruption and Good Governance in Asia**
Nicholas Tarling

31 **US–China Cold War Collaboration, 1971–1989**
S. Mahmud Ali

32 **Rural Economic Development in Japan**
From the nineteenth century to the Pacific War
Penelope Francks

33 **Colonial Armies in Southeast Asia**
Edited by Karl Hack and Tobias Rettig

34 **Intra-Asian Trade and the World Market**
A. J. H. Latham and Heita Kawakatsu

52 **Pre-Communist Indochina**
R. B. Smith, edited by Beryl Williams

53 **Communist Indochina**
R. B. Smith, edited by Beryl Williams

54 **Port Cities in Asia and Europe**
Edited by Arndt Graf and Chua Beng Huat

55 **Moscow and the Emergence of Communist Power in China, 1925–30**
The Nanchang Rising and the birth of the Red Army
Bruce A. Elleman

56 **Colonialism, Violence and Muslims in Southeast Asia**
The Maria Hertogh controversy and its aftermath
Syed Muhd Khairudin Aljunied

57 **Japanese and Hong Kong Film Industries**
Understanding the origins of East Asian film networks
Kinnia Shuk-ting

58 **Provincial Life and the Military in Imperial Japan**
The phantom samurai
Stewart Lone

59 **Southeast Asia and the Vietnam War**
Ang Cheng Guan

60 **Southeast Asia and the Great Powers**
Nicholas Tarling

61 **The Cold War and National Assertion in Southeast Asia**
Britain, the United States and Burma, 1948–1962
Matthew Foley

62 **The International History of East Asia, 1900–1968**
Trade, ideology and the quest for order
Edited by Antony Best

63 **Journalism and Politics in Indonesia**
A critical biography of Mochtar Lubis (1922–2004) as editor and author
David T. Hill

64 **Atrocity and American Military Justice in Southeast Asia**
Trial by army
Louise Barnett

65 **The Japanese Occupation of Borneo, 1941–1945**
Ooi Keat Gin

66 **National Pasts in Europe and East Asia**
P. W. Preston

67 **Modern China's Ethnic Frontiers**
A journey to the West
Hsiao-ting Lin

68 **New Perspectives on the History and Historiography of Southeast Asia**
Continuing explorations
Michael Aung-Thwin and Kenneth R. Hall

69 **Food Culture in Colonial Asia**
A taste of empire
Cecilia Leong-Salobir

70 **China's Political Economy in Modern Times**
Changes and economic consequences, 1800–2000
Kent Deng

71 **Science, Public Health and the State in Modern Asia**
Edited by Liping Bu, Darwin Stapleton and Ka-che Yip

72 **Russo-Japanese Relations, 1905–1917**
From enemies to allies
Peter Berton

73 **Reforming Public Health in Occupied Japan, 1945–52**
Alien prescriptions?
Christopher Aldous and Akihito Suzuki

74 **Trans-Colonial Modernities in South Asia**
Edited by Michael S. Dodson and Brian A. Hatcher

75 **The Evolution of the Japanese Developmental State**
Institutions locked in by ideas
Hironori Sasada

76 **Status and Security in Southeast Asian States**
Nicholas Tarling

77 **Lee Kuan Yew's Strategic Thought**
Ang Cheng Guan

78 **Government, Imperialism and Nationalism in China**
The Maritime Customs Service and its Chinese staff
Chihyun Chang

79 **China and Japan in the Russian Imagination, 1685–1922**
To the ends of the Orient
Susanna Soojung Lim

80 **Chinese Complaint Systems**
Natural resistance
Qiang Fang

81 **Martial Arts and the Body Politic in Meiji Japan**
Denis Gainty

82 **Gambling, the State and Society in Thailand, c. 1800–1945**
James A. Warren

83 **Post-War Borneo, 1945–1950**
Nationalism, empire and state-building
Ooi Keat Gin

84 **China and the First Vietnam War, 1947–54**
Laura M. Calkins

85 **The Jesuit Missions to China and Peru, 1570–1610**
Ana Carolina Hosne

86 **Macao – Cultural Interaction and Literary Representations**
Edited by Katrine K. Wong and C. X. George Wei

87 **Macao – The Formation of a Global City**
Edited by C. X. George Wei

88 Women in Modern Burma
Tharaphi Than

89 Museums in China
Materialized power and objectified identities
Tracey L-D Lu

90 Transcultural Encounters between Germany and India
Kindred spirits in the 19th and 20th centuries
Edited by Joanne Miyang Cho, Eric Kurlander and Douglas T. McGetchin

91 The Philosophy of Japanese Wartime Resistance
A reading, with commentary, of the complete texts of the Kyoto School discussions of "The Standpoint of World History and Japan"
David Williams

92 A History of Alcohol and Drugs in Modern South Asia
Intoxicating affairs
Edited by Harald Fischer-Tiné and Jana Tschurenev

93 Military Force and Elite Power in the Formation of Modern China
Edward A. McCord

94 *Japan's* Household Registration System and Citizenship
Koseki, identification and documentation
Edited by David Chapman and Karl Jakob Krogness

95 Itō Hirobumi – Japan's First Prime Minister and Father of the Meiji Constitution
Kazuhiro Takii

96 The Non-Aligned Movement and the Cold War
Delhi – Bandung – Belgrade
Edited by Nataša Mišković, Harald Fischer-Tiné, and Nada Boškovska

97 The Transformation of the International Order of Asia
Decolonization, the Cold War, and the Colombo Plan
Edited by Shigeru Akita, Shoichi Watanabe and Gerold Krozewski

98 Xinjiang and the Expansion of Chinese Communist Power
Kashghar in the early twentieth century
Michael Dillon

99 Colonial Counterinsurgency and Mass Violence
The Dutch Empire in Indonesia
Edited by Bart Luttikhuis and A. Dirk Moses

100 Public Health and National Reconstruction in Post-War Asia
International influences, local transformations
Edited by Liping Bu and Ka-che Yip

101 The Pacific War
Aftermaths, remembrance and culture
Edited by Christina Twomey and Ernest Koh

102 **Malaysia's Defeat of Armed Communism**
The Second Emergency, 1968–1989
Ong Weichong

103 **Cultural Encounters and Homoeroticism in Sri Lanka**
Sex and serendipity
Robert Aldrich

104 **Mobilizing Shanghai Youth**
CCP internationalism, GMD nationalism and Japanese collaboration
Kristin Mulready-Stone

105 **Voices from the Shifting Russo-Japanese Border**
Karafuto/Sakhalin
Edited by Svetlana Paichadze and Philip A. Seaton

106 **International Competition in China, 1899–1991**
The rise, fall, and eventual success of the Open Door Policy
Bruce A. Elleman

107 **The Post-war Roots of Japanese Political Malaise**
Dagfinn Gatu

108 **Britain and China, 1840–1970**
Empire, finance and war
Edited by Robert Bickers and Jonathan Howlett

109 **Local History and War Memories in Hokkaido**
Edited by Philip A. Seaton

110 **Thailand in the Cold War**
Matthew Phillips

111 **Early Modern Southeast Asia, 1350–1800**
Ooi Keat Gin and Hoang Anh Tuan

112 **Managing Famine, Flood and Earthquake in China**
Lauri Paltemaa

113 **Science, Technology, and Medicine in the Modern Japanese Empire**
Edited by David G. Wittner and Philip C. Brown

114 **Street Performers and Society in Urban Japan, 1600–1900**
Gerald Groemer

115 **Suicide in Twentieth-Century Japan**
Francesca Di Marco

116 **Treaty Ports in Modern China**
Law, land and power
Edited by Robert Bickers and Isabella Jackson

Suicide in Twentieth-Century Japan

Francesca Di Marco

Routledge
Taylor & Francis Group
LONDON AND NEW YORK

First published 2016 by Routledge

2 Park Square, Milton Park, Abingdon, Oxfordshire OX14 4RN
711 Third Avenue, New York, NY 10017

Routledge is an imprint of the Taylor & Francis Group, an informa business

First issued in paperback 2018

British Library Cataloguing in Publication Data
A catalogue record for this book is available from the British Library

Library of Congress Cataloging-in-Publication Data
A catalog record for this book has been requested

ISBN: 978-1-138-93776-5 (hbk)
ISBN: 978-1-138-35150-9 (pbk)

Typeset in Times New Roman
by Apex CoVantage, LLC

Contents

Acknowledgments

Writing this book was an eventful journey full of unexpected detours, a mental iteration that constantly pushed my limits further. This book grew out of my PhD dissertation at SOAS. Large sections of my doctoral thesis in fact constitute Part II of this book. Part I, the analysis of prewar Japan, was researched and written at a later stage. I produced an initial articulation of Part I for the refereed *Journal of Japanese Studies*. My article "Act or Disease? The Making of Modern Suicide in Early Twentieth-Century Japan" appeared in the summer 2013 issue. Since that point, I have relentlessly worked to integrate the results of my latest research with the work carried out for my doctoral thesis, with the final aim of producing an overarching study of the Japanese suicide phenomenon between 1900 and the 1980s.

In writing this book, I owe a tremendous debt to friends, family, former colleagues, and institutions. I would like to express my gratitude to those who saw me through this book: to those who road-tested certain chapters and offered comments and support, to those who assisted with the editing and proofreading, and to those who financially supported its completion.

I owe a special thanks to the Council on East Asian Studies at Yale University; their extraordinary academic community along with their care and funding encouraged me to get more ambitious and radically revisit the scope and aim of my book. I am also grateful to the Center for East Asian Studies at Stanford University, which granted me the opportunity to work in a vibrant intellectual environment and have access to invaluable resources during the final stages of the manuscript. Finally, this project would have been impossible without the generous financial help of the Japanese Ministry of Education (Monbushō, now Monkashō), the Kayoko Tsuda Bursary, the Japan Foundation Fellowship, and the British Central Research Funds, which allowed me to spend long fieldwork periods in Japan throughout the years.

I wish to personally thank the following people for their contributions of inspiration and knowledge in creating this book. Thanks to my supervisor, Angus Lockyer, who patiently read the same paragraphs over and over and provided me with insightful comments. Akihito Suzuki deserves extra special mention for his many contributions to this project. I can never fully thank him for helping me navigate through the fieldwork in Japanese psychiatry and for enabling me through his insightful comments on my writing to raise my work to a higher level. Thanks too to many academics who have informed my thinking, whether consciously or not, and encouraged me to make this possible: Kitanaka Junko, Ian Marsh, Fabian Drixler, Daniel Botsman, Aaron Gerow, Karen Nakamura, Shigehisa Kuriyama, Susan Morrissey, and Susan L. Burns. I am deeply grateful to the friends and colleagues who offered their support throughout the years. Thanks to Yumi Kim and Stephen Poland for reading chapters, providing critical feedback, and letting me quote their remarks. Thanks to Alyssa Park, Youn-mi Kim, Naoki Yamamoto and Roberta Strippoli, who helped me navigate the difficulties of being an independent researcher. Thanks also to Julia Deems and Matt Gleeson, who meticulously helped me shape the book in its final form not only by catching mistakes, but also by suggesting additions that I would never have thought to include but which made all the difference. I cannot thank Routledge enough for their commitment to this book, and all the technical and anonymous reviewers who worked on this project and who have patiently and efficiently guided me through the production process.

Making a book is a long-term affair. I would have never finished this project without Massimo's encouragement and unique sense of humor, which accompanied me everywhere throughout the years, along with his merciless incitement to get things done, to cut old chapters and leave only what really matters. Finally, I would never have started this project and I could never have finished it without listening carefully to my father's lifetime silence, which first inadvertently and then undeniably made me want to break the taboo and talk about suicide without shame. I dedicate this book to his silence.

Introduction

> Only Japanese people can understand the suicide of the Japanese. Foreign scholars can look at statistical numbers on suicide, but they will not understand the phenomenon.
>
> Ōhara Kenshirō, *Nihon no Jisatsu* (Tokyo: Seishin Shobō, 1965), p. 142

A frightening statistical wave of suicides peaked in Japan in 1958 (in total 25.7 per 100,000 inhabitants, with 30.7 for men and 20.8 for women). That year, Japan ranked as the nation with the highest suicide rate in the entire world for all age groups.[1] In fact, the rate was so high that the late 1950s were identified as "the era of suicide heaven" [*jisatsu tengoku*] by national newspapers.[2] Apropos of such tragic statistical data, an anonymous writer commented in *Bungei Shunjū*, "Japanese people shed tears, and foreigners think they are strange." However, the author added, "Japan is a Suicide Nation [*jisatsu no kuni*]. And this is why it happens that in the rest of the world the suicide rate is decreasing, while Japan is showing a rapid increase. [. . .] Japan is a literary nation [*bunkakokka*]."[3] A deeply troubling social phenomenon had just spread throughout the country, but rather than a pathologizing narrative, a cultural discourse tinged with narcissistic and nationalistic nuances came to the fore, wrapping suicide in a romantic aura; voluntary death was proudly acknowledged as a peculiar feature of Japanese society, as part of the national character.

Twenty years later, in 1978, Takeda Katsuhiko, a professor of English literature at Waseda University and a researcher curious about Japan's mysterious notoriety as a 'Suicide Nation,' retraced the genealogy of the label, identifying its origins in the 1958 suicide peak. It was then, according to Takeda, that both Japanese and Western countries came to know Japan for its high suicide rate and began to associate Japan with voluntary death, without any attempt to understand or assess the phenomenon. More importantly, he clarified, Japan was also known as a 'Suicide Nation' because the motive behind the majority of suicides committed was a quality central to Japanese character: altruism.[4] In 2005, Ueno Kayoko, professor of sociology at Tokushima University, explained the so-called Japanese suicide culture [*Nihon jisatstu bunka*] by reiterating the thesis of an allegedly high number of altruistic suicides.[5] These conceptualizations of suicide became the dominant narrative even though scientific findings called them into question. First of all, when comparing the prevalence of suicide in all industrialized countries, with the exception of 1958, Japan has consistently ranked between 9th and 14th. Furthermore, motives for suicide have been labeled differently at different times in Japan; it is misleading to say that all suicides in Japan are examples of 'altruism.' Finally, the origins of the stereotype that associates Japan with suicide – in fact, the entire idea of the 'Suicide Nation' – can be traced to the early 1900s, and the idea continued to be burnished both within and outside of the country throughout the twentieth century. How could Japan be proudly proclaimed a 'Suicide Nation' when the statistics proved otherwise? How could science – a potent principle in organizing knowledge and in constructing suicide as a bio-pathological force – be silenced by the idea of voluntary death as a national feature? Is suicide the outcome of biological factors or a collective and socially negotiated construction, a disease or a subjective act? What different discourses shaped this conceptualization of suicide?

This book explores how the concept of suicide in Japan was shaped, interpreted, and reinvented from the 1900s to the mid-1980s, interrogating the assumption that Japan is a 'Suicide Nation.' Although Japan's suicide phenomenon has fascinated both the media and academics, many of the aforementioned questions, as well as the complexity and paradoxes embedded in the debate on suicide, have remained unaddressed in the existing literature, causing common misconceptions about the phenomenon and its features. This book explores the genealogy and development of modern suicide in Japan by examining the ways in which beliefs about the nation's character, historical views of suicide, and the cultural legitimation of voluntary death acted to influence even the scientific conceptualization of suicide in Japan. It thus unveils the way in which the language on suicide was transformed throughout the century according to the fluctuating relationship between suicide and the discourse on national identity, the pathological and the cultural narratives. It proposes a new path to understanding the norms and mechanisms of the process of the conceptualization of suicide itself, filling in a critical gap in three particular fields of historical study: the history of suicide, the history of death, and the cultural history of twentieth-century Japan.

The reasons for writing this book are twofold. First, this book seeks to rescue suicide in Japan from the broad cultural generalizations to which it has so far been subject, generalizations which see suicide as a typical and traditional index of a homogeneous society, thereby marking Japan off from the rest of the world. Instead, it supports ideas from more recent research, which insist on the 'ordinariness' of the phenomenon. The work produced on suicide in Japan is essentially simplistic and profoundly biased. The vast majority of research on the subject in both English and Japanese was published in the 1970s in a flurry after Mishima Yukio's spectacular suicide. A large proportion of this academic work was built on a number of unwarranted assumptions influenced by the revival of cultural nationalism and the *nihonjinron* debate, which glorified the specificity of Japanese culture – and suicide – as a positive model.[6] It constructed what I call 'the conventional story of suicide in Japan.' Such scholarship on the history, sociology, psychiatry, and psychology of suicide claimed that (a) Japan has one of the highest suicide rates – if not the highest – in the world; (b) the Japanese are predisposed to commit suicide; (c) every facet of suicide in Japan is formalized by a long-standing tradition of particular patterns; and (d) suicide is a cultural phenomenon peculiar to Japan that only Japanese people can understand. Western studies written in the 1970s and continuing through the 1990s share this tendency, explaining all aspects of Japanese culture as based on a unique psychology that also entails a downside: a predisposition to suicide.[7] Social scientists who were engaged in a quest to define 'Japanese people's suicide' described voluntary death in Japan as 'exceptionally traditional.'[8] Even the ambitious study by the French literary scholar Maurice Pinguet, entitled *Voluntary Death in Japan* (1993), which examined the history of suicide from the Kamakura period (1185–1333) to Mishima's *harakiri*, concentrated uniquely on the suicides of samurai warriors, of *kamikaze* fighter pilots, and of artists and lovers, aiming to exalt the uniquely Japanese nature of these voluntary deaths.[9] Historical studies produced by Japanese scholars between the 1970s and the 1990s mainly focused on the history of lovers' suicides and family suicides as the patterns most explanatory of Japanese uniqueness.[10] These works insisted on the idea that in Japan there is a historical continuity of suicide committed for romantic reasons and for the sake of taking responsibility for members of one's own group, an attitude that at some level standardized the society. To sum up, the histories of suicide by both Western and Japanese scholars influenced by the *nihonjinron* were not written as rigorous, objective studies of the Japanese, their culture, and their national character, but rather as works of popular sociology intended to portray a peculiar society, explain its economic success, and rationalize its despicable wartime history.

Recent works on suicide in Japan, influenced by the work of suicidologists and media studies researchers in the 1990s, have focused on specific aspects of suicide. Much of this scholarship seems to aim to separate itself from the *nihonjinron* debate but does not seem unsympathetic to it. Some scientific studies have challenged the validity of the *nihonjinron* assumptions and have proven that the suicide patterns, the level of predisposition to suicide, and the motivations behind suicide in Japan are absolutely 'ordinary' and do not deviate from the universal norms of suicidology.[11] Several Japanese scholars, including Ogino Masahiro and Ueno Masahiko, have focused in particular on youth suicide and bullying [*ijime*] from historical, clinical, and socio-legal perspectives.[12] These studies are quite specialized, commonly covering a single decade, and imply that youth suicide is the outcome of the peculiar type of education received in Japanese schools – thus they do not depart from the *nihonjinron* narrative. No contemporary book-length historical study influenced by the work of suicidology has been written by any Western scholar. However, the legal, sociological, and anthropological studies by Mark D. West, Susan Long, Adrienne Carey Hurley, and Chikako Ozawa-de Silva have proven to be extremely innovative within the field of suicide research.[13] Regrettably, while many scholars – in particular Ozawa-de Silva – have highlighted the need to facilitate collaborative research projects on cross-cultural understandings of voluntary death in Japan, these studies have so far been limited in their capacity to speak to each other's findings or even to generalize about the phenomenon.

Where does this book stand then? While acknowledging many debts to the existing historiography, this book rethinks the grand narrative of suicide in Japan. It is my hope that the broad strokes I describe can serve as a fresh point of departure to launch new debates about the meaning of suicide. A *longue durée* approach can provide bold clarity and contrast by shifting our attention from the finer details of small studies to the commonalities inherent across longer time frames. This book separates itself from the *nihonjinron* narrative and from those medical and cultural history books on twentieth-century Japan that focus on the ways in which national culture and national features have shaped the notions of health, life, and death. It also distances itself from those works that describe the history of psychiatry in Japan as a process of mimicry, culminating in the adoption of Western practices, essentially using allegedly advanced Western science as a yardstick. This book positions itself between a cultural narrative that identifies suicide as a uniquely sociocultural outcome and suicidology's claim that suicide is universal. It tells the critical history of the idea of suicide and its sociocultural formation. It thus relativizes the inherent nationalistic issues of the notion of suicide, while also acting as a counterbalance to the more universalizing tendencies of modern suicidology. This book aims to be part of the so-called second wave of history on psychiatry in Japan, a series of classics in the history of psychiatry that have been published since the 1980s. However, many of these works have been written by practicing psychiatrists, not by professional historians, and as Suzuki Akihito claims, "some of them have the shortcomings familiar to [the] history of psychiatry in the West three decades ago: they are anecdotal, judgmental and partisan."[14] In addition to the fact that these works are rarely published in languages other than Japanese and are therefore isolationist, Suzuki continues, no dialogue has occurred with the post-antipsychiatry and post-Foucault historiographical reflections developed in English-speaking countries in the last several decades. This current book is deeply indebted to the recent English-language works *Foucault, History and Truth* by Ian Marsh (2010) and *Depression in Japan: Psychiatric Cures for a Society in Distress* by the anthropologist Kitanaka Junko (2011).[15] By challenging the assumptions embedded in our process of conceptualizing suicide, Ian Marsh opens a path toward the examination of the norms, practices, and policies behind the notion of suicide and its construction. This book draws from his provocative study the need to grow an intellectual awareness of the complexity of talking about suicide: there are infinite possible ways to construct the notion of voluntary death. Kitanaka Junko pioneers one of the grand narratives on the evolution of medical notions in twentieth-century Japan by examining the genealogy and development of the concept of depression and by combining medical history, ethnography, and sociology. As is true of *Depression in Japan*, this book pursues answers about a complex medical concept by navigating among the conflicting forces of Japanese society.

The second reason for writing this book, then, is to inquire how and why 'the conventional story of suicide' consolidated inside and outside Japan in the first place, and to seek to provide a more accurate picture of the forces that contributed to this conceptualization. In defying the stereotyped interpretations of suicide as a unique feature of the Japanese, this book narrates a 'cultural history' through a decidedly nonlinear procession of problematization and solutions. Rather than looking at the problems created by progress (and by historical events), the book focuses on the norms and mechanisms of the debate itself. In so doing, it aims to help the reader better understand the ways in which the notion of suicide has been conceptualized. An important part of the value of writing this story about the construction of the notion of suicide is that the other versions have left out or rendered invisible other sides. In order to explain how suicide has commandeered such a central place in the modern imagination of Japan and the Japanese, we need to understand the medical science that has gradually revealed the biological pathways between suicide and mental illness, as well as the shifting political and cultural contexts that have invested that scientific knowledge with meaning and authority. Suicide is a historical and cultural construction in which multiple discourses converge, and the ongoing conversation among these discourses is dynamic, changing over time and through space. This book sees the historical and cultural construction of suicide as the result of a dialectical relationship – rather than a dichotomous one – among structure, discourse, and agency: society and discourse shape the individuals who in turn create discourse and society, forming a continuous loop. Therefore, discursive context and social structure do not unidirectionally guide or influence the individual's behavior; rather, social and environmental factors, along with the presentation of the act of suicide and its representation by the media, engage in an endless exchange in which act and representation mirror each other and simultaneously contribute to each other's formation. By speaking about the conceptualization of suicide, we make the phenomenon visible.

In that sense, this book offers a fresh perspective, with research based on new and original sources. It explores the conceptualization of voluntary death in Japan, encompassing a range of fields and employing suicide as the key analytical construct. However, the main investigation focuses on two particular realms – medical (by which I mean the discourse produced by medical science, leaving aside medical practice) and cultural narratives about suicide – and the interaction between the two. The book primarily analyzes the formulation of the medical notion of suicide by academic psychiatrists and its development throughout the twentieth century, as well as the popular romanticization of suicide within the media and by the nation. It finally examines how the medical theories of suicide as organic *disease* intersected with the notion of suicide as an individual *act*, and suggests how throughout the century, at various times, some narratives became more influential than others in conceptualizing and managing the problem. The examination of medical discourse serves as a useful counterweight to the all-too-frequent idealization of the notion of suicide, which tends to emerge from an uncritical perusal of popular text alone. The scope and importance of the history of medicine is thus immense. This book engages with the work of various actors – epidemiologists, statisticians, doctors, and academics, primarily active in the psychiatric field, but also in the psychological and sociological ones – and with popular narratives such as those presented by the press, or fictional productions about suicide. It engages with the dissemination of such sources, all of them problematic reflections of their times, via multiple channels (textbooks, journals, periodicals, books, newspapers), and it addresses the problems of how the meaning of suicide gradually came to be redefined and to what extent expert accounts informed or failed to inform non-expert ones. The book concerns itself with the evolution of discourses on suicide in order to map the tides, so to speak, of the debate on voluntary death. By constructing a dialogue between the medical and the cultural narratives, the book seeks to understand which discourses came into play in the conceptualization of suicide and how they contaminated one another. Additionally, it seeks to understand how concepts of suicide as an individual act and as a 'peculiar feature' of the nation became more salient than the universalizing biological discourse on suicide. Two theoretical frameworks, however, are not tackled in this book. Firstly, I have deliberately chosen not to address the question of the diffusion and reception of ideas on suicide, as this would have entailed methodological tools other than discourse analysis. Secondly, although a theorization of the relationship among doctors, social scientists, journalists, and the state would be central to understanding the nature of their interactions, the sources I researched and analyzed did not substantiate any of my hypotheses. I might be able to speculate on such a theorization, but I would not be able to offer a supported argument.

The book addresses these questions following a chronological format and is divided into two parts: Part I covers the prewar period, from the early 1900s to 1939; Part II covers the postwar period, from 1946 to 1985. Part I begins by narrating the story of the conceptualization of suicide that commenced in Japan in the early twentieth century with the drive to adopt and adapt Western medicine, and sketches its development up to the late 1930s. Chapter 1 introduces the genealogy of the biological narrative on suicide in Japan and explores how psychiatry came to be the dominant discourse; this development demanded negotiation among multiple discourses, eventually incorporating many forms of reasoning and working to satisfy a variety of needs and agendas.[16] Describing the role of Westernization and the emergence of new medical concepts, Chapter 1 addresses when and how medicine conquered cultural authority, the origins of the Japanese medical community's fascination with suicide, and the historical significance of that fascination. The chapter traces the origins of the tension between the psychiatric discourse and the cultural anti-discourse that romanticized and glorified voluntary death. The dialectic of suicide as a pathology versus suicide as a voluntary act crystallized in 1903 around the well-known suicide of Fujimura Misao, which fired up a debate among psychiatrists, intellectuals, and journalists that went on for over two decades. The chapter illustrates how a medically heterogeneous response conflicted with the alternative response of romanticizing suicide. By the early 1920s, the biochemical explanation of suicide dominated, and psychiatry had emerged victorious: the discipline had embraced biological language, had identified suicide as the outcome of mental illness, and had established the primacy of its knowledge over sociology and psychology.

Psychiatry's lead in conceptualizing suicide was brief, however. In the late 1920s, under pressure from rampant nationalism, psychiatrists gradually bent to cultural expectations in reconceptualizing voluntary death. Despite efforts to acknowledge suicide as a disease, intensifying nationalistic propaganda and war mobilization ultimately claimed the cult of voluntary death and celebrated it as an expression of 'Japaneseness.' This led to the integration of sociocultural explanations. Japan came to be described in academia and in popular culture as a 'Suicide Nation.' Chapter 2 examines how the myth of a 'Suicide Nation' was built by jingoistic propaganda, and asks under what norms the interaction between medical authority and the nationalistic discourse developed. Systematic attempts to reconcile the patriotic narrative with the psychiatric theoretical apparatus were carried out by a narrow yet eminent group of psychiatrists, who had the twofold intention of popularizing the concept of suicide and embracing its nationalistic roots. Once their authority was publicly acknowledged, Japanese psychiatrists incorporated notions like public anxiety, economic hardships, and sociocultural features as factors that triggered the suicide phenomenon; suicide was thus not only an internal disease but a collective one. In the attempt to resolve their approach with conflicting views of suicide as an act of national pride, and in order to maintain their authority, psychiatrists progressively integrated not only social factors but also 'cultural features' into their theoretical apparatus. For example, they described the same suicide cases using inconsistent language and disharmonious terms, providing heterogeneous responses that varied from pathologization to criminalization to the romanticization of suicide as a peculiar feature of Japanese culture. By examining the debate over a well-known suicide on Mihara Mountain in 1933, Chapter 2 explains how several psychiatrists successfully reconciled the biological universality of suicide with the nationalistic ideal of cultural uniqueness, and how psychiatrists exempted some demographic categories (such as women) from the process of 'culturalization' of suicide, isolating those cases as biological anomalies. In other words, psychiatrists saw the suicide of men as indicative of their moral superiority, but that of women as indicative of their biological weakness. By the 1940s, psychiatrists had elaborated a conception of suicide less as a biological disease and more as a sociocultural act, to the detriment of their theoretical coherence, reinforcing the nation's idea of 'suicide as a characteristic of the Japanese.' Part I thus argues that the ethnocentric narrative legitimized the proliferation of an inconsistent biological narrative, and the lack of scientific integrity indirectly reinforced the myth of the 'Suicide Nation.' This circularity and reciprocal contamination between the nationalistic and the psychiatric discourse produced an incongruous and at times contradictory response to suicide.

Part II, consisting of Chapters 3 and 4, examines the postwar period until the mid-1980s. During the years of the American occupation, Japan witnessed a decreased interest in biopsychiatry. With the nation being punished for war crimes once thought 'scientifically' justified, biopsychiatry, with its biological roots, became understandably unpopular. Also, the collective emotional postwar trauma radically influenced the way the medical community perceived, comprehended and conceptualized voluntary death. 'Orthodox' Japanese psychiatrists, for example, offered little resistance to American psychoanalytical psychiatry, with its attempt to 'psychoanalyze' suicide and to unveil its social dimension. The end of the American occupation witnessed a temporary resurgence and revamping of biological reductionism, but soon psychiatrists returned their focus to the ecological and collective aspects of suicide, rediscovering its 'human' side. The public anxiety about the dramatic statistical suicide peak of 1958 suggested to the medical community that a monodisciplinary approach to the phenomenon was undesirable. Chapter 3 thus delves into the history of the conceptualization of suicide in terms of sociocultural pathology. By discovering the intimate relationship between individuals and social conditions – that is, by humanizing the meaning of suicide – the 1950s paved the way to the restoration of a romantic and glorifying discourse on suicide as a peculiar feature of the Japanese. The association between suicide and Japaneseness thus survived the war and raised a voice seeking to rehabilitate the past and to revitalize the historical continuity of Japanese values and traditions.

Some psychiatrists have argued that the burgeoning scientific research that followed the postwar period should have led to the triumph of the biological approach to mental illness once and for all. However, from the late 1960s on, when a new wave of cultural nationalism along with the *nihonjinron* debate engulfed Japan, and the antipsychiatry movement hit the medical community, the Japanese once again became fascinated with the idea of suicide as part of the national character. The recovery from extreme poverty and the return to strong economic growth rehabilitated the nation's shattered image and ignited rampant cultural nationalism. The ingrained ethnocentrism that then dominated every professional field challenged the paradigms of biomedical science, rejecting biological reductionism and emphasizing sociocultural variables that tended to exalt the national character. Chapter 4 focuses on this turbulent era and on the re-energized cultural discourse that helped establish the concept of medicine as a cultural system. The chapter investigates the forces that pushed psychiatrists to become critical of their own discipline's tendency to medicalize social problems like suicide; these forces generated disruption and opened a conceptual vacuum that was conveniently filled by the cultural notion of suicide.

For the second time in the twentieth century, Japan was described as the 'Suicide Nation' within the media, and voluntary death was publicly rehabilitated as a unique feature of the Japanese. Such a notion led to the increased visibility and popularity of the phenomenon both inside and outside of Japan. Voluntary death was thus explained culturally rather than biologically, as an action toward which the Japanese had a peculiar propensity: in this light, the system of values and beliefs that molds an individual was considered a more meaningful influence than his/her neurobiological predisposition. The jump from 'suicide as a cultural feature of the Japanese' to 'Japan as Suicide Nation' was thus short. If individuals committing suicide were victims of social forces, biopsychiatry – which professed that suicide was physical in origin, and thus medically treatable – was theoretically inadequate to explain the phenomenon. What happened then to the notion of suicide as illness, and how was it overshadowed by the notion of suicide as a feature of the Japanese? That is, how was the concept of suicide as the symptom of a deeper disease transformed into an action undertaken by the community?

All these questions are at the core of Chapter 4, which, to find answers, delves into the dichotomy between those suicides that were reckoned to be typically and uniquely Japanese, conceived as cultural artifacts and as products of social and historical forces situated outside the mental state of isolated individuals, and those suicides described as pathological expressions of mental illness.

In the wake of this nationalistic euphoria, psychiatrists exalted and condoned suicides committed for altruistic reasons, and exonerated indefatigable male workers and nostalgic novelists from clinical intervention in the name of culture. On the other hand, medical professionals continued to medically treat 'the outcasts': women, who were seen as physically and neurologically weak, and irrational young people, whose suicides were not seen as appropriately reflecting Japanese culture. Medical treatment was urged for these outliers because the origins of their illness were considered to lie in physical defects or individual failings. How could the idea of certain de-culturalized demographic categories, victims of pathological conditions, be reconciled with the idea of Japanese values and beliefs played out in the suicides performed by working males and novelists? Psychiatrists proved that the romanticization of suicide could quietly coexist alongside its pathologization. The incoherent yet resolute psychiatric approach envisioned two categories of suicides – one representative of the nation and one non-representative – and this dichotomous approach served to secure the position of psychiatrists within the medical community while simultaneously satisfying the powerful nationalistic and cultural discourses that were pushing suicide further and further into the province of ethnocentrism. More importantly, the nationalistic and cultural discourses revealed themselves to be extremely appealing to the psychiatric one: they helped psychiatrists to normalize suicide and make it familiar to the Japanese by creating an emotional attachment to their 'cultural features,' by simplifying the discourse on mental health, and by aestheticizing Japaneseness. Part II thus claims that the resilient association between suicide and Japan was inherently promoted by medical professionals' concern for preserving their personal and political prestige.

In the chronological story of the conceptualization of suicide throughout the twentieth century, underlying questions eventually emerge: in the 1930s and the 1970s, why were psychiatrists so eager to reject biological reductionism and to reformulate their discipline in the wake of a scientifically fallacious discourse on the 'Suicide Nation'? What made them willing to misrepresent the phenomenon as a 'Japanese' rather than a human behavior? The hypothesis here is that medical institutions and social practices intentionally supported the association between national 'uniqueness' and voluntary death. Such a policy was first deployed in the 1930s and later in the 1970s when Japan was described as the 'Suicide Nation.' It is crucial to deploy a comparative analysis of clinical assessments on voluntary death in order to understand the similarities that brought an analogous approach to the conceptualization of suicide during disparate time periods, and to shed light on the process of appeasement with the emerging and emotionally charged idea of the nation. In the Conclusions, the main arguments advanced in the core chapters are briefly reviewed and a summary is offered of this 'unconventional story of suicide in Japan.'

By exploring a long historical span and by unveiling hidden similarities between the 1930s and the 1970s, for example, in the way Japanese thoughts on life and death, health and wealth, group and gender, and the value of the individual were conceptualized, the book asks the reader to rethink the controversial and still vehemently debated periodization of twentieth-century Japan. Rather than challenging or redefining the labels of twentieth-century periodization, this book re-presents the narrative for what it is: a story after all, and as such a human artifact. By returning to this story, we can interrogate it, to understand how it works and what purposes it serves, and to come to know how the principles and constraints of its textuality produce further meaning. Instead of accepting a consolidated periodization produced by a 'derivative discourse' linked to major historical events, this book proposes the application of interpretative strategies to the subject of suicide and reinterprets the historical flow of the twentieth century accordingly.

The significance of this strategy is that it ultimately provides an unorthodox periodization of twentieth-century Japan. In the process of seeking to turn seemingly disconnected suicide events into a historical narrative, a quite unusual periodization emerges, a periodization produced – and not given – by its cultural usage, which insists on the complexity of the twentieth century. The prewar period begins with the advent of the modernization of several medical concepts, suicide among them, and witnesses a meaningful rift in the early 1930s, when the phase of exploration and gradual sedimentation of the scientific narrative was interrupted by the growth of authoritarian state power that engulfed every province of knowledge. The division set in the early 1930s does not correspond to the usual prewar periodization, which sees the beginning of the Showa period (1926) as the eve of a new historical phase, nor to the usual periodization in the history of Japanese medicine that sees the beginning of the Taisho period (1912) as the eve of the development of psychotherapeutic treatments inspired by new scientific and medical ideas absorbed from the West.[17] This story instead traces the development of the conceptualization of suicide in dynamic terms, identifying significant social and intellectual implications in the early 1930s that triggered a rupture in historical continuity, and not merely considering the development of medicine as an isolated discipline.

The postwar periodization of this book further challenges the rigid periodization of the so-called stage theories. This book assumes that between the end of World War II and 1960, the period explored in Chapter 3, a consistent rationale stands behind suicide's conceptualization, in contrast with those historians who claim that a significant rift occurred in 1949 and/or 1952. Such a phase overlaps with the so-called era of ideals or "era of hierarchy," first conceptualized by the sociologist Mita Munesuke and then reassessed by Ōsawa Masachi and Azuma Hiroyuki.[18] According to Mita, this phase is reminiscent of imperial Japan, in which a dominant discourse with optimistic expectations regarding technological progress and social reforms emerged. The period dealt with in the fourth chapter of this book, from 1960 to 1985, covers a longer span of time than the one suggested by several Japanese scholars, who identify 1975 as a watershed. The book assumes that throughout these 25 years there was a cultural, political, and economic continuity to the conceptualization of suicide and suggests that the mid-1980s represent a rupture with the past. Many historians consider 1989 to be the year in which the disintegration of the Cold War system, the death of the Emperor Shōwa, and the Bubble Economy brought drastic changes to Japanese society, as well as the first shadows of new poverty and social inequalities. However, this book identifies 1985 as the actual watershed. This periodization shares the arguments of Hara Hiroyuki, Narita Ryū, Kobayashi Yōichi, and Kitada Akihiro, who believe that a turning point occurred in 1985, when the Plaza Accord, the advent of Mikhail Gorbachev, and the emergence of the *Nyū Aka*[19] brought radical changes to the political, economic, social, and intellectual landscape. In other words, 1985 marked the collapse of the blind certainty of 'Japan as number one' and paved the way for a new kind of nationalism.[20] I argue that 1985 marks the beginning of a meaningful new narration on suicide in the postwar period, a phase not covered here. Since 1985, psychiatrists' widespread medicalization has described suicide as a medical condition caused by accumulated anxiety and prolonged depression. The absence of a mitigating cultural discourse has retransformed the narrative on suicide into a merely neurochemical account, and suicide into a treatable disease.

This unconventional periodization of twentieth-century Japan reveals a rhythmic flow, manifested in the alternation of medical and cultural narratives, ongoing in both the prewar and postwar periods. The prewar period witnessed a phase of independent scientific progress that pushed suicide into the sphere of pathology, followed by a decade of scientific resources mobilized to clothe suicide in an aura of nationalistic glory. The postwar period presented a similar alternation of discourses: a decade of biologized views on suicide followed by a long phase of romanticization. The recurrence of alternating discourses produces a sort of historical 'beat' in the account of the conceptualization of suicide. The question that arises here is: does it then make sense to acknowledge 1945 as a watershed in the history of twentieth-century Japanese medicine? Or, considering the alternation of a disease-centered narrative on suicide with a culture-centered narrative on suicide, would it be more useful to label the century a 'transwar period' – denoting an era that bridges wartime and exhibits consistent features across it? This book acknowledges World War II as a significant watershed in the conceptualization of suicide in the twentieth century for the simple reason that the war and the fervent nationalism associated with it imposed a temporary halt to efforts to medicalize the discourse on voluntary death, instead reinvigorating the cultural discourse that glorified the so-called traditional suicide patterns. When the war was over, the medical community leveraged the domestic and international consensus against the glorification of voluntary death so as to recover their dominant position in suicide's conceptualization. Whereas the war fractured the twentieth century in two, it did not stop the prewar pattern of alternation between pathologization and romanticization from being repeated. This is why the book defines the period that runs from the early 1900s to 1985 as a 'transwar period,' and the periodization and the chronological division in the chapters of the book are structured upon this assumption.

While a variety of definitions of the term 'suicide' have been suggested, this book will use the definition proposed by Margaret Pabst Battin in *Ethical Issues in Suicide*, in which she condones suicide ethically and morally: "a suicide is any death in which the proximate cause of death is deliberately (not accidentally) inflicted upon oneself whatever its moral character."[21] This classification of suicide is close to that of Ōhara Kenshirō, who claims that the act implies a desire to die and involves an action or several actions tending to provoke one's death (throwing oneself from a terrace because of being convinced of being able to fly is not suicide, he elucidated).[22] Accordingly, in this book, the term 'voluntary death' is used as a synonym for suicide; 'voluntary death' is a neutral term that implies a certain degree of tolerability. The term 'self-murder' is avoided, on the other hand, as it has an aggressive connotation. A careful use of language with regard to suicide is in fact necessary. Some references from old articles contain language that may be considered inappropriate today. In this regard, I also refrain from using the locutions 'successful' or 'failed' in reference to suicide, as these carry connotations on the value of finishing the acts noted.[23] I have found it useful to distinguish between suicide linked to biological factors and suicide as an act of free will. To clarify this distinction, I use the terms *disease* and *act*. *Disease* is used when referring to suicide framed within the biopsychiatric discourse on objectivity (wherein suicide is a disease of the mind, and individual agency plays no role). *Act* is used when referring to suicide framed within the cultural anti-discourse (wherein suicide is seen as a free and even romantic choice and the individual is seen to have sovereignty over such choices). Finally, this book contemplates the existing distinction between sacrifice and suicide. Several historical works on voluntary death in Japan share the tendency to not distinguish between sacrifice and suicide. Sacrifice or self-sacrifice was defined by Durkheim as the act inspired by the attitude in which individuals are so integrated into social interests as to be willing to give up even their own lives.[24] Since the late 1960s, several works on Durkheim and his study of suicide have highlighted the ambiguity of the concept of 'altruistic suicide' and the need to draw a distinction between suicide and sacrifice. A debate emerged between those who recognized the usefulness of a distinction between suicide and sacrifice and those who rejected the distinction.[25] In this book, suicide and sacrifice are acknowledged as two different categories: will and intention are fundamental to defining an act of 'suicide,' while the existence of constraint and obligation of any sort (social, political, etc.) defines an act as a sacrifice. The careful use of language related to suicide here assumes that speaking about voluntary death entails choosing among the array of concepts offered by a cultural system, and that the selection and recombination of these elements assigns different meanings to death. It is an extremely sensitive activity that gradually and naturally constitutes the vocabulary of death, and a profound awareness of the power of this vocabulary to shape social meaning is therefore required.

In conclusion, this study hopes to offer a narrative on suicide for a specific regional reality. This type of narrative is crucial in order to develop a future comparative analysis of the histories of suicide in different countries, and to detect fundamental similarities or dissimilarities among them. Such regional histories of suicide (not only this Japanese one), which seek to map the circulation of ideas as a historical and cultural formation, will be especially valuable in promoting the interrogation of unquestioned contemporary assumptions and practices. In place of the idea of suicide as an unchanging object of study, this book seeks to enable us to explore the constant evolution of suicide's conceptualization.

Notes

1 Ministry of Health, Labor and Welfare, *Dai 5 Kai Jisatsu Shibō Tōkei: Jinkō Dōtai Tōkei Tokuchō Hōkoku* [5th Statistics Concerning Suicide Deaths: Special Report on Demographic Statistics] (Tokyo: Ministry of Health, Labor and Welfare, 2005), p. 42.

2 *Asahi Shinbun*, "Wakamono Jidai no Jisatsu no Tengoku" [The Suicide Paradise for the Young Generation], April 25, 1956; Yoshitomo Takahashi, *Gunpatsu Jisatsu* [Suicide Clusters] (Tokyo: Chūkō Shinsho, 1998), p. 26.

3 Anonymous, "Shi wo Isogu Wakamono ga Oosugiru" [There Are Too Many Young People Rushing to Die], *Bungei Shunjū*, 36(2), 1958, pp. 74–83, p. 74 and pp. 78–79.

4 Takeda Katsuhiko, "Nippon ha Jisatsu Tengoku ka" [Is Japan a Suicide Nation?], *Ushio*, 233, October 1978, pp. 238–248, p. 248.

5 Ueno Kayoko, "Suicide as Japan's Major Export? A Note on Japanese Suicide Culture," *Revista Espaco Academico*, 44, 2005, retrieved July 27, 2014, from www.espacoacademico.com.br/044/44eueno_ing.htm.

6 *Nihonjinron* literally means 'theories regarding the Japanese.' The term refers to discourses on the distinctiveness of the society, culture, and national character of the Japanese. The literature is vast, ranging over such varied fields as sociology, psychology, history, linguistics, philosophy, and even science. As such, *nihonjinron* have manifested periodically from the Meiji era to the present while continually undergoing changes in form. In its narrower and most recent sense, the term refers to the vogue of such discourses during the 1970s and the early 1980s, when a very large quantity of works on the unique qualities of the Japanese inundated bookstores – the so-called *nihonjinron* boom. The debate emphasized the uniqueness and homogeneity of shared Japanese blood, culture, and language. In turn it has had a large impact on the ways in which Japanese society and culture continue to be discussed today. Though the genre is published predominantly in Japan by the Japanese, notable examples have also been penned by foreign scholars, journalists, and residents.

7 George A. DeVos, *Socialization for Achievement. Essays on the Cultural Psychology of the Japanese* (Berkeley: University of California Press, 1973); Iga Mamoru, *The Thorn in the Chrysanthemum: Suicide and Economic Success in Modern Japan* (Los Angeles: University of California Press, 1986).

8 Yagiri Tomeo, *Seppuku Ronkō* [Debates on Seppuku] (Tokyo: Chūō Kōron, 1970), pp. 6–32; Stuart D. B. Picken and Hori Taoko, *Nihonjin no Jisatsu: Seio to no Hikaku* [Japanese Suicide, a Comparison with the West] (Tokyo: Saimaru Shuppankai, 1979); Fuse Toyomasa, *Jisatsu to bunka* [Suicide and Culture] (Tokyo: Shinchōsha, 1984).

9 Maurice Pinguet, *Voluntary Death in Japan* (London: Polity Press, 1993).

10 Ōhara Kenshirō, *Shinjūkō – ai to Shi no Byōri* [On Shinjū – The Pathology of Love and Death] (Tokyo: Taiyō Shuppan, 1973); Susumu Iizuka, "Michizure Jisatsu, Konjaku" [The Double Suicide, Past and Present], *Bulletin of Momoyama Gakuin University*, 15(2), 1982, pp. 207–208; Kunimitsu Shirō, *Jōshi no Rekishi* [The History of Lovers' Suicide] (Tokyo: Gonzai Eibunshō, 1995).

11 Steven Stack, "Media Impact on Suicide," in David Lester (ed.), *Current Concepts of Suicide* (Philadelphia: The Charles Press Publishers, 1990), pp. 108–119; George Domino and Takahashi Yoshitomo, "Attitudes Toward Suicide in Japanese and American Medical Students," *Suicide and Life-Threatening Behavior*, 21(4), Winter, 1991, pp. 345–359; Takahashi Yoshitomo, *Gunpatsu Jisatsu*, pp. XXX.

12 Ogino Masahiro, *Kaihatsu Kukan no Boryoku: Ijime Jisatsu o Umu Fukei* [Developmental Violence – an Atmosphere that Produces Suicides for Bullying] (Tokyo: Shin'yosha, 2012); Ueno Masahiko, *Jisatsu no Kyūwari wa Tasatsu de Aru* [Nine out of Ten Suicides Are Homicides] (Tokyo: Kanzen, 2012).
13 Mark D. West, *Law in Everyday Japan: Sex, Sumo, Suicide, and Statutes* (Chicago and London: University of Chicago Press, 2005); Susan Long, *Final Days: Japanese Culture and Choice at the End of Life* (Honolulu: University of Hawai'i Press, 2005); Adrienne Carey Hurley, *Revolutionary Suicide and Other Desperate Measures* (Durham, NC: Duke University Press, 2012); as well as the anthropologist Chikako Ozawa-de Silva's recent articles on Internet suicide forums, which carefully analyze the language and forms used by participants on these sites: Chikako Ozawa-de Silva, "Too Lonely to Die Alone: Internet Suicide Pacts and Existential Suffering in Japan," *Cultural Medical Psychiatry*, 32, 2008, pp. 516–551; Chikako Ozawa-de Silva, "Shared Death: Self, Sociality and Internet Group Suicide in Japan," *Transcultural Psychiatry*, 47(3), July 2010, pp. 392–419.
14 Suzuki Akihito, "A Brain Hospital in Tokyo and Its Private and Public Patients, 1926–45," *History of Psychiatry*, 14(337), 2003, pp. 337–360, p. 338.
15 Ian Marsh, *Foucault, History and Truth* (Cambridge: Cambridge University Press, 2010); Kitanaka Junko, *Depression in Japan: Psychiatric Cures for a Society in Distress* (Princeton, NJ: Princeton University Press, 2011).
16 I call the psychiatric discourse 'dominant' as it established its authoritative knowledge over alternative discourses that I call 'counter-discourses' (meant in the sense used in the Foucauldian tradition), as they contested the dominant habits of mind and expression of the hegemonizing psychiatric discipline. Michel Foucault, *The History of Sexuality*, Vol. 1 (Harmondsworth: Penguin, 1981), pp. 92–102.
17 Christopher Harding, "Religion and Psychotherapy in Modern Japan – a Four Phase View," in Christopher Harding, Iwata Fumiaki, and Yoshinaga Shin'ichi (eds.), *Religion and Psychotherapy in Modern Japan* (New York: Routledge, 2015), p. 25.
18 Munesuke Mita, *Shakaigaku Nyūmon* [Introduction to Sociology] (Tokyo: Iwaba Shoten, 2006), pp. 70–72; Masachi Ōsawa, *Fukanōsei no Jidai* [The Era of Impossibility] (Tokyo: Iwaba Shoten, 2008), pp. 33–34; Hiroki Azuma, *Dōbutsuka Suru Posutomodan* [Otaku: Japan's Database Animals] (Tokyo: Kōdansha, 2001), p. 8.
19 *Nyū Aka* or *Nyū Akademizumu* is an intellectual trend that emerged in the early 1980s in Japan, and more precisely in 1983 with Asada Akira's *Kōzō to Chikara* [Structure and Power]. The appellation implied that members of the *Nyū Aka* and their works transgressed the established boundaries of academic specialization and affiliation, in contrast to the high seriousness of faculty seminars and research groups. The current was born within structuralist and semiotics schools, but it refused the postwar dichotomy between intellectuals and the masses. The *Nyū Aka* was acclaimed outside universities as a fashionable mode of thought for the younger generation but was then subsequently forgotten with the era. As a theoretical fad, *Nyū Aka* was often referred to as 'post-modernism.' However, after *Nyū Aka* disappeared from Japan, theories on post-modernism remained a subject of study and affected subsequent academic trends.
20 Hiroyuki Hara, *Baburu bunkaron – 'Posuto-sengo' toshite no 1980 Nendai* [Theories on the Bubble Era – The 1980s and the Postwar] (Tokyo: Keio Daigaku Shuppankai, 2006), pp. 13, 216; Narita Ryū, Kobayashi Yōichi, and Kitada Akihiro, "Gaido Mappu 80–90 nendai" [A Guide Map of the 80s and 90s], in Iwasaki Minoru (ed.), *Sengo Nihon Sutadizu 3* [Studies on Postwar Japan 3](Tokyo: Kinokuniya Shoten, 2008), pp. 6–42.
21 Margaret Pabst Battin, *Ethical Issues in Suicide* (Upper Saddle River, NJ: Prentice-Hall, 1995), p. 20.
22 Ōhara Kenshirō, *Nihon no Jisatsu – Kodoku to Fuan no Kaimei* [Suicide in Japan – Understanding Solitude and Anxiety] (Tokyo: Seishin Shōbo, 1966), pp. 4–6 and 33.

23 For further references in regard to sensitive terms about suicide, see Loren Coleman, *The Copycat Effect: How the Media and the Popular Culture Trigger the Mayhem in Tomorrow's Headlines* (New York: Paraview Pocket Books, 2004), pp. 2–3.
24 Émile Durkheim, *Suicide: A Study in Sociology* (New York: The Free Press Corporation, 1951), pp. 110–121.
25 See C. Davies and M. Neal, "Durkheim's Altruistic and Fatalistic Suicide," in W.S.F. Pickering and G. Walford (eds.), *Durkheim's Suicide: A Century of Research and Debate* (New York: Routledge, 2000), pp. 38–39; Steve Taylor, *Durkheim and the Study of Suicide* (New York: The Macmillan Press, 1982), pp. 132–136; Steve Taylor, "Suicide, Durkheim, and Sociology," in David Lester (ed.), *Current Concepts of Suicide* (Philadelphia: The Charles Press Publishers, 1990), pp. 195–200.

Bibliography

Suzuki Akihito, "A Brain Hospital in Tokyo and Its Private and Public Patients, 1926–45," *History of Psychiatry*, 14(337) (2003), pp. 337–360.
Anonymous, "Shi wo Isogu Wakamono ga Oosugiru" [There Are Too Many Young People Rushing to Die], *Bungei Shunjū*, 36(2) (1958), pp. 74–83.
Hiroki Azuma, *Dōbutsuka Suru Posutomodan* [Otaku: Japan's Database Animals] (Tokyo: Kōdansha, 2001).
Margaret Pabst Battin, *Ethical Issues in Suicide* (Upper Saddle River, NJ: Prentice-Hall, 1995).
Loren Coleman, *The Copycat Effect: How the Media and the Popular Culture Trigger the Mayhem in Tomorrow's Headlines* (New York: Paraview Pocket Books, 2004).
George A. DeVos, *Socialization for Achievement. Essays on the Cultural Psychology of the Japanese* (Berkeley: University of California Press, 1973).
George Domino and Takahashi Yoshitomo, "Attitudes Toward Suicide in Japanese and American Medical Students," *Suicide and Life-Threatening Behavior*, 21(4) (Winter, 1991), pp. 345–359.
Émile Durkheim, *Suicide: A Study in Sociology* (New York: The Free Press Corporation, 1951).
Michel Foucault, *The History of Sexuality*, Vol. 1 (Harmondsworth: Penguin, 1981).
Hiroyuki Hara, *Baburu Bunkaron – 'Posuto-Sengo' Toshite no 1980 Nendai* [Theories on the Bubble Era – The 1980s and the Postwar] (Tokyo: Keio Daigaku Shuppankai, 2006).
Christopher Harding, Iwata Fumiaki, and Yoshinaga Shin'ichi (eds.), *Religion and Psychotherapy in Modern Japan* (New York: Routledge, 2015).
Adrienne Carey Hurley, *Revolutionary Suicide and Other Desperate Measures* (Durham, NC: Duke University Press, 2012).
Susumu Iizuka, "Michizure Jisatsu, Konjaku" [The Double Suicide, Past and Present], *Bulletin of Momoyama Gakuin University*, 15(2) (1982), pp. 207–208.
Kitanaka Junko, *Depression in Japan: Psychiatric Cures for a Society in Distress* (Princeton, NJ: Princeton University Press, 2011).
Takeda Katsuhiko, "Nippon ha Jisatsu Tengoku ka" [Is Japan a Suicide Nation?], *Ushio*, 233 (October, 1978), pp. 238–248.
Ueno Kayoko, "Suicide as Japan's Major Export? A Note on Japanese Suicide Culture," *Revista Espaco Academico*, 44 (2005), retrieved 27 July 2014, from www.espacoacademico.com.br/044/44eueno_ing.htm
Ōhara Kenshirō, *Shinjūkō – ai to Shi no Byōri* [On Shinjū – the Pathology of Love and Death] (Tokyo: Taiyō Shuppan, 1973).

Ōhara Kenshirō, *Nihon no Jisatsu – Kodoku to Fuan no Kaimei* [Suicide in Japan – Understanding Solitude and Anxiety] (Tokyo: Seishin Shōbo, 1966).
David Lester (ed.), *Current Concepts of Suicide* (Philadelphia: The Charles Press Publishers, 1990).
Susan Long, *Final Days: Japanese Culture and Choice at the End of Life* (Honolulu: University of Hawai'i Press, 2005).
Iga Mamoru, *The Thorn in the Chrysanthemum: Suicide and Economic Success in Modern Japan* (Los Angeles: University of California Press, 1986).
Ian Marsh, *Foucault, History and Truth* (Cambridge: Cambridge University Press, 2010).
Ueno Masahiko, *Jisatsu no Kyūwari wa Tasatsu de Aru* [Nine out of Ten Suicides Are Homicides] (Tokyo: Kanzen, 2012).
Ogino Masahiro, *Kaihatsu Kukan no Boryoku: Ijime Jisatsu o Umu Fukei* [Developmental Violence – an Atmosphere that Produces Suicides for Bullying] (Tokyo: Shin'yosha, 2012).
Ministry of Health, Labor and Welfare, *Dai 5 Kai Jisatsu Shibō Tōkei: Jinkō Dōtai Tōkei Tokuchō Hōkoku* [5th Statistics Concerning Suicide Deaths: Special Report on Demographic Statistics] (Tokyo: Ministry of Health, Labor and Welfare, 2005).
Iwasaki Minoru (ed.), *Sengo Nihon Sutadizu 3* [Studies on Postwar Japan 3] (Tokyo: Kinokuniya Shoten, 2008).
Munesuke Mita, *Shakaigaku Nyūmon* [Introduction to Sociology] (Tokyo: Iwaba Shoten, 2006), pp. 70–72.
Masachi Ōsawa, *Fukanōsei no Jidai* [The Era of Impossibility] (Tokyo: Iwaba Shoten, 2008).
Chikako Ozawa-de Silva, "Too Lonely to Die Alone: Internet Suicide Pacts and Existential Suffering in Japan," *Cultural Medical Psychiatry*, 32 (2008), pp. 516–551.
Chikako Ozawa-de Silva, "Shared Death: Self, Sociality and Internet Group Suicide in Japan," *Transcultural Psychiatry*, 47(3) (July, 2010), pp. 392–419.
Stuart D. B. Picken and Hori Taoko, *Nihonjin no Jisatsu: Seio to no Hikaku* [Japanese Suicide, a Comparison with the West] (Tokyo: Saimaru Shuppankai, 1979).
W.S.F. Pickering and G. Walford (eds.), *Durkheim's Suicide: A Century of Research and Debate* (New York: Routledge, 2000).
Maurice Pinguet, *Voluntary Death in Japan* (London: Polity Press, 1993).
Kunimitsu Shirō, *Jōshi no Rekishi* [The History of Lovers' Suicide] (Tokyo: Gonzai Eibunshō, 1995).
Yoshitomo Takahashi, *Gunpatsu Jisatsu* [Suicide Clusters] (Tokyo: Chūkō Shinsho, 1998).
Steve Taylor, *Durkheim and the Study of Suicide* (New York: The Macmillan Press, 1982).
Yagiri Tomeo, *Seppuku Ronkō* [Debates on Seppuku] (Tokyo: Chūō Kōron, 1970). Fuse Toyomasa, *Jisatsu to Bunka* [Suicide and Culture] (Tokyo: Shinchōsha, 1984).
Mark D. West, *Law in Everyday Japan: Sex, Sumo, Suicide, and Statutes* (Chicago and London: University of Chicago Press, 2005).

Part I

1 Biologizing the meaning of suicide (1880s–1930s)

A theoretical approach to suicide in the West

As Japan's encounter with Western medicine deepened and accelerated in the nineteenth century, the country's attitude was an enthusiastic embrace of the newly arriving scientific knowledge, with the ultimate ideological justification of strengthening the foundations of its own imperial rule. In the government's eyes, improving the health of its citizens would help Japan survive in the face of vigorous imperial competition and resist the Europeans' desire to 'civilize the barbarian nations.' To this end, the country's priority was to learn from Western teachers how to improve national efficiency so as to modernize while at the same time avoiding Western colonization. Between 1868 and the Russo-Japanese War of 1904–05, imperial programs were developed to support a public policy of hygiene [*eisei*] that would ensure physically and spiritually healthy civilians and soldiers, and in a climate of 'biological optimism' [*seibutsugakuteki rakkanron*] resulting from the extensive medical knowledge arriving from the West, Japan witnessed the establishment of a professional medical community. This new medical profession defined itself by the desire to scientifically quantify its techniques and prove them correct, and through the promise of a safe society, one that would eliminate dangers arising from the threat of physical and mental disturbance. Suicide was identified as one of these threats.

Influences from the West's evolving conceptions of suicide were brought to bear on Japan during this period, and are essential to understanding the discourse that subsequently developed. In the West, research on suicide has not been confined to one field: on the contrary, anthropologists, philosophers, psychologists, psychiatrists, sociologists, and theologians have all studied the phenomenon. Since Socrates, suicide has been viewed by many as a 'moral' problem. Theologians have devoted attention to suicide and morality as a question of religious doctrine, while philosophers have dedicated attention to suicide and morality as a question of ethics. In the early Christian tradition, suicide was defined as a crime against life and God, a process that culminated with Thomas Aquinas' conceptualization of suicide as "a clear sin against God." However, as early as the publication of *Biathanatos* by John Donne in 1609, and again with *Essay on Suicide* by David Hume in 1783, this strict definition of suicide as a sin was challenged by philosophers. The existential writings of David Hume, Søren Kierkegaard, Friedrich Nietzsche, Martin Heidegger, Jean-Paul Sartre, and Albert Camus have all argued that suicide can be an expression of freedom and responsibility and, as such, may represent an existential choice.

The problem of determinism versus free will was taken up to some extent by the philosophical and theological approaches to suicide, but the issue was considered secondary to the problem of the morality of suicide until the nineteenth century. The change in concerns that occurred at this point was due in general to the triumph of rationalism and specifically to the development of the empirical approach to the study of suicide, which included psychology, psychiatry, sociology, and various forms of official statistics.

From the seventeenth century on, secular laws were developed to prohibit suicide, and scholars such as J. B. Merian in 1763 and Jean-Étienne Dominique Esquirol attempted to define it as an illness. In 1812, Esquirol, pioneer of the intensive study of insanity and of clinical nosology in psychiatry, defined the act of suicide as indicative of mental illness, and blamed social stress for alterations to the brain that purportedly predisposed individuals to the act. Observing socially maladaptive personality types in clinical settings, Esquirol claimed with unshakable conviction: "I think I have proved that no man takes his own life unless he is in delirium, and that all suicides are deranged."[1]

Epidemics of youth suicide allegedly caused by the publication of Goethe's *The Sorrows of Young Werther* prompted the Vienna Psychoanalysis Society to hold the world's first conference on youth suicide prevention in Vienna in 1910. Sigmund Freud organized the conference. In his opening and closing remarks, the psychologist – drawing from Goethe's story in which the hero shoots himself over an unrequited love – argued that the main risk factor for adolescent suicide was love conflicts. This initial hypothesis was followed by years of intermittent research on suicide by Freud, which culminated in *Mourning and Melancholia* (1917), the classic text for psychoanalytic discussion of suicide. The book located the etiology of suicide in intrapsychic conflicts, portrayed the phenomenon in terms of moral crisis, and acknowledged it as an extension of melancholic behavior. Freud conceptualized suicide as the murder of one's self resulting from the internalization of aggressive forces. He also believed that suicide was more likely in advanced civilizations, because they required greater repression of sexual and aggressive energies.

At the same time, the German psychiatrists Emil Kraepelin (1921) and Ernst Kretschmer (1925) observed suicide symptoms mainly in connection with "manic-depressive illness" (a term coined by Kraepelin, which originally referred to all kinds of mood disorders). Kraepelin and Kretschmer offered alternative explanations that diverged from the cultural narrative. They interpreted suicide not as a symptom of mental disease but of individual character type, and defined character types as biogenetically related variants of paranoid and affective psychoses. Kraepelin drew a distinction between single-episode depressions such as melancholia and recurrent depressive disorders, which he labeled "maniacal-depression." The maniac-depressive was in great danger of committing suicide "because he displays great fluctuations in emotional equilibrium, [. . .] falls into outbursts of boundless fury, [. . .] sheds tears without a cause, gives expression to thoughts of suicide, and brings forward hypochondriacal complaints."[2] Kraepelin ascribed these symptoms to metabolic anomaly; they all thus had a biological foundation. In believing that organic disturbances underlay depressive disorders, Kraepelin totally rejected psychological and sociological interpretations of external pressures. Twenty-one years later, in 1925, Kraepelin commented on certain differences in the incidence and presentation of psychopathological phenomena that he considered to be caused by ethnic-cultural characteristics or social conditions. These observations on the pathogenic effects of cultural and social factors demonstrated the emergence of a reciprocal exchange among disciplines, which would influence the development of social and transcultural psychiatry in the following decades.[3] Kretschmer contributed to the process of suicide pathologization by developing the concept of "personality disorder." He defined "personality" as the subjective aspects of the self, while "personality disorder" meant an alteration of consciousness, or loss of coherence between the cognitive and emotional functions. Kretschmer's theory initially considered suicide to be the result of the individual's personality, and thus a form of attenuated insanity.

Meanwhile physiological and biological theories had been emerging which viewed personality as forming primarily on the basis of physical factors; interest in suicide had gradually taken a statistical bent, and statistics became increasingly considered to be the 'proper' data to be used in studying suicide. Through these data (known as 'moral statistics'), it emerged that the 'morality' of suicide varied from society to society and from one historical period to another.[4] This variation attracted the attention of sociologists, who explored social – rather than medical – explanations for the act. The differing approaches of psychiatry and sociology were framed by their responses to the two general questions that they tackled: What characteristics distinguish individuals who commit suicide from those who do not? And secondly: Why does the suicide rate vary from one population to the next?

Although sociology and psychiatry became engaged in a long-standing controversy, the two disciplines also greatly influenced each other. The debate, which began in the mid-nineteenth century with André Michel Guerry, Pierre Égiste Lisle, Alfred Legoyt, Thomas Masaryk, and Enrico Morselli, peaked during the interwar period following Durkheim's contribution to the sociology of suicide. Durkheim insisted on seeing suicidal actions as the result of social factors, explaining suicide by studying variations in the suicide rate between different groups and within different contexts.[5] He attempted to demonstrate that social factors such as norms, institutions, and the division of labor have a decisive influence on the acts of individuals. Society is a system of rules, external to the individual, that constrain and regulate the individual's behavior. The explanation of suicide rates, according to Durkheim, thus lies in the nature of society, not in an individual's psychological or biological attributes. Durkheim saw social integration and regulation as variables that could explain variations in suicide rates. Too little integration leads to egoistic suicide and too much integration to altruistic suicide. Too little regulation produces anomic suicide; too much regulation, fatalistic suicide.

Indeed, for several decades Durkheim's account dominated the field of suicide studies. His ideas, however, opened a breach between social and psychiatric analyses of suicide. Leading psychiatrists who researched suicide remarked that Durkheim had dismissed mental illness too quickly and had taken for granted that constituent features of the suicidogenic current – that is, egoism, altruism, anomie, and fatalism – were societally determined. Durkheim had insisted that the nature and the intensity of the suicidogenic current were factors independent of psychological conditions. In other words, he defied any psychological theory that identified the individual as the source of social phenomena; Durkheim determined only the rate at which the population was affected, not the identity of those to be affected. Rifts between sociological and psychiatric approaches became universal and persistent. Little was done to integrate psychiatrists' observations and findings with sociological studies until the 1970s, by which point specific contributions came primarily from works by psychiatrists who studied suicidal actions as social phenomena.[6]

In sum, by the beginning of the twentieth century, the consensus on the causes of suicide was in flux as biological psychiatry and the rise of social sciences jointly called into question specific causes and explanations of the phenomenon. Freud, Kraepelin, Kretschmer, and Durkheim were no closer to finding a satisfactory answer as to why certain individuals committed suicide and others did not. The major impediment to resolving such a dilemma was, reiterating Howard Kushner's argument, the very professionalization and specialization of the knowledge that grew from the theories offered by these emerging disciplines.[7] Not until the 1950s did more complex research on suicide come into bloom, research that gradually moved away from an orthodox, field-related approach to the phenomenon and slowly but continuously incorporated the notion that suicide varies both culturally and historically.

This specialization within disciplinary boundaries in the West was mirrored in Japan. Although a relatively sustained philosophical dialogue among disciplines did occur, the members of the emerging Japanese medical community showed more eagerness to firmly establish their disciplines than to communicate across these disciplines' borders. They too began to narrate suicide along the lines of their European teachers: that is, according to specific, fragmented subject areas.

A disease: Western-style psychiatry in Japanese academia

Japanese historians and academic psychiatrists have rightly described the history of psychiatry in early-twentieth-century Japan mainly as a succession of highly influential specialists who, due to their personal charisma, intelligence, acumen, or political skill, utilized their power in such a way that they had decisive historical impact. They have also described the history of psychiatry in Japan as a process of mimicry resulting in the adoption of Western practices, essentially gauging the progress of the Japanese discipline against the allegedly advanced Western model.[8] However, evidence proves that the indigenous medical community had already set in motion a process of 'modernization' – even if it was somewhat disorganized – of the nosology, diagnosis, and treatment of suicide before encountering Western science. When in the late nineteenth century Western-style psychiatry established itself in Japanese academia, the newly trained Japanese psychiatrists gradually absorbed the Western conceptualization of suicide, and then departed from it, by welcoming universal, biological norms and tempering them with local ones.

The introduction of Western medicine into Japanese academia is a topic that has been discussed at length by Ann B. Jannetta, Hoi-Eun Kim, and Alexander R. Bay.[9] The earliest introduction of European medicine to Japan was by Jesuit missionaries in the sixteenth century, and then Dutch physicians in the seventeenth century. Translations of European books on anatomy and physiology subsequently flocked into Japanese libraries. In 1857, a group of Dutch-trained Japanese physicians founded a medical school in Edo (later Tokyo) that is considered the precursor of the medical faculty of the Imperial University of Tokyo. The introduction of the smallpox vaccine in 1849, fifty years after the advanced disease prevention technique had been developed in Europe, was a crucial event that increased the credibility and honor of Western medicine in Japan. This event also unveiled the obsolescence of *kanpō*, or customary Asian medicine. *Kanpō* had remained the backbone of Japanese medicine for more than 1500 years; it perceived disease as something sent by the gods or produced by the influence of evil spirits. Treatment and prevention were based on religious practices, such as prayers, incantations, and exorcism. The absorption of scientific medicine arriving from the West inaugurated its desuetude.

Nonetheless, even before the introduction of Western medicine, indigenous forces had pushed early modern Japan toward the demystification of the theory of possession and exorcism.[10] As early as the mid-eighteenth century, Japanese physicians had recognized suicide as the result of a disordered mind [*ranshin*], challenging the established belief that it was the outcome of fox possession [*kitsuneki*].[11] Kagawa Shūtoku (1683–1785), disciple of Gotō Konzan and physician in *kanpō*, insisted that suicide – like every other disease – was caused by the stagnation of vital energy [*ki*]. Kagawa divided mental disorders [*kan*] into psychosis [*kyō*], fright disorder [*kyo*], epilepsy [*ten*], and mental retardation or dementia [*chigai*], and further argued that only people who had a predisposition toward mental disorders could become possessed by a fox. Kagawa identified suicide as a mental disorder, but he ultimately fell prey to confusion in categorizing it, inconsistently describing it in terms of the psychopathological classifications he used, such as depression, persecution, obsession, phobia, etc. Nevertheless, despite his confusion over its labeling, Kagawa aimed at identifying suicide as a 'disease,' and at explaining it as something determined by biological norms.[12] When the ongoing debate regarding the medicalization of suicide that was already taking place in European academic circles reached Japan, it suggested looking at suicide through the eyes of medical professionals. This instigated a systematic passage from regarding mental illness as the result of superstitious forces to a more refined stance of understanding it medically. In this shift from the priest to the doctor, a central passage in the history of secularization of medicine in Japan, Kagawa's endeavor was a crucial forerunner, one that may have even helped to facilitate the acceptance of Western medicine.

Soon after the Restoration, the Meiji government began to exert control over medical knowledge, practices, and institutions as part of its larger program of modernization. It fully endorsed Western medicine as the most desirable method of diagnosis and treatment, and excluded *kanpō* from the official medical education system as obsolete and valueless in strengthening the nation's health. With the passage of the Medical Act [*Isei*] in 1874, new medical schools and a system of national licensing examinations for physicians based on European medicine were established. The new examinations focused on chemistry, anatomy, physiology, pathology, pharmaceutics, internal medicine, and surgery, with the intended goal of instituting a change that gave preference to so-called Western medicine over *kanpō*. In 1883, the government required that even those who wished to practice *kanpō* and use traditional medical treatments such as herbs and acupuncture had to pass the new examinations. The Office for Medical Affairs [*Imu-ka*] (created within the Ministry of Education in 1872) and the Bureau of Hygiene [*Eisei-kyoku*] coordinated a number of measures that aimed to standardize practices in order to improve public health, claiming a binding link between individual health and the health of the state. Under this hygiene policy, the notions that human biology is universal and that individuals must learn to achieve hygiene and health by following scientific procedures were popularized within the country. Hospitals and laboratories were designed to become the new loci where scientific medicine investigated signs and symptoms of diseases, and where doctors treated and ensured the health of patients. The Japanese government's increasing attention in assessing the health of its citizens, including that of mental patients both at home and in psychiatric institutions, reached its apex with the establishment in 1916 of the Health Inspection Committee [*Hoken'eisei Chōsakai*] as an advisory body to the Ministry of Home Affairs [*Naimushō*].

In 1869, the Meiji government opted to introduce German rather than British medicine in order to modernize the national medical system of Japan and make it 'scientific.' Between 1871 and 1881, thirteen teachers from Germany and Austria were invited to teach at medical schools in Tokyo, Kyoto, Nagoya, and other Japanese cities, propelling unprecedented transnational medical encounters.[13] By 1880, apart from some exceptions, higher education in medical science in Japan was conducted in the German language. In 1877, the Faculty of Medicine, the first Western-style medical school, was established at the University of Tokyo, which remained the only university in Japan until 1897. With the ambition of producing highly qualified physicians and researchers, elite Japanese students were taught by foreign authorities, sent to Europe to study at the government's expense, and trained as professors to replace their European tutors. Japanese students flocked to medical schools in Berlin, Heidelberg, Munich, and Freiburg. By 1900, the Japanese medical profession had changed drastically, absorbing and mastering German scientific knowledge and practices until Western missionary doctors and their hospitals had seemingly become unnecessary.

The first Department of Psychiatry, established within the Faculty of Medicine of the renamed Imperial University of Tokyo in 1886, was described by the historian Suzuki Akihito as "the undisputed intellectual center, from which almost all professors in other university psychiatric clinics graduated."[14] This department acted as the center of production of scientific knowledge as well as verification of the data produced by non-affiliated researchers. Control over the evaluation of scientific production was maintained by a community of Western medical practitioners who colonized the department. It was in the very same Faculty of Medicine too that neuropathology – a recent mania among German psychiatrists at the time – and biological psychiatry were soon introduced. The essential difference between the two disciplines could be found in their distinct conceptions of mental illness. Neuropathology conceived of 'insanity' as untreatable mental derangement, and the proper techniques for dealing with it revolved around custodial care in an asylum. Biological psychiatry, or biopsychiatry, was based on the belief that insanity was a mental disorder, physical in origin, due to heredity and compounded by bad habits such as masturbation or homosexual practices. In this conception, madness was thus a degenerative condition that passed from generation to generation, threatening the sanity of the entire country, but it nevertheless could and should be treated scientifically and medically.

Biopsychiatry made its entrance into Japan in the 1870s and 1880s through translations of the first German neuropsychiatric textbooks of Henry Maudsley, Heinrich Schule, and Richard von Krafft-Ebing. German psychiatrists had rejected the notion of suicide as an untreatable mental disease (which Japanese psychiatrists translated as *seishin shikkan*) linked to the individual character type, and instead argued that it was a disorder [*shōgai*] linked to the individual's personality and thus treatable. The shift blurred the knife-edge distinction between sanity and insanity and identified a much higher number of potential patients who could be treated. This transformation guaranteed psychiatrists greater possibilities for their emerging discipline, with a prominent role in the diagnosis and treatment of mental illnesses and a decisive role in the process of the modernization of suicide. The newly professionalized Japanese medical community was promptly engaged by the government to lead health and social-policy debates. For example, psychiatrists were asked to investigate the regions where fox possession incidents were occurring, a phenomenon that had allegedly threatened social order ever since the Edo period.[15] Mental illness and suicide – acknowledged during the Edo period as phenomena of an unhealthy and rebellious mind – had begun to be treated in the same manner as infectious disease. The healing authority was charged with detecting, containing, and curing it.

In the transition from pre-scientific to scientific medicine, the conception of a balanced bodily economy, formerly understood through magical, mystical, alchemical, and naturalistic explanations, gradually turned to chemical explanations. The contact with Western medicine compelled the Japanese academic establishment to reconceptualize knowledge about the mind and the body, and to promptly adopt notions like brain [*nō*], nerves [*shinkei*], neurasthenia [*shinkei suijaku*], and so forth.[16] This language began to modernize the identity of mental illness and suicide in Japan.[17] Sakaki Hajime, the first government-financed student to study overseas in psychiatry, and the first appointed professor of psychiatry at the Imperial University of Tokyo, extensively contributed to the diffusion of German biopsychiatric norms and practices. After his graduation from the University of Tokyo in 1880, Sakaki had been dispatched by the Ministry of Education to study neuropathology and biological psychiatry for four years at the University of Berlin. During his stay in Europe, Sakaki toured several asylums in Germany and Austria and acquired innovative neuroanatomical techniques. On his return, he worked continuously to establish the theoretical apparatus of the new discipline. He reeducated the students of the faculty, encouraging them to familiarize themselves with the imported neologisms, newly developed norms, and new practices of German psychiatry.[18]

An essay by Kure Shūzō in 1894, *Seishinbyōsha no Jisatsushō ni Tsuite* [On Suicide in Mentally Ill Patients], was the first psychiatric work on suicide published in Japan.[19] Kure's neurobiological research paved the way for the 'biologization' of voluntary death, defining suicide (which he referred to as *jisatsushō*) as a mental disease [*seishin shikkan*] that was genetic [*iden ari*], symptomatic, and dangerous.[20] Widely distributed and highly persuasive, the paper demonstrated the first experimental deployment of biopsychiatric techniques (statistical analysis and clinical observation of 521 women and 830 men in the Public Asylum of Tokyo) to diagnose suicidal patients. The research indicated that anyone who showed anti-social behaviors (for example, anyone inclined to have love affairs alienating family or children, or to become an alcoholic or psychotic) or who had physical impairments (Kure listed a number of physical disabilities, including dyspepsia and other generic digestive disorders) was more prone to commit suicide. Kure further argued that patients who were inclined toward suicide displayed symptoms, suggesting that psychiatrists could spot those suicidal indicators and confine the patients.[21] In viewing suicide as mainly a genetic disease, observable by dangerous and anti-social behaviors, Kure claimed that suicidal patients were victims of mental disorder and thus had a diminished responsibility for their actions. For this reason, the psychiatrist suggested that patients should be kept under observation for at least six months, preferably one year, if an attempted suicide had occurred or if a psychiatrist had detected any suicidal symptom.[22] There was an additional effect created by considering suicide as the result of one's inherited physiological and neurological constitution and as the outcome of an observable organic pathology: this allowed psychiatrists like Kure to gain patients who might otherwise be treated by general practitioners. Claiming responsibility for suicide's diagnosis and treatment helped psychiatrists demonstrate the social value of their discipline, which was still greatly marginalized.

Kure further declared that suicide was a pressing public health problem that required vigilance, and that asylums were the best places to ensure this. As early as 1898, in his *Seishinbyōgaku-shūyō* [Textbook of Psychiatry], the first anthology of materials related to psychiatry and mental illness, Kure claimed that sanity was a fundamental condition for a strong nation, thus reinforcing the significance of mental hospitals and of the profession of psychiatrists as guarantors of the health of the country.[23] Until the eve of the twentieth century, given that suicides and attempted suicides were seen as dangerous behaviors for society, families of potential victims had the duty to help the 'disordered mind' or the 'unable' by agreeing to keep them detained at home. Such duties were codified in the 1900 Mental Patients' Custody Act, which Kure strongly opposed. In 1902, he chose to directly put pressure on the government, writing: "The country does not need to gather mental patients in private institutions, but in public, or better, prefectural institutions [. . .]."[24] Kure supported the Mental Hospitals Act in 1919, which regulated the confinement of the mentally ill to institutions, rather than to cells at home, thus framing it as a problem of illness rather than public safety or order. This enabled prefectures to build public asylums and brought the locus of confinement from private homes to public hospitals governed by doctors.[25] Commenting on the restricted growth of asylum accommodation in Japan compared with Western countries, Kure criticized the inadequacy of Japanese psychiatric provision as a sign of the hidden backwardness of the state. Thus, he tacitly assumed that hospitalization of the insane was an inevitable step in the evolution of psychiatric social policy.

Kure's effort was primarily directed toward three goals: gaining a scientific grasp of suicide and opening up possibilities for constituting suicidal identities; encouraging the surveillance ward to bring and hold suicidal cases under the gaze of the doctors, who ultimately could incorporate them into the fold of psychiatric nosology; and 'popularizing' the biological language on suicide. This last goal, that is, the diffusion and the dissemination of a simplified form of knowledge from the learned to the uneducated, was successfully achieved thanks to his active participation in public debates. Between 1891 and 1921, Kure wrote fairly regularly for the Yomiuri and Asahi Newspapers. Using a simple but effective vocabulary, the psychiatrist maintained that mental illness would have to be cured in order to avoid further victims of suicide. He firstly explained to the Japanese readership what the new discipline of psychiatry was, how professional psychiatrists were trained, what they did in clinics and mental institutions, and what kind of treatments they deployed. Then he reformulated the scientific narrative on problematic diseases into a lay version using unpretentious language and self-explanatory metaphors. For instance, Kure described the propensity to mental illness, a precursory symptom of suicide, as the outcome of an extensive and prolonged "nervous consumption" [*shinkei no shohi*], "material fatigue" [*hirō busshitsu*], and contextual pressure. He wrote, for instance, "The civilizing progress changed social conditions and made life competitive, as it is for those students who have to face exams too often."[26] In addition to the creative use of metaphors, Kure was inclined to organize knowledge within a limited number of categories. In a series of 20 articles published in the Yomiuri Newspaper in 1906 on the causes of mental illness, Kure divided the reasons for mental imbalance into two groups: physical, such as menstruation or menopause for women and alcoholism for men; and non-physical, such as a sense of anxiety and restlessness caused by modern society.[27] Kure's explanation was benevolent and demonstrated confidence that he would be able to help patients recover their underlying sanity. Furthermore, the blurring of the definition of insanity gave greater authority to physicians like him to identify a greater number of potential patients within the realm of psychiatry.

The reformulation and recontextualization of psychiatric language aimed at expanding medical practice within the realm of everyday life, and served as a rhetorical device to break down competing popular narratives. However, the actual psychiatric contribution – that is, the creation and dissemination of knowledge – continued to work at the academic level through activities in teaching, research, and knowledge transfer. In 1902, Kure inaugurated the first medical journal devoted to psychiatry, *Shinkeigaku Zasshi*, together with Miura Kinnosuke, professor of internal medicine at Tokyo Imperial University. Numerous essays on suicide, including mother/child suicide, were published in this journal in the following years. Kure's eminent reputation within academia (he became successor to Sakaki Hajime and professor of the Department of Psychiatry of the Tokyo Imperial University between 1901 and 1925), his leading role in the public debate on the establishment of asylums, and his productive activity in academic and public journals amplified the resonance of his theories and even bestowed on him the name of 'father of psychiatry' [*Nihon no seishin igaku no kusawake*].

Kure's work marked the birth of a new psychiatric theory on suicide in Japan. By biologizing and pathologizing voluntary death, Kure's was the first crucial enterprise undertaken by the Japanese medical community in the twentieth century that aimed at modernizing suicide. He pressured the government to take a more responsible attitude toward mental health and tried to standardize the clinical assessment of suicide, thereby intrinsically marginalizing contextual factors such as cultural and historical issues. However, while the magnitude of his biological theories resonated even outside of the medical field, a deeply rooted popular discourse on suicide was confronting psychiatry's early foundations. Journalists and literati were revivifying premodern images of romantic and noble suicides, challenging and contaminating the biological language on voluntary death. By doing so, though, they unintentionally encouraged the medical community to push suicide pathologization further.

A symptom: the consolidation of the cultural narrative

As the Meiji government aggressively colonized health and hygiene, the state-authorized medical orthodoxy began to trigger folk resistance. The more medicine became scientific, the more the popular discourse contested it. As a result of the increasing tendency to identify a patient with the neurobiology of his or her brain, and the medical community's willingness to overlook the patient's subjectivity, at the beginning of the twentieth century a long-standing popular narrative in defense of individual sovereignty and in support of suicide as a free and romantic choice intensified.

For centuries, Japanese legend, literature, and drama had portrayed suicide in a positive and romantic light, and enshrouded it in a passionate and glamorous aura. Suicide was described as an act of dedication and commitment, related to a deep sense of responsibility or profound love, and thus deserving of social appreciation. In other words, voluntary death was not condemned as an act of escapism or cowardliness; it was rather glorified according to a peculiar aesthetics of death.

Newly emerging societal factors and institutions also reinforced the intensification of this customary romantic narrative of voluntary death. The increasing number of statistical reports on suicide, the establishment of the journalistic industry and of newspapers as an arena of public opinion, and the remarkable role of intellectuals within the emergent mass media amplified the resonance of the discussion on voluntary death in the public sphere. This discussion concentrated predominantly on three themes: first, the consolidation of the notion of suicide as a romantic act; second, the identification of suicide as a unique feature of the Japanese; and third, a view of suicide as a reflection of modernity, and thus a *symptom* of the contemporary cultural transition.

The growing awareness of suicide as a 'problem' was undoubtedly enabled not only by the introduction of Western theories, but also by the increasing number of statistical reports on the phenomenon. Under the aegis of the empirical approach being developed for the study of suicide in the West, the interest in suicide had increasingly taken a statistical bent in Japan as well. Despite often questionable methodological categorization, the Meiji government began to systematically collect suicide data in 1899.[28] According to official statistics, Japan experienced its first peak in the documented suicide rate immediately before and during the first year of the Russo-Japanese War. In 1903 and 1904, the suicide rate was on average 19.4 per 100,000 people.[29] Comparative analyses with Western countries, which situated Japan among industrialized nations, distinctly demonstrated that Japan's suicide rate was fairly high. These statistical data indicating an elevated suicide rate propelled numerous reports informing the public about urban misery, working conditions, delinquent children, the plight of prostitutes, and so forth. The 'suicide as a problem' perspective opened up a space for public discussion on the phenomenon. For example, middle-class intellectuals began to engage in lengthy informative writings on hygiene education, and psychiatrists began to popularize their discipline by writing in popular magazines and featuring health advice. It was precisely during these years that the psychiatric movement gathered momentum because of the concern over the 'new' phenomenon of an increase in the suicide rate.

The press was the country's loudest arena for the discussion of the suicide phenomenon: it both popularized and sensationalized suicide, and catalyzed the attention of scholars and men of culture.[30] The turn of the century saw the rapid establishment of a newspaper industry that, thanks to progress in printing technology, quickly made newspapers a staple of everyday life. Presses, which since the late eighteenth century had shifted their focus to news-centered journalism, played a central role in making the discussion of suicide public. Newspapers were the platform in which worrisome statistics were reported, and they also became the platform where the romanticism of voluntary death and nostalgia for 'traditional patterns of suicide' were overtly voiced. For example, the Ministry of Home Affairs [*Naimushō*] hypothesized that two-thirds of the suicides committed in Japan in 1905 were caused by mental illness, whereas one-third were caused by economic difficulties (unemployment, illness or incapacity to work, bankruptcy, etc.). As a result, the ministry contemplated the possibility of increasing the number of psychiatric institutions within the country.[31] Reporters and men of culture reacted by arguing that the emerging asylums were aseptic and alienating loci of retreat from a larger society. They instead insisted on the exploration of suicide as a collective phenomenon, and as the expression of a 'cultural' feature.[32] Journalists reaffirmed the beauty and the nobility of suicide committed in an unpolluted and uncorrupted past, and glorified in particular two patterns inherited from the Tokugawa period: the ascetic, warrior-centered pattern – which will be explored in the following chapter – and the romantic one. Newspapers ran endless reportorial accounts of the suicides of heartbroken lovers and brave men fulfilling social functions such as complimenting a host, expressing gratitude, bidding farewell, or redeeming a serious offense that had shamed someone. In a disquisition on the renowned attraction of Meiji poets and novelists toward *jōshi* [love suicide], an anonymous writer stated, "Stars are in the sky, flowers are on the soil, and love is in human beings. Is there anything more beautiful than this? When it is accomplished for noble reasons, such as true love, death as well becomes fascinating. [. . .] Among all kind of deaths, *jōshi* is the death that most resembles a recuperation of life. It puts an end to a miserable existence and makes death joyful and beautiful."[33] This idea of the beauty of voluntary death, along with the notion of the act of reappropriation of the individual's subjectivity, lay at the very core of the public discussion of suicide.

It was not just in providing a channel of communication, however, that newspapers spurred a sense of nostalgia for the proclaimed 'traditional patterns of suicide.' The language itself employed by presses in talking about suicide was often enriched by symbolic formulas and conventional rhetoric, by emotions and melancholic reminiscences. Such linguistic 'attachment' to the traditional metanarrative and its terminology was justified by a strategy of rationalization: given patterns of suicide were described as appealing to the legality of enacted rules and the sanctity of immemorial customs. Claims were embedded in stories that recounted the past and regenerated the present as part of a timeless and cherished tradition. Examples included accounts romantically narrated as pure cases of unforgettable beauty, or tales of lovers honorably destroying their irksome relationships. The narration of one young girl's suicide, for instance, reached its apex of exquisiteness when she "bound her extremities to her partner's hands and feet. She then let death embrace her, tied up to Kintarō for eternity."[34] Another young woman's suicide was exaltedly portrayed by describing her "shining, ebony black, loose hair at her last final breath."[35] The beauty of suicide could even rehabilitate allegedly irrational actions. In one case, two high school girls from Kyoto left a long suicide note that stated that life was difficult to deal with at their age; a reporter concluded that the reason for the act was ridiculous, but he absolved it romantically, stating that "the two girls will not be separated for eternity."[36] Such a romantic account evoked a close bond between the two students, and the emotional advocacy, *pathos*, and sentimental appeal of the narration triggered collective sympathy for the victims. In the popular 'Shinagawa case' [*Shinagawa jōken*] of 1903, suicide motives too were reinterpreted and enshrouded in a romantic aura.[37] Despite the fact that seven letters proved that the man involved had managed to convince his lover to commit suicide with him because of the economic hardship they were enduring, the reporter sentimentalized their joint suicide, concluding, "It is always respectable to embrace death for love."[38] This improper speculation on the romanticism at the heart of the couple's suicide was embedded in a historically negotiated construction: if the very same suicide case had occurred in the 1990s on the wave of the Bubble Economy, it would likely have been interpreted as a suicide for economic reasons. However, at the beginning of the twentieth century, suicide was glorified by reporters as a romantic act, both in its details and in its perceived or proclaimed *purity* of motivations.

A resistance against the march of modernity was implicitly embedded within journalists' glamorization of proclaimed 'traditional' norms and practices of suicide. Their evocative portrayal, however, did not always explicitly contest psychiatrists' conceptualization of suicide as a disease – that is, as a biological event characterized by a set of symptoms – that needed to be managed, controlled, and regulated. Rather, journalists and the intelligentsia disregarded this biological notion of suicide. When commenting on the suicide of a 17-year-old girl who was warned by her mother not to marry a man far out of her social league, the reporter glamorized her act, stating, "When the passion of a 17-year-old girl, fresh as a blossoming flower, was rationalized by her mother, it faded like petals from a tree. This is why the young lady committed such an act: because of a grudge [*enkon*]."[39] The use of the flower metaphor to signify unpolluted love was contrasted with the adults' rationalization of feelings. It stood for the consequences endured by Japanese society as the emerging process of the pathologization of suicide threatened to obliterate the romantic aura of the act. By redeeming the purity of motives through sensational accounts, the press contributed considerably to reaffirming immortal premodern suicide paradigms.

Thus, as modernity encroached on Japan, journalists mobilized a historicized narrative on voluntary death by evoking old suicide cases, and propagated a sense of nostalgia for an uncontaminated past. By reasserting the romanticism of premodern suicide aesthetics and of ascribed motivations, they were inherently conceptualizing voluntary death as the repository of an 'imagined' historical continuity that could appease the anxiety of this destabilizing moment. Suicides were subsumed within old paradigms, aiming to 'normalize' and 'naturalize' a new Japanese universality. The notion that there was a Japanese proclivity toward suicide, the co-opting of traditional linguistic terminology, and the reassertion of suicide as an age-old social expression were all elements that discounted, and even inherently undermined, the narrativization of suicide by the new biological language and new medical patterns.

This romantic narrative of suicide increasingly took a cultural bent. The importance of culture in determining suicide as a behavior was publicly discussed, and the capacity to find great beauty, passion, and nobility in the act was vigorously glorified as a peculiarly Japanese trait. One such example was the notorious case of the actress and singer Matsui Sumako. Sumako had already been divorced twice when she fell in love with the *shingeki* director Hogetsu Shimamura. Two months after he died, on January 5, 1919, she hanged herself. Although in general she was publicly portrayed as a despicable female model, the *Asahi Shinbun* commented, "Sumako is the Japanese image of a typical passionate woman."[40] A series of newspaper reports and articles by intellectuals covered every aspect of the eccentric artist's life, romanticizing 'exaggerated Japanese passion' and the Japanese propensity to love profoundly. Sumako's distinctive ardor was viewed as a sentiment unique to the Japanese. Her suicide also inspired many movie directors, who produced films on this 'unique act' until the late 1980s. As pointed out by Fukushima Shirō, a professor of family law, a few days after Sumako's suicide, the case strongly attracted readers because "while [Sumako] embraced the difficulties of social morality, she glorified the beauty of human feelings and compassion. Her act did not stand uniquely as an example of individual thought, but as a social example too. She unified social ethics with individual sincerity."[41] In other words, Sumako's death was glorified not simply because she was a passionate woman, but because she was a passionate *Japanese* woman. Another suicide case highly romanticized and sensationalized by the media was the so-called Chiba *shinjū* [double suicide at Chiba] that occurred on March 6, 1917. In this case, Yoshikawa Kamako and her lover threw themselves in front of an express train in Chiba station. Both were seriously injured, but whereas Kamako was hospitalized and survived the incident, her lover, Kuramochi Rokusuke, was convinced that the love of his life had died, and he killed himself with a short *katana*. The incident revealed an adulterous relationship: Kamako, the fourth daughter of bureaucrat, statesman, and cabinet minister Yoshikawa Akimasu, was married to Sone Arasuke, adopted by her father as a younger son, while the lover Kuramochi was her chauffeur. Because of this, the minister Yoshikawa was forced to resign his positions and retire from public life, and Kamako was officially divorced, expelled, and disinherited from the Yoshikawa house. Interestingly enough, this case of scandalous adultery brought not only vehement condemnation by Yoshikawa's peers, but also passionate absolution by the press. Kamako's love for an outcast was labeled as a "liberal love" [*jiyūshugi ren'ai*] and she was represented within national newspapers as an independent woman who exposed herself to public shame by living life in its fullness rather than according to knighthood's canons. The romanticized narration of her love affair and the attempted suicide not only aimed at glorifying the brave attitude of the Japanese in defying social rules when inspired by an uncontrollable passion. It also became the vehicle of a larger discourse that humanized the medical, and that philosophically and emotionally mediated the rampant popularization of scientific language.[42]

Remarkable were the pseudo-scientific reports that sought to explain the cultural matrix of romantic suicides. A small, educated elite that included writers, translators, officials, and civil servants was concerned about the rapid increase in suicide cases recorded soon after the Russo-Japanese War. Ōmichi Waichi, for instance, compiled a study on double suicides committed between 1909 and 1911. Ōmichi examined 501 cases, firstly framing them within a long-standing tradition that extended from samurai ritual acts to Chikamatsu Monzaemon's masterpiece *Sonezaki Shinjū* [Double Suicide at Sonezaki]; secondly he explored 29 cases of double suicide (interestingly enough, none was a male-male suicide), deploying a somewhat questionable observational analysis. Overlooking the economic and social motivations that might stand behind an act of suicide, the journalist advocated that indigenous cultural values (such as freedom, suicide as an act of free will and of social rehabilitation, etc.) made voluntary death in Japan "traditional," "ethical," and "historical."[43] In fact, according to Ōmichi, the highly romanticized pattern of *jōshi* was performed within the entire nation because all people [*kokumin*] shared the same cultural values. In his reports, Ōmichi appeared as a patriotic propagandist for a cultural discourse. His stories dramatized issues of national character and surely attracted nationalistic readers.

The same cultural logic was profoundly embodied in the suicides of famous literati as well, including Kawakita Bizan, Arishima Takeo, Akutagawa Ryūnosuke, and Makino Shin'ichi. The voluntary deaths of members of the literati symbolized Japanese romantic uniqueness and the sense of displacement of a society overwhelmed by Western values. Being one of the Japanese literati did not mean being a *déraciné* or lacking social functionality; on the contrary, it meant being romantic, passionate, and visionary. In Europe, early medical studies had highlighted the increased likelihood of suicide for literati who were mentally ill. Researches concluded that psychosis and other forms of mental disturbances were actually associated with creative work (the nowadays well-known Sylvia Plath effect) and were the price paid for creativity.[44] Despite a lack of statistical support, Japanese intellectuals claimed that Japan had the highest suicide rate for novelists and intellectuals in general, crystallizing the inexact notion of 'uniqueness' and enshrouding it in a romantic aura.[45] One might wonder why, despite the elaboration of universal theories already in motion, in Japan the link seemed to take a nationalistic turn.

Such an inaccurate portrayal of the Japanese intelligentsia was also enabled by the idea that literati were the ones most exposed to Western influences; their suicides were seen as a reaction to stimuli such as industrialization, urbanization, and modernization in general. As argued by Kōsaka Masaaki, an established philosopher of the School of Kyoto, literati "were sinless. Society was sinful." Kōsaku maintained that Japanese intellectuals experienced *in primis* the overwhelming cultural changes occurring on the eve of the twentieth century; further, he collectively dubbed them "Hamlet," after the way in which their combination of narcissism and empathy for a rapidly evolving society resulted in the suicides of many.[46] In a distinguished column about society for the Yomiuri Newspaper, a reporter commented on Arishima Takeo's suicide in 1923. Takeo had hanged himself in his villa in Karuizawa along with his lover. The reporter firstly premised that voluntary death is the logical and respectful way in which a man should face the end of his life. Then, despite acknowledging suicide as the individual's choice, the journalist reproached Arishima because he "spent his whole life staring at himself, and he did not avert his eyes from himself even in death, when he committed double suicide with his lover." He eventually concluded that the individualism and the narcissism Arishima had demonstrated in his life, in his profession, and even in his death were artifacts of his long exposure to Western influences. In other words, what was despicable in Arishima was the attitude he absorbed from European culture. Similarly, Fukushima Shirō morally condemned Arishima for being egotistical and irresponsible toward his children; nonetheless, he redeemed the novelist for "having glorified his life through death."[47]

Contrary to psychiatrists' conviction that suicide was a disease, the popular discourse asserted that voluntary death was instead a symptom of the new era. This discourse mourned the loss of communal spirit, reciprocity, and altruism. Journalists and intellectuals perceived suicide as the indicator of a chronic and debilitating phenomenon caused by modernity and Western individualism. The literary critic Takayama Rinjirō bluntly demonized Japan's Westernization, arguing that individualistic developmentalism [*kojinsei hattenshugi*], "an unprecedented feature for the Japanese," was the major cause of suicide.[48] The translator Hasegawa Tenkei reiterated Takayama's argument, criticizing the serious social changes caused by Westernization, but absolving the act of suicide, calling it "fascinating" [*miryokuteki*].[49] Similarly, the intellectual Ōtsuka Sokō condemned suicide (which he said should be called "self homicide") as an individualistic act (subtly suggesting that it was a value 'adopted' from the West) that should be illegal. The act was, according to Ōtsuka, anti-utilitarian, because the person who commits it has received much from society but has not returned anything.[50] In other words, modernists too started to problematize modernity, questioning its sociocultural costs, which they saw becoming visible in social alienation and a high number of suicides. Intellectuals envisioned suicide as the most direct outcome of the breakdown of social bonds and family values, and of the sense of disempowerment and dissatisfaction that came with Westernization. Suicide thus was interpreted as the cost paid for social dislocation and was portrayed as an emblematic image of the consequences of the ideologies of progress.

The meaning of suicide as a symptom of a society witnessing the vanishing of long-established values was widely explored in fictional production too. Suicide epitomized the image of the disease of a civilization absolutely ineffectual against sweeping social changes. It also epitomized the consequences of a myopic pursuit of European models. Some noteworthy novels of the early twentieth century, such as *Abe Ichizoku* [The Abe Family, 1913] by Ōgai Mori, and *Kokoro* (1914) by Natsume Sōseki, published soon after Nogi Maresuke's anachronistic suicide, told stories of the search for symbolizing continuities that could be traced back to premodern suicide patterns. Other novels romanticized suicide as the individual resolution to a widespread sense of social displacement caused by the new era. *Doku to Yaku* [Poison and Medicine, 1918], by Katai Tayama, was a sort of autobiographical confession of the antithetical attraction toward life and death that culminated in reconciling the two: poison with which to commit suicide was the cure for a miserable life. Other literary works envisioned suicide as an act of reconciliation with the past. The characters of Nagai Kafū's *Sumidagawa* [The River Sumida, 1911], for instance, personified two cultural spheres: the marginalized Edo culture, and the modernized Meiji one. In this work, it was the character who symbolized 'tradition' who – overwhelmed by social malaise and decadent human conditions – commits suicide. In the psychological novel *Minage Kyūjogyō* [The Suicides' Rescuer, 1916], Kikuchi Kan elegantly portrayed an old woman saving potential suicides who were ready to jump into canals in Kyoto. Thus, as the country marched toward the future, fiction revealed the impact of modernization on social roles and cultural values and mirrored a visceral need to reconnect with the premodern period. It pictured suicide not only as an act of authority and independence performed by the individual that aimed at placating his own anxiety, but also as an anchor that could reconcile the community with the past.

Whereas academic psychiatry's writings embraced a biological language in the early twentieth century, and sought to define, debate, and persuade others of the relevance of acknowledging suicide as a pathology, popular literature reenacted archetypal images of romantic and noble suicides. Japanese writers had engaged with questioning the validity of the pursuit of Western models since early in the Meiji period.[51] By portraying suicide as a dysfunctional product of civilization, their works inherently turned the discourse on mental disturbance in general, and voluntary death in particular, into a social critique. The revivification of narratives of premodern patterns of voluntary death was very much embedded in other discourses about nostalgia for pre-Westernized Japan and about historical continuity. Ancient portrayals of suicide heroes and heroines replete in Tokugawa sources gained new momentum, and their renaissance in modern contexts can explain the force driving particular habits of representing beauty, aesthetics, and proclaimed 'Japanese values.' Deeply rooted in the popular discourse, such notions of suicide did not make the process of psychiatric popularization any easier. Latent traces of the popular images of suicide slowly but gradually permeated the academic literature, contaminating the biological language. The clash that occurred between the two separate discourses in the early twentieth century would eventually translate in the 1930s into an overlap between the medical and popular narratives.

A crime: the Fujimura case

The public attentiveness to the decline in health and vitality in Japanese society opened up a space for a long-standing dialectic between the medical view of suicide and the romantic cultural discourse. An open debate fired up in May 1903, when Fujimura Misao, an enthusiastic 18-year-old student of philosophy at Dai-ichi High School in Tokyo, jumped from the top of Kegon Falls in Nikkō. Before committing suicide, he carved on a tree trunk a farewell poem infused with references to Shakespeare's Hamlet and to the Latin poet Horace.[52] Fujimura's death was overwhelmingly portrayed by the media[53] as a philosophical suicide [*tetsugakutekina jisatstu*], and newspapers asserted that it deserved the same respect as a samurai's *harakiri*.[54] Miyatake Kameshirō, founder of the newspaper *Yorozu Chōhō*, writing under the pseudonym Miyatake Gaikotsu, defined Fujimura's suicide as a "historical accident" [*rekishitekina jiken*], an act that garnered "respect for the freedom of the individual who unified simultaneously singularity and universality." He further glorified the young man's act as the gesture of a free individual [*jiko no jiyū*], commenting, "In my country there are no philosophers, but in this young man I saw one. Or better, there might have been some philosophers, but no one ever challenged death for the sake of philosophy."[55]

Fujimura immediately became a national celebrity and the waterfall a popular destination, particularly attracting young people who attempted to follow his model. Between 1903 and 1907, the spot witnessed about 40 suicides and 140 attempted ones, and over the next twenty years, several cases were still identified as imitative of Fujimura's philosophical rejection of life. Yamana Shōtarō, a journalist for the *Asahi Shinbun* from 1911 onward and someone who wrote extensively on suicide and euthanasia, noted that Fujimura's case not only triggered copycat suicides but also led to increasing interest in philosophical essays and treaties, as well as foreign countries and customs. In particular, Yamana opined that Fujimura's death was the direct cause of the exponential increase in sales of the 1904 essay *Ten'ninrom* [A Discourse on the Universe and Human Beings] by the journalist Kuroiwa Shuroku.[56] The essay advocates that there is a 'soul' [*reikon*] in every being of the universe, and all souls form a 'great spirit' [*tairei*]. Death, in this view, is thus not the beginning of the inexistence of the individual, but rather the continuation of one's being, with one's spirit and memories stored in the universe's greater soul.

A few months after Fujimura's suicide, the novelist and Waseda professor Tsubouchi Shōyō wrote a long reflection on suicide in the journal *Taiyō*, in which he inaugurated the so-called theory of support for voluntary death [*yōgoron*].[57] Tsubouchi defined Fujimura's suicide as an avenue of freedom for those newly contending with the impossible demands of modernity: "suicide is the outcome of the progress of human intellect, as well as a form of conservative self-defense. In other words, [suicide] is the peculiar creation of a civilized world."[58] Thus, he saw modernity as causing internal conflicts. He further argued: "suicide does not necessarily harm others; it rather brings relief to others. Seen in these terms, it is evident that *bushidō* precepts have not dissipated in my country. [. . .] However, we must shed some light on those suicides that are not justified and are perceived as dishonest, irrational and insincere."[59] Tsubouchi's *yōgoron* epitomized the cultural discourse that confronted the medicalization of suicide as detrimental to the indigenous culture. He mourned the 'eradication of history' by Western science, and invoked the cultural and ethical foundations of Japanese identity by romanticizing Fujimura's suicide. Tsubouchi advocated that the completion of his final act of free will was noble in that it eased the individual's burden on society and evoked a samurai's *bushidō*; he also urged academia to more thoroughly explore the reasons behind the act, including its psychological and social meanings. In a sense, Tsubouchi rebelled against medical science, which discriminated against or excluded those found biologically abnormal or defective; thus, he refrained from accepting biology as fate and reassessed the high degree of subjectification of an individual's actions.

Similarly, the intellectual Fujihara Sei sharply criticized the medical community's attitude toward suicide, raising the question, "Why do scholars reckon that suicide is unacceptable? [. . .] And why are some suicides considered unethical or immoral?" Fujihara hypothesized that the reason behind such an attitude was what he called *gimuron* [theory of duty]. According to him, people perceive their lives as a sequence of duties toward family, partners, and ultimately society. Consequently, societies are inclined to misjudge anyone who contests or retreats from such a utilitarian system and opts for a less functional path. In defense of Fujimura's act of free will, Fujihara stated that for a society, death is sometimes more beneficial than life: "[S]uicide should not be rejected as an awful sin; suicide resembles a virtuous action [*dōtoku kōi*] and an admirable and noble act." He further added, "suicide is often despised as being committed by a person with a feeble will and frail capacity to act [*hakushi jakkō*]. However, we should not overvalue duty over death; and we should not be scared of death."[60] With this, Fujihara implicitly condemned psychiatrists for treating suicide victims solely according to the paradigms of biology and the *gimuron*, aiming in their treatment at reconstituting functional members of a society. In doing so, physicians were neglecting the true significance of suicide. At times voluntary death might be more functional than life for the collectivity, while at other times it was exclusively a beautiful performance, empty of any social function.

The medical community's response was prompt and trenchant.

In 1906, Katayama Kuniyoshi, authority in forensic medicine and a former acting chair of psychiatry at the Imperial University of Tokyo, stated that suicidal individuals were "dispersing poison in society" and that the nation must "strengthen its body and mind so that it can eliminate such pathological molecules [*byōteki saibō no jikō hakai*]."[61] In the same year, at a gathering of psychiatrists, Ōkuma Shigenobu, a highly influential statesman and a central figure in the hygiene movement, reasserted the validity of Kure's interpretation of the act. Kure had assessed Fujimura's case as the act of a young student affected by mental disease, a pathological condition threatening the entire nation, which strictly required close medical attention. Ōkuma proclaimed, "Students talk about philosophy of life. [. . . But someone who] jumps off a waterfall or throws himself in front of a train is weak-minded. [. . .] Weak-minded people would merely cause harm if they remain alive."[62]

Ōkuma's assessment of the degenerative nature of suicide was pushed further a few years later by Sawada Junjirō and Mita Sadanori, who, eager to catch up with the march of science, tinged biopsychiatry with eugenics, a movement emerging in the West.[63] Sawada and Mita, encouraged by this new science, moved away from the notion of suicide as pathology, and labeled Fujimura's act a *crime*.

Medical doctor and intellectual Sawada argued, "There are no motives other than the disposition and the character behind a suicide," and thus it was a person's genetic character that contributed to his or her disposition to suicide and crime.[64] Sawada drew an identikit of the suicidal person/criminal as a person who suffered physically from migraines, frequent epistaxis, and stomach disorders, or mentally from chronic manic-depressive disease, anxiety, neurasthenia, and androgyny [*chūkansei*]. He also noted that cases of both suicide and crime were observable within the same families, along with cases of epilepsy, dementia, and alcoholism. Referring to Fujimura, he added that a person who suffered from brain abnormalities would easily feel angry, jealous, and desperate, and would tend to act irrationally. In other words, Sawada pushed Kure's description of Fujimura as a patient suffering from brain abnormalities to one in which he was a potential criminal.

Mita Sadanori, a professor of forensic medicine, was the first to scientifically apply Kure's theoretical apparatus; by concentrating on bedside observation, he aimed to provide standardized examination techniques. However, what began as a promising attempt to prove the biological and genetic roots of suicide ended in the specter of degeneration and criminalization. Essentially, Mita combined the anatomical-pathological model he had formulated during his studies in Germany with the discourse of degeneration and eugenics, creating an original framework to diagnose and 'treat' suicidal tendencies. The concept of degeneration was picked up by Japanese eugenicists and social hygienists to support the argument that society and culture were doomed unless action was taken to control threatening medical phenomena. By associating the term 'degeneration' with suicide, Mita asserted that mental illness caused a progressive decline within families and the population, and that medical care was needed to avoid further decline.

Between 1893 and 1912, Mita examined the corpses of 443 males and 152 females who had committed suicide, in a study widely cited by later psychiatrists. Mita found that 81 percent of males and 29 percent of females showed signs of pathological or abnormal constitutions, and that 48 percent of females were menstruating or pregnant when they committed suicide. In 1915, he concluded that the deviations that led to voluntary death were located most typically in the central nervous system for men and in the reproductive system for women. Based on these findings, Mita claimed that a pathological constitution, whether neurological or gynecological, was an underlying cause of suicide.

Considering these pathological constitutions to be inherited, Mita backed Kure's theory of suicide as a genetic disease, and drew the conclusion that eugenics was the solution: "[Like] criminals, those who committed suicide were losers in the struggle for survival or natural selection. The ideal means for the prevention of suicide is to keep such persons from being born."[65] Like many leading geneticists of the time, he supported the practice of neutering 'mentally defective' individuals to relieve the public of the cost of caring for future generations of the mentally ill. In this way, Mita represented that generation of enthusiastic medical professionals who adopted and promoted the science of eugenics along with their political leaders. The newly established psychiatric community's alignment with the political authority over the eugenics movement revealed a general obsession with modern reforms, and a desire to align their policies with those of their European peers.

With the Fujimura case, which catalyzed extensive attention within different fields and triggered a vivid debate between intellectuals and the medical community, Japanese psychiatry witnessed another pivotal achievement in the process of the making of modern suicide: suicide became associated with crime. This association developed firstly because of the acceptance of eugenic science, and secondly because psychological and social interpretations had not yet been included in the diagnostic picture. Despite resilient cultural resistance, Fujimura's case was framed within the province of *transgression*, the degenerative and criminal bent propounded in Sawada and Mita's conceptualization of suicide, through which human capacity was reduced by the constraints of abnormal or defective biological inheritance. Thus the authoritative role – as well as the romantic voice – of the individual who voluntarily chooses death was silenced.

A biocultural phenomenon: the convergence of disciplines[66]

The debate over Fujimura's case fired up again in 1921 when Sugita Naoki, a psychiatrist specializing in adolescent sexual disorders, commenting on Fujimura and the young men who imitated his suicide, wrote that "youthful philosophical agony over the purpose of life and the future of the universe results from abnormal congestion in the brain."[67] By denying legitimacy to any potential philosophical motives, Sugita trivialized both the deeds and the concerns of the youths in question, rejected any potential agency in their acts, and dismissed the idea of a possible suicide epidemic.

Sugita's remark was not oblique, and it provoked angry rebuttals that led to an animated debate that lasted a year. The debate moved from the specialized medical journal *Ikai Jihō*, which had hosted Sugita's original comments, to the popular journal *Fujin Kōron*. Undoubtedly referring to the copycat phenomenon surrounding Fujimura's suicide, the physicist and essayist Terada Torahiko defended individual suicides as a form of self-assertion: by exercising control over the time and means of their death, "the young show their weakest and their strongest side."[68] Hinting at Fujimura's case, Hasegawa Nyozekan – social critic and journalist, pro-liberalist and active democrat – further added that self-killing showed strong will [*ishi*] and rationality [*gōrisei*]. However, if the psychological side were omitted from the investigation of voluntary death, suicide would result in an incomprehensible act, entirely dominated by biological rules. Hasegawa openly criticized the medical community for demonizing self-killing as unhealthy [*fukenkō*] and rebellious [*hankōteki*].[69] The debate continued three years later in 1924 when legal doctor Tanaka Kōgai claimed that despite the complex moral and ethical issues involved in suicide, "life belongs to the individual," and therefore Fujimura's act was totally legitimate and correct.[70] Yamana Shōtarō defended Fujimura, polemicizing, "[Our society perceives the one] who subjectively wants to die as worse than one who thinks he has to die; he who dies of illness is less deplorable than he who dies of suicide; he who kills himself in older age is more forgivable than he who kills himself in youth."[71] In contrast, Hoashi Riichirō, professor of philosophy at Waseda University, wrote that no suicide pattern (referring to Fujimura's philosophical suicide) can be poetically aestheticized or ethically justified. According to Hoashi, all suicides are a sheer expression of pusillanimity and the reluctance to take responsibility toward society and oneself.[72] The psychiatrist Sugie Kaoru, employed by the Metropolitan Police at the time, warned that the leap in the suicide rate was doomed to rise due to newly adopted modern lifestyles that worsened the conditions of those who suffered from physiological imbalances and abnormalities. He invited forensic pathologists to delve deeply into the contemporary European medical literature on suicide to grasp scientific means for diagnosis and treatment of the phenomenon.[73]

The response to Sugita's remark was thus heterogeneous. Whereas journalists and literati portrayed Fujimura's suicide in a romantic light or showed compassion, medical professionals tended to pathologize and ethically demonize it. Why was the debate so heated eighteen years after this particular suicide? Interestingly, Sugie's analysis hinted at two reasons. First, the suicide rate had been constantly high since 1913 (at a rate of 20.2 per 100,000 people in 1913, and 20.0 in 1921 when the debate fired up again), and since 1917 the media had given much attention to the alarming leap, leading readers to consider the phenomenon in ecological terms.[74] Second, Sugie suggested that the debate might have been reignited because sociological and psychological discourses were gaining strength vis-à-vis the pathological models suggested by Sugita and others. While Sugie did not discount the role of brain abnormalities in suicidal individuals, he considered psychological and sociological factors pivotal to a full understanding of Fujimura's death. Psychiatry and its descriptive approach had restricted the possibilities for a richer understanding of suicide beyond biological explanations, but new circumstances were calling for the integration of socio-psychological interpretations. It was in the early 1930s that a gradual sociological and psychological contamination of psychiatry led to the genesis of a biocultural narrative on suicide.

As early as 1907, a reporter for *Kyōto Nisshutsu Shinbun*, Ōmichi Kazuichi, had addressed a plea to academics to explore the sociology of suicide. However, because of popular prejudice that associated sociology with socialism and because of Japanese academic sociologists' inability to do more than simply 'import' modern Western sociological theories, sociology did not acquire influential status within Japanese academia and did not show a significant impact on the clinical assessment of suicide. Only in the late 1920s did it encounter a brief moment of popularity.[75] Thanks to the strong and enthusiastic influence of the so-called sociological positivism [*sekkyokushugi*][76] that emerged in the US soon after the Wall Street crisis and brought attention to the social effects caused by a sense of displacement, discomfort, and economic hardship, a first generation of Japanese sociologists led by Matsumoto Junichirō and Tanabe Suketoshi engaged in the understanding and acceptance of Western sociological scholarship. In particular, they actively introduced Durkheim's body of work to Japan. *Le Suicide* was translated relatively early on for the Japanese public by Suzuki Munetada and Tobisawa Ken'ichi in May 1932.[77] Later that year, Tanabe founded the journal of sociological studies *Shakaigaku*, in which he extensively explored the solidity of Durkheim's theories.[78] Although there is no evidence of a Durkheimian theoretical base or of the use of the Durkheimian paradigms – such as individualistic, altruistic, anomic, and fatalistic suicide – in the literature published before the end of World War II, Durkheim's sociological explanation of suicide showed a certain ascendancy among literati and men of culture, and among some psychiatrists such as Sugie. From the late 1920s onward, slowly but increasingly, factors like industrialization, urbanization, and Westernization were defined by Japanese newspaper reports and specialized medical journals as sweeping changes in the social fabric that were influencing behaviors. Suicide was perceived as a social pathology, a by-product of the tumultuous transformations that had produced profound and pervasive losses on multiple fronts: cultural, social, personal, spiritual, and material.

By the early 1920s, psychology too reached the apex of its unimpressive prewar historical narrative with the establishment of Morita therapy and the success of the Uchida-Kraepelin psycho-diagnostic test, both of which had proven to have a certain amount of influence on psychiatrists.[79] Some of the most popular Freudian concepts had been introduced into Japan between 1912 and 1918 by the psychologists Kimura Kyūichi and Otsuki Kaison in the academic journal *Shinri Kenkyū* [Psychological Research]. Comprehensive examination of Freud's work and of his method of psychological interpretation appeared in the 1917 *Seishin bunsekihō* by Kubo Yoshihide, and in the 1918 *Shinrigaku yōryō* by Ueno Yōichi. In the same years, the psychiatrist Morooka Son sought to fight the myopic view of psychoanalysis as strictly medical therapy for the treatment of neurosis and encouraged its reception as a theoretically valuable method of analysis per se. Academic interests in psychology came first, followed by clinical interests. Even so, psychology was still looked on with suspicion. The first efforts to popularize psychological theories occurred in the early 1920s, when the new discipline was in the throes of proposing a more 'customized' and less universal interpretation of Japanese life in its cultural and social aspects. Once again, intellectuals played a significant role in popularizing psychological texts and translating them into lay versions for an inexpert public. Intending to minimize the process of erasure exerted by modernization upon 'Japanese peculiarities,' the literati encouraged the inclusion of a psychological inquisition exploring the phenomenon of suicide. The interest they demonstrated in a more holistic approach to exploring voluntary death was, as Okonogi Keigo hypothesized, because "they were the ones dealing with their own neurasthenia and anxiety." In other words, the literati were reading Freud and other texts arriving from the West for their own sake.

Not satisfied with the commonly accepted argument that reduced suicide to a physical pathology, psychologists had departed from the dictum of Esquirol to pursue an alternative framework to understanding the suicide phenomenon. Clinical psychologists such as Marui Kiyoyasu, Kosawa Heisaku, and Ōtsuki Kinji insisted that many cases of suicide lay in the gray area between the normal and the abnormal. Therefore, in order to unveil the act's complexity, potential victims would have to be psychoanalyzed deploying Freudian techniques. Other clinical psychologists, such as Matsuhara Saburō, Ishida Noboru, and Mori Michitomo, deeply inspired by Adolf Meyer and Sigmund Freud, focused on prevention of some of the conditions leading to suicide, such as schizophrenia, solipsism, madness, and neurosis. Unlike psychiatrists, these psychologists dismissed any form of judgment or discrimination toward 'biologically defective individuals' and rejected the idea of permanent institutionalization for the mentally disabled. Instead they prioritized the development of a therapy capable of rescuing needy patients.[80]

However, while advocating a broader, overarching investigation of suicide, and despite investing great effort in popularizing its discipline, psychology failed, remaining isolated within the walls of academia, labs, and hospitals.[81] After a brief moment of ascendancy in the early 1920s, clinical psychology waned when the Great Depression hit hard in 1929 and the national government could no longer support science. Physicians were progressively mobilized into the army and navy and enrolled in state indoctrination programs.[82] Psychologists promptly channeled their energy into the state's priorities of the time, aligning themselves with the mental hygiene movement in hopes of offering an alternative to somatic theories of mental illness, innatism, and heredity-based policies of confinement and sterilization. However, the psychological approach was not embraced, and the emerging psychoanalysis of suicide cases similar to Fujimura's was pushed into the background. Once psychological exploration was eliminated from the picture, suicide cases were interpreted merely as the outcomes of brain abnormalities.

Nevertheless, the diverse disciplines of psychiatry, sociology, and psychology had begun to converge and contaminate each other. Other psychiatrists besides Sugie began to reach beyond what they felt was a reductive somatic explanation of suicide. Some suggested looking to Kretschmer's theory on personality types or Freudian psychoanalysis; others suggested cultural and social considerations of suicide. In a 1928 paper, the psychiatrist Ihara Shigehiko asserted the need for a more psychological approach to suicide in a clinical setting, criticizing the one-sided focus on the body involved in the anatomico-pathological approach. Ihara conducted possibly the first detailed psychological study of a person who had attempted suicide and was hospitalized to a university clinic.[83] Another critic of biological reductionism was Naka Shūzo, an early advocate of Morita psychotherapy and a professor of psychiatry at Kyūshū Imperial University. Naka asserted that modern materialistic science had impoverished the 'metaphysical' thought inherited from the past and that it failed to comprehend the full complexity of the individual. To enrich our understanding of humanity, psychiatry should be better integrated with psychology.[84] Some suicide cases, Naka noted with particular interest, did not demonstrate observable symptoms of insanity. If psychological tools had not been able to detect anomalies in life, he felt there was little hope of discovering them postmortem via the anatomico-pathological approach: these cases, according to him, showed the need for combined psychological and biological techniques. Kusakari Haruitsu pursued an alternative framework to understanding suicide; contrary to Esquirol's dictum inflexibly associating suicide with derangement, he asserted that many cases of suicide did not occur within the realm of madness.[85] Even Sugita Naoki made an eventual about-face, criticizing the simplistic mapping of suicide onto mental illness found in the work of Kraepelin, and proposing a more overarching approach to understanding the phenomenon.[86]

Such a move toward a sociological and psychological framework resulted not only from the discursive convergence of a variety of discourses, norms, values, and practices associated with health, illness, and medicine, but also from new conceptualizations of mental illness that gradually reduced the gap between sanity and insanity. Though psychiatry and its descriptive approach originally identified suicide as a fixed and unchanging biological condition, thus restricting more diverse possibilities of understanding it, eventually several discourses came together. For more than 30 years, diverse narratives operated around the body in its social, political, cultural, and scientific aspects, proceeding in a somewhat uncoordinated manner. But by the late 1920s the gradual contamination of psychiatry by sociology and psychology timidly prompted the genesis of a biocultural narrative of suicide, in which both biology and culture were seen as shaping and influencing an individual's behavior. Thus what had been exclusively explained as a biochemical imbalance was now reexamined by many psychiatrists in a more complex light. Guided by a theoretical framework that aimed at transcending the dichotomy between the biological and socio-psychological explanations of suicide – along with other dichotomies such as voluntary death and sacrifice, nature and culture – the biocultural approach to suicide represented a deliberate attempt to utilize the potentials offered by a set of discourses and a promise to fully comprehend the phenomenon of suicide in its complexity.

With the advent of a biocultural narrative, it became evident that there was little room left for an orthodox, simplistic study of suicide. It was also at this moment, though, that some psychiatrists bitterly responded to the attempts to popularize the psychological and sociological discourses. They vividly reasserted the imperative necessity to diagnose and treat suicidal patients, framing the conceptualization of voluntary death within the realm of legal condemnation.

Popularizing the criminalization of suicide: uncooperative psychiatry

The reaction by dissenting psychiatrists to the emergence of a biocultural language took several forms. Firstly, the process of associating suicide with crime in the popular narrative accelerated, aimed at suggesting that the phenomenon threatened the entire society. Secondly, many psychiatrists uncompromisingly reasserted that it was essential to contextualize suicide within a universal theoretical framework phrased in biological language. They continued to establish biological norms and practices within academia, and at the same time worked to serve the political interests of the nation. The influence of the eminent professor Kaneko Junji was particularly noteworthy.

A remarkable effort to associate suicide, crime, and degeneration in the popular imagination can be seen in the sensationalistic literature. By the early 1920s, the line between medicine and sensationalistic journalism had become increasingly tenuous. Psychiatrists achieved success in popularizing the association of suicide and crime by participating in debates in newspapers and popular medical magazines, reporting on suicide cases in a lurid manner, and offering portrayals of suicidal-homicidal maniacs who were intolerably harmful to themselves and to society. One example was the notorious Sakakibara suicide case. Sakakibara Shikasaburō was a convicted murderer who escaped twice from psychiatric confinement, once in 1916 and again in 1923, and ultimately hanged himself in a high-security cell. The case was largely portrayed as the inexorable result of mental abnormality, something that could result in any number of perilous outcomes if the individual were not confined and treated.[87]

The marriage of suicide, crime, and degeneration started to appear in specialized magazines as well. *Hentai Shinri* [Abnormal Psychology], for example, which was published between 1917 and 1926, offered a platform for psychiatrists to explore a wide range of topics, from nervous diseases to split personality, from abnormal psychological phenomena to the introduction of psychoanalysis. The series' leitmotif was to investigate the dark side of modern individuals, whether this be their oneiric life or their antisocial behavior, and to debunk superstitions in favor of 'true' psychotherapy. Several articles were dedicated specifically to love suicides and their entanglement with crime. Psychiatrists explained complex biological theories of the mechanisms that led people to commit love suicides and homicides through the use of unnecessary gory metaphors and redundant gruesome details. Ōto Tessei, a psychiatrist who reported the case of a woman who begged her brother to kill her and her partner after their families opposed their marriage, offers just one example among many. The detailed descriptions of the disemboweled victims and of the smell of blood were utterly irrelevant in an article that aimed at explaining psychiatric theories on inhibition and the externalization of feelings.[88] Nonetheless, such portrayals were surely useful in the construction of a memorable narrative that popularized the psychiatric jargon and established a connection between suicide and crime. It can be argued that in a set of conscious, imaginative strategies, psychiatrists used the trajectory of a horror narrative to vulgarize the connection between suicide and crime.

Homosexuality-related slayings and suicides of the Edo period provided ready fodder for the popular criminology press too. In the journals *Hanzai Kagaku* and *Hanzai Kōron*, which specialized in the scientific study of sexuality and crimes, a newly emerging class of sexual 'experts' offered up an extensive number of articles discussing 'perverse sexuality,' which principally included double suicides. While female homosexuals were considered liable to commit dual suicide, killing oneself over a lover was itself considered to be *hentai* [perverse] even if the partner was of the other sex. Miyagawa Mangyo was a writer for both journals who, with refined psychological sophistication, portrayed perverse sexual relationships, macabre suicides, and wild exploits of jealousy, titillating and at the same time educating the reader with fascinating stories.[89] Miyagawa's adventurous sexual ethics and macabre details were designed to shock and disgust readers, as well as to create a climate of suspense and chaos that presented the world as a dangerous place. Miyagawa deployed a figurative and metaphorical language that aimed to explore the unconscious and at the same time to undermine traditional narrative progression. He delved into the criminal's mind, teasing out the underlying driving force toward crime, and emphasized psychiatric logic as the unique tool able to solve the unexpected described in his sensationalistic fiction. Through psychiatric reasoning, he gave a coherent appearance to a fragmented and inscrutable reality.

Even journals whose audience consisted of medical professionals published accounts intended to shock readers with their lurid details. In 1932, Asada Hajime, a professor of medicine at Nagasaki School of Medicine, published a series of articles in the reputable medical journal *Chiryō Oyobi Shohō* [Therapy and Prescription]. These consisted of gruesome, outré accounts of suicide and murder, and often included graphic photographs of corpses intended to have downright pornographic appeal. One characteristic example of Asada's articles regaled readers with the detailed description of a grisly incident in which a deceased prostitute wearing clothes and makeup was found in a shed following an attempted double suicide. Another was accompanied by photographs of the dead body of a woman whose lover had coerced her into double suicide.[90] Thanks to a skillful exploitation of the multitudinous trappings of horror, physicians like Asada fabricated thrilling stories of suspense that validated and promoted current progress in medical knowledge. Such sensationalistic treatment of cases of suicide in a medical journal stood in stark contrast to earlier representations of the subject.[91] Placed in the framework of degeneration and criminal pathology, some part of the medical account of suicide was assimilated into the non-medical culture of Gothic horror and decadent fascination.

While some psychiatrists colonized the popular discourse to reaffirm the criminalization of suicide, a remarkable academic contribution contesting the incorporation of psychological and sociological narratives into the psychiatric discourse was provided by Kaneko Junji. In 1927, Kaneko, a fervent disciple of biopsychiatry and leading authority on criminal psychiatry, published some of his initial thoughts on suicide in the journal *Taiyō*.[92] The psychiatrist, obliquely referring to Fujimura's philosophical suicide and the copycat cases it triggered, firstly responded to the sociological and psychological counter-discourses, repudiating any potential interpretation of suicide as an act of freedom through which an individual might exercise self-sovereignty by disposing of his/her own life. Secondly, he identified these suicide cases as obvious symptoms of a diseased and criminal mind. Kaneko premised that during the Tokugawa period, voluntary death had been associated with aesthetics and will, and in recent times the media had superficially tended to categorize the act as political, altruistic, religious, philosophical, and much more. However, a close clinical observation of those who attempted suicides and/or "extended suicides" [*kakushō jisatsu*, or suicide-homicide] revealed that their motivations could be caused by brain abnormalities, which led the patient to exhibit anomalous behaviors (such as dependence on alcohol, hysteria, proclivity to abortions, or inertia).[93] Kaneko explained that "suicide by inertia" [*kansei jisatsu*], for example – a very common suicide pattern according to him – was motivated by the victim's deep identification with an event or another person. Kaneko saw this as a result of the disinterest in one's own life caused by clinical apathy; therefore the victim did not have an internal motivation that could be classified as political, aesthetic, or anything else. Rather, it was his or her biomedical structure that pushed him or her to commit suicide. For Kaneko, biomedical factors were fundamental, whereas any adduced romanticism, aestheticism, or strong will was a trivial, cultural construction.

Kaneko pushed his argument even further, relating the degenerate bodily conditions of suicide victims to rebellion and tumult in Japanese society.[94] When in

1925 the government established the Peace Preservation Law designed to crush communists and other dissidents, Kaneko seized the moment to express his concerns over a potential link between insurgency and the constitutional defects he believed led to mental illness. While the authorities unhesitatingly established organizations and censorship laws to combat the thought and activities of political leftists, Kaneko tried to convince them that diseases of the mind and body warranted the same attention. He argued that anarchism, communism, and insurgent activity – like suicide – were signs of degeneracy in people who had abnormal bodily constitutions. He stated that "the problem of psychopaths or the mentally abnormal is like a cancer in the state" [*seishinijōsha no mondai wa kokka no ganshu de aru*], showing a clear intent to serve the imperialistic cause of his country and simultaneously to reassert the pivotal role of the psychiatrist.[95] For Kaneko, the suicidal patient was a psychopath, prompt to under- or overreact to average stimuli because of pathological deficiencies, and therefore a potential political criminal. In order to prevent criminality in general, and leftist uprisings in particular, Kaneko argued that the mentally disordered had to be placed and kept in hospitals. Despite some of his colleagues' fascination with emerging sociological and psychological explanations of suicide, Kaneko welcomed eugenic science because it reinforced the pathologization, and consequently the criminalization, of suicide.[96] When the government later adopted the National Eugenics Law [*Kokumin yūseihō*, 1940], however, which allowed for sterilization of the mentally abnormal, Kaneko objected to the enactment of sterilization legislation and insisted that permanent institutionalization was a more reliable means of prevention. He claimed that more studies on heredity should be conducted, and in addition argued that consideration must be given to environmental factors in the development of mental and physical disorders. Like many of his colleagues, he was skillfully negotiating between the contingent needs of Japanese psychiatrists and the state agenda. Most psychiatrists working in hospitals were not interested in the ultimate goals of eugenics. They reassured the government that doctors could confine 'degenerates' and safeguard the health of the Japanese race; this would ensure a considerable need for their services and a long mandate for mental institutions.

Thus, with the first debate over Fujimura's case in 1903, psychiatry had gradually tried to exert moral and bodily control over the self-sovereignty of the individual, rendering the 'free disposal of life' an illegitimate act and silencing the authoritative role of the patient. With the second debate in 1921, some psychiatrists went further in equating the criminalization of suicide with scientific, moral, and social progress and with an intention to serve the nation. The acceleration of this narrative happened when, under the aegis of Social Darwinism and the ideology of the nation-as-family, a diagnosis of the individual was considered to cast judgment on the whole family, in other words on the whole nation. The treatment of the suicidal mind was thus functional in two ways in the determination of the modern Japanese state: first, it contributed to enabling Japanese doctors to professionalize; second, it contributed to reinforcing the autocratic patriarchal order, despite the acceleration of modernity.

Notes

1 Jean-Étienne Dominique Esquirol, *Dictionnaire des Sciences Médicales* (Paris: C.L.F. Panchouch, 1812), p. 213.
2 Emil Kraepelin, *Lectures on Clinical Psychiatry* (New York: Wood, 1904), pp. 130–131. See also Théodore Millon and Seth Grossman, *Personality Disorders in Modern Life* (New York: John Wiley and Sons, 2004), p. 489.
3 Wolfgang G. Jilek, "Emil Kraepelin and Comparative Sociocultural Psychiatry," *European Archives of Psychiatry and Clinical Neuroscience*, 245(4–5), 1995, pp. 231–238.
4 Joseph Fletcher, "Moral and Educational Statistics of England and Wales," *Journal of the Statistical Society of London*, 10, 1847, pp. 193–221; André-Michel Guerry, *Essai sur la Statistique Morale de la France* (Paris: Crochard, 1833); Enrico Morselli, *Il Suicidio: Saggio di Statistica Morale Comparata* (Milano: Dumolard, 1879).
5 See the chapter "Suicide and Cosmic Factors" in Émile Durkheim, *Suicide: A Study in Sociology* (New York: The Free Press Corporation, 1951).
6 See David Lester, *Suicide Prevention: Resources for the Millennium* (New York: Taylor and Francis, 2001), p. 22; Steven Stack, "Suicide: A Comparative Analysis," *Social Forces*, 57(2), Special Issue, 1978, pp. 644–645.
7 Howard I. Kushner, *American Suicide: A Psychocultural Exploration* (New Brunswick, NJ: Rutgers University Press, 1991), p. 8.
8 Suzuki Akihito, "A Brain Hospital in Tokyo and Its Private and Public Patients, 1926–45," *History of Psychiatry*, 14, 2003, pp. 337–360.
9 Ann Bowman Jannetta, *The Vaccinators: Smallpox, Medical Knowledge, and the "Opening" of Japan* (Stanford, CA: Stanford University Press, 2007); Hoi-Eun Kim, *Doctors of Empire: Medical and Cultural Encounters between Imperial Germany and Meiji Japan* (Toronto: University of Toronto Press, 2014); Alexander R. Bay, *Beriberi in Modern Japan: The Making of a National Disease* (Rochester, NY: University of Rochester Press, 2012).
10 Susan Burns, "Constructing the National Body: Public Health and the Nation in Meiji Japan," in Timothy Brook and André Schmid (eds.), *Nation Work: Asian Elites and National Identities* (Ann Arbor: University of Michigan Press, 2000), pp. 17–50; Hyōdō Akiko, *Seishinbyō no Nihon Kindai: Tsuku Shinshin Kara Yamu Shinshin he* [Mental Disease and Japanese Modernity: From the Possessed Mind/Body to the Diseased Mind/Body] (Tokyo: Seikyūsha, 2008).
11 It was commonly believed that the fox had an evil spirit and the supernatural power to bewitch and possess people. See Hayami Yasutaka, *Tsukimono Mochi Meishin* [Superstition of Tsukimono Mochi] (Tokyo: Akashi Shoten, 1999); Hiruta Genshirō, "Nihon no Seishin Iryōshi" [History of Psychiatry in Japan], in Matsushita Masaaki (ed.), *Rinshō Seishinigaku Kōza* [Clinical Psychiatry Course] (Tokyo: Nakayama Shoten, 1999); Hyōdō Akiko, *Seishinbyō no Nihon Kindai: Tsuku Shinshin Kara Yamu Shinshin he*, pp. 5, 22.
12 Kagawa Shūtoku, "Ippondo Gyoyo Igen" [My Extra Medical Commentary], in Kure Shuzō (ed.), *Kureshi Iseido Sōsho* [Kure Collection of Great Physicians' Texts], pp. 579–601 (Tokyo: Shinbunkaku, 1970).
13 Hashimoto Akira, "Invention of 'Japanese Gheel,'" in Waltraud Ernst and Thomas Mueller (eds.), *Transnational Psychiatries, Social and Cultural Histories of Psychiatry in Comparative Perspective, c. 1800–2000* (Cambridge: Cambridge Scholars Publishing, 2010), pp. 142–171, p. 147.
14 Suzuki Akihito, "Global Theory, Local Practice: Shock Therapies on Japanese Psychiatry, 1920–1945," in Waltraud Ernst and Thomas Mueller (eds.), *Transnational Psychiatries, Social and Cultural Histories of Psychiatry in Comparative Perspective, c. 1800–2000* (Cambridge: Cambridge Scholars Publishing, 2010), pp. 116–141, p. 127.
15 Kitanaka Junko, *Depression in Japan* (Princeton, NJ: Princeton University Press, 2012), p. 42; Ōtsuki Yasuyoshi, "Hyōi to Seishinka Rinshō" [Spirit Possession and

Clinical Psychiatry], *Rinshō Seishingaku Kōza*, Vol. 23 (Tokyo: Nakayama Shoten, Tabunkakan Seishinigaku, 1998), pp. 335–356.

16 See Kuriyama Shigehisa, "Between Mind and Eye: Japanese Anatomy in the Eighteenth Century," in Charles M. Leslie and Allan Young (eds.), *Paths to Asian Medical Knowledge* (Berkeley: University of California Press, 1992), pp. 21–43; Kitanaka Junko, *Depression in Japan*, pp. 18, 55.

17 For an account of how the language of modernization developed simultaneously with the progress of science, see Suzuki Akihito and Christopher Aldous, *Reforming Public Health in Occupied Japan, 1945–52*, p. 41.

18 Etsuro Totsuka, "The History of Japanese Psychiatry and the Rights of Mental Patients," *Psychiatric Bulletin*, 14, 1990, pp. 193–200.

19 Kure Shūzō, "Seishinbyōsha no Jisatsushō ni Tsuite" [On Suicide in Mentally Ill Patients], in *Kure Shūzō Chōsakushū*, 2 vols. (Kyoto: Shibunkaku, 1982), Vol. 2, pp. 255–301.

20 Kure studied under Sakaki first, and then beginning in 1897 he specialized in psychiatry and neuropathology for four years in Austria and Germany under the mentorship of Emil Kraepelin and Richard von Krafft-Ebing.

21 For a complete list of symptoms, see Kure Shūzō, "Seishinbyōsha no Jisatsushō ni Tsuite," Vol. 2, pp. 278–279.

22 Ibid., p. 301.

23 Kure Shūzō, *Seishinbyōgaku-shūyō* [Textbook of Psychiatry] (1894), 2nd ed. (Tokyo: Tohōdō, 1916).

24 Akimoto Haruo, *Seishin'igaku to Hantai seishin'igaku* [Psychiatry and Anti-psychiatry] (Tokyo: Kongō Shuppan, 1976), p. 19.

25 Suzuki Akihito. "Family, the State and the Insane in Japan, 1900–1945," in Roy Porter and David Wright (eds.), *The Confinement of the Insane: International Perspectives 1800–1965* (Cambridge: Cambridge University Press, 2003), pp. 193–225.

26 *Yomiuri Shinbun*, "Bunmei to Shinkei Suijaku" [Civilization and Neurasthenia], Kure Shūzō, May 20, 1913.

27 *Yomiuri Shinbun*, "Seishinbyō to Ki'in" [Mental Illnesses and Causes], Kure Shūzō, May 8, 1906.

28 Ōmichi Waichi, a journalist fascinated by *jōshi*, rightfully lamented the unreliability of official statistics and in particular the non-methodical categorization of suicide patterns by the Meiji government, which overlooked and failed to consider cases of joint suicide. Ōmichi provided his own statistical data on *jōshi*, in which he counted cases based on newspaper articles, which did not lead to improvements in data compiling. Years later, the psychiatrist Komine Shigeyuki pointed out Ōmichi's own methodological weakness and theoretical confusion, but a methodological fallacy emerged in his work too: Komine gathered data from mental hospitals and newspaper articles (he argued that newspapers reported two or three new cases of *jōshi* every day). The numbers he provided were problematic because they were not collected systematically and presumably were the result of specific personal agendas. See Ōmichi Waichi, *Jōshi no Kenkyū* [A Study on Lovers' Suicides] (Tokyo: Dobunkan, 1911), p. 236; Komine Shigeyuki, "Jōshi ni Taisuru Igakuteki Kōsatsu" [Medical Considerations on Lovers' Suicides], *Komine Kenkyūjo Kiyō*, 6, 1938, pp. 1–301, p. 118.

29 The male suicide rate was, however, extremely high compared with the female rate (24.1 for males vs. 14.7 for females). See Ministry of Health, Labor and Welfare, *Dai 5 Kai Jisatsu Shibō Tōkei: Jinkō Dōtai Tōkei Tokuchō Hōkoku* [5th Statistics Concerning Suicide Deaths: Special Report on Demographic Statistics] (Tokyo: Ministry of Health, Labor and Welfare, 2005), p. 42.

30 *Yomiuri Shinbun*, "Jisatsu ni Kan Suru Tōkei: 1901nendo ha Zenkoku de 8458nin ni mo" [Statistics on Suicide: 8,458 Suicide Cases in the Whole Country in 1901 Alone], September 9, 1903; *Yomiuri Shinbun*, "Doitsu no Jisatsusha Tōkei" [Suicide Statistics in Germany], May 19, 1905; *Asahi Shinbun*, "Ichinenkan no Jisatsusha" [Suicide Cases

in One Year], May 12, 1906; *Asahi Shinbun*, "Jisatsusha no Zōka" [The Increase in the Suicide Rate], September 24, 1906; *Asahi Shinbun*, "Jisatsusha no Koto" [On Suicide Victims], February 15, 1907; *Asahi Shinbun*, "Nennen Zōka Suru ha Naze ka" [Why Does the Suicide Rate Increase Year by Year?], May 19, 1908.

31 Anonymous, "Seikatsunan to Jisatsu" [Life Difficulties and Suicide], *Taiyō*, 12(8), June 1906, pp. 28–34.

32 For fictional works contrasting the idea of asylum as an institution to protect the nation, see Susan Burns, "Constructing the National Body: Public Health and the Nation in Meiji Japan," in *Nation Work: Asian Elites and National Identities*, pp. 45–46.

33 Anonymous, "Bungaku Jiji" [Literary Affairs], *Taiyō*, 2(18), September 5, 1896, pp. 158–168, 158–159.

34 *Yomiuri Shinbun*, "Satsuma-fu Yori Jōshi Ikken Hakken" [Discovery of a Double Suicide in Satsuma], January 31, 1901.

35 *Yomiuri Shinbun*, "Senju no Jōshi" [Double Suicide in Senju], March 24, 1901.

36 *Yomiuri Shinbun*, "Dōseiai Shinjū no Jogakusei no Kisho Hakken Saru" [Discovery of the Note of Two High School Girl Students Who Committed Same-Sex Suicide], December 1, 1920.

37 The suicide of the two lovers occurred in Shinagawa, Tokyo, in 1903. The case attracted widespread popular attention, partly because newspapers debated whether it was a double suicide or a suicide-homicide, and partly because of its similarities to the eighteenth-century *rakugo* entitled *Shinagawa Shinjū* [The Love Suicide at Shinagawa]. See also David Pollack, "The Love Suicides at Shinagawa: A Sort of Love Story," *Monumenta Nipponica*, 57(1), Spring 2002, pp. 73–89.

38 *Yomiuri Shinbun*, "Shinagawa no Jōshi Zokuhō – Kyaku ga Saki ni Shōgi wo Koroshi Waribara Jisatsu" [A Follow-up on the Shinagawa Case – He First Killed Her and Then Committed *Harakiri*], October 20, 1903.

39 *Yomiuri Shinbun*, "Joshi no Higeki – Jisatsu 2ken ha Jitsubo no Mujō ga gen'in" [A Girl Drama – a Mother's Heartlessness behind Both Suicides], May 28, 1907.

40 *Asahi Shinbun*, "Yahari Nihonjin no Onna" [A Typical Japanese Woman], January 6, 1919.

41 Fukushima Shirō, *Fujinkai Sanjūgonen* [Thirty-five Years of a Woman's Life] (Tokyo: Fuji Shuppan, 1984), p. 582. This section on Matsui Sumako was written on January 10, 1919, five days after her suicide.

42 The dialectic between the reproachful voices raised against the desecration of social rules and the forgiving gaze of an audience fascinated with a love *sans-frontières* was vividly portrayed in a short novel titled *Chiba Shinjū* [Double Suicide in Chiba]. *Chiba Shinjū* appeared in the newspaper on March 25, just nineteen days after the incident. Along with the romantic love that transcends all obstacles, the anonymous novelist suggested that the affair was nothing but the last hope of an indebted chauffeur to redeem himself economically by seeking refuge under Kamako's family. For more details, see the article by Yorimatsu Tamao, professor at the Law Department of Tokyo Denki University and specialist in legal history of Japan: "Taishōki no Jitsuroku shōSetsu ni Kakareta Shinjū Jiken to hōTeki Mondai," *Hōshigaku Kenkyūkai Kaihō*, 8, 2003, pp. 55–58.

43 Ōmichi Waichi, *Jōshi no Kenkyū* [A Study on Lovers' Suicides] (Tokyo: Dobunkan, 1911), pp. 232–236.

44 Several early studies carried out in European universities (the most important were Terman's survey in 1925 and Ellis' survey in 1926) demonstrated high rates of mental disorders in creative or gifted people. Several causes leading to artists' premature suicides were identified: specifically, the studies identified that creative people tend to have a weaker sense of daily life, less conventional forms of interaction with people in general (thus tending to suffer from solitude), unstable lifestyles, dependence on alcohol and sleeping pills, and attraction to deviation.

45 Without proper evidence, Ōhara Kenshirō argued that Japan was the country with the highest suicide rate for novelists (p. 13). To the question 'Why do they kill themselves?',

Ōhara offers several reasons that could be summarized under the Durkheimian category "lack of integration" (pp. 16–17). Ōhara Kenshirō, *Nihon no Jisatsu* [Suicide in Japan] (Tokyo: Seishin Shobō, 1965). See also Kataguchi Yasufumi, *Sakka no Shindan* [Analysis of Novelists] (Tokyo: Shibundo, 1966).

46 Kōsaka Masaaki, *Nihonjin no Jisatsu* [Suicide of the Japanese] (Tokyo: Sōbunsha, 1966), pp. 360, 369.

47 Fukushima Shirō, *Fujinkai Sanjūgonen* [Thirty-five Years of a Woman's Life] (Tōkyō: Fuji Shuppan, 1984), pp. 586–588.

48 Takayama Rinjirō, "Jiji Hyōron – Bukkyō no Kanka to Jōshi" [Essay on Contemporaneity – Buddhism and Lover Suicide], *Taiyō*, 5(6), March 1899, pp. 63–71.

49 Hasegawa Tenkei, "Jinsei Mondai no Kenkyū to Jisatsu" [Research on Problems of Living and Suicide], *Taiyō*, 9(9), August 1903, pp. 174–176.

50 Ōtsuka Sokō, "Jisatsu to Seinen" [Suicide and Teenagers], *Taiyō*, 9(8), July 1903, pp. 207–213.

51 See more on novelists and the depiction of neurasthenia in: Christopher Hill, "Exhausted by Their Battles with the World – Neurasthenia and Civilization Critique in Early Twentieth-Century Japan," in Nina Cornyetz and Keith Vincent (eds.), *Perversion and Modern Japan: Experiments in Psychoanalysis* (London: Routledge, 2009), pp. 242–258.

52 Bessho Naoki, *Jisatsu no Bigaku* [The Aesthetics of Suicide] (Tokyo: Nichigei Shuppan, 1972), pp. 219–221.

53 Ōhara Kenshirō explains that Fujimura's suicide drew media attention because "Japanese people were attracted by the aesthetics of Fujimura's poem." Ōhara argues that Fujimura's death can be defined as a pure suicide [*junsuina jisatsu*] because it enhanced the beauty of the individual's choice. Ōhara Kenshirō, *Nihon no Jisatsu* [Suicide in Japan] (Tokyo: Seishin Shobō, 1965), p. 87.

54 *Harakiri* or *seppuku* is the ritual disembowelment by a sword or a dagger committed by samurai. See Asakura Kyōji, *Jisatsu no Shisō* [Thoughts on Suicide] (Tokyo: Ōta Shuppan, 2005), p. 20.

55 Miyatake Kameshirō, "Shōnen Tetsugakusha wo chōSu" [Begrudging the Death of a Young Philosopher], *Yorozu Chōhō*, May 27, 1903. See also *Asahi Shinbun*, "Tetsugaku Chindan – Kegon Taki Kara no tōShin Seinen wo Saguri, Biteki Seikatsu Ronsō" [Philosophical Stories – a Young Student Jumps into Kegon Falls – Debating the Aesthetics of Life], August 4, 1903.

56 Yamana Shōtarō, *Nihon Jisatsu Jōshiki* [Records on Japanese Suicide] (Tokyo: Shichō Bunken, 1928), p. 98.

57 Tsubouchi Shōyō, "Jisatsu no Zehi" [Suicide Approval], *Taiyō*, 9(9), 1903, pp. 56–71.

58 Ibid., p. 56.

59 Ibid., pp. 59, 68.

60 *Yomiuri Shinbun*, "Jisatsu to Kyōiku" [Suicide and Education], July 29, 1909.

61 *Tōkyō Asahi Shinbun*, "Jisatsu to Shakai" [Suicide and Society], Katayama Kuniyoshi (October 22, 1906). See also Kitanaka Junko, *Depression in Japan*, p. 59.

62 Ōkuma Shigenobu, "Seishinbyō ni tai Suru" [Impressions on Mental Illness], *Shinkeigaku Zasshi*, 4(12), 1906, pp. 614–625, p. 616.

63 Despite the fact that early Japanese medical reformers revealed racist tendencies, they seemed hesitant about German racial hygiene until 1930, when the Japanese Society for Racial Hygiene was established. Before 1930, it is more appropriate to define Japanese medical reforms as influenced by eugenics, rather than German racial hygiene. Michael Shiyung Liu, *Prescribing Colonization: The Role of Medical Practices and Policies in Japan-ruled Taiwan, 1895–1945* (Ann Arbor, MI: Association for Asian Studies, 2009), pp. 38–39.

64 Sawada Junjirō, "Jisatsu to Jisatsu Kishitsu" [Suicide and Disposition to Suicide], *Taiyō*, 19(16), December 1913, p. 118.

65 Mita Sadanori, "Jisatsuron" [On Suicide], *Kokka Igaku Zasshi*, 343, 1915, pp. 1–31, p. 1.
66 This section includes several references to Akihito Suzuki's article, "Psychiatry in the Land of Suicide: Medicalization of Self-killing in Early Twentieth-Century Japan," *Nihon Ishigaku Zasshi*, 59, 2013, pp. 3–15. Similar arguments resonate both here and in Suzuki's article, as the same literature and core compendium of texts have been scrutinized.
67 Sugita Naoki, "Jidaibyō to Sono Ryōhō" [Illness of an Era and Its Treatment], *Ikai Jihō*, 1921, pp. 1429–1436, p. 1436.
68 Terada Torahiko, "Jisatsu ni Yoru Manzoku – Jisatsusha no Shinriteki Kōsatsu" [A Sense of Satisfaction from Suicide – Psychological Considerations of Suicide Victims], *Fujin Kōron*, 9, September 1921, pp. 26–34, p. 34.
69 Hasegawa Nyozekan, "Jisatsu no Kenkyū – Shakai Genshō Toshite no Jisatsu" [On Suicide: Suicide as a Social Phenomenon], *Fujin Kōron*, 9, September 1921, pp. 22–25.
70 Yamana Shōtarō, *Nihon Jisatsu Jōshiki*, p. 373.
71 Ibid., p. 337.
72 Hoashi Riichirō, "Jisatsu no Rinriteki igi" [The Ethical Significance of Suicide], *Fujin Kōron*, 9, September, 1921, pp. 39–45.
73 Sugie Kaoru, "Jisatsu no Dōki to Hōhō" [Trends and Patterns on Suicide], *Fujin Kōron*, September 1921, pp. 35–38.
74 Between 1917 and 1921, an average of one article on suicide statistics every other month appeared in the Japanese press. Here is a selected list of relevant articles on suicide statistics published between 1917 and 1921: *Yomiuri Shinbun*, "Jisatsu – Nennen Zōka Shite Iku" [Suicide Rate Increasing Year by Year], October 5, 1921; *Asahi Shinbun*, "Sennin ni Nijūsannin no Shiboritsu" [Twenty-three Suicides Every 1,000 People], October 22, 1921; *Asahi Shinbun*, "Wakai Fujin no Jisatsu ga ooi" [High Rate of Suicide among Young Ladies], April 16, 1917.
75 Kawamura Nozomu, "Sociology and Socialism in the Interwar Period," in Thomas Rimer (ed.), *Culture and Identity: Japanese Intellectuals during the Interwar Years* (Princeton, NJ: Princeton University Press, 1990), pp. 61–82.
76 The psychiatrist Moriyama Kimio argued that sociological 'positivism' originated in the US with the work of H. S. Sullivan soon after the Wall Street crisis and had a strong impact on Japanese academia. Moriyama Kimio, *Gendai Seishin Igaku Kaitai no Ronri* [Criticism of Modern Psychiatry] (Tokyo: Iwasaki Gakushutsu Shuppansha, 1975), pp. 243, 245–247.
77 A Spanish translation of *Le Suicide* was published in 1928, and an unofficial English one was available in 1933. Émile Durkheim, *Le Suicide: Étude de Sociologie* (Paris: F. Alcan, 1897).
78 See the scholarship published on Durkheim during the prewar period: Matsumoto Junichirō, "Dyurkeemu no Shakaigakuron ni Tsuite" [Durkheimian Theories on Sociology], *Shakaigaku Zasshi*, December 10, 1925, pp. 25–60. See also the historian Miyanaga Takashi, *Meiji Taishō shōWa no Nihon Shakaigakushi* [Considerations on the Heredity of Sociology – Japanese Sociology in the Meiji, Taishō, and Shōwa Period] (Tokyo: Kadokawa Gakugei Shuppan, 2007), p. 280.
79 Morita Masatake (1874–1938), also known as the father of Japanese psychoanalysis, was a contemporary of Sigmund Freud and the founder of Morita therapy, a branch of clinical psychology strongly influenced by Zen Buddhism. In his capacity as the head of psychiatry for a large Tokyo hospital, Morita began developing his methods while working with sufferers of neurasthenia and anxiety disorders with a hypochondriac foundation. On a different note, the Uchida-Kraepelin test was a questionnaire that measured abilities in terms of task performance speed and task performance accuracy. The results provided an estimate of the individual's character. See Satō Tatsuya, "Rises and Falls in Clinical Psychology in Japan: A Perspective on the Status of Japanese Clinical Psychology," *Ritsumeikan Jinbungaku Kenkyū*, 2007, pp. 83–84. For the history of the

introduction and development of the psychological discipline in Japan, see Okonogi Keigo, *Gendai Seishin Bunseki Volume 1 and Volume 2.*
80 Akimoto Haruo, *Meisai no Dohyo: Hyoden Nihon no Seishin Iryō* [Camouflaged Signs: A Critical Biography of Japanese Emotional Healing] (Tokyo: NOVA Shuppan, 1985).
81 Okonogi Keigo, *Gendai Seishin Bunseki Volume 1*, p. 94.
82 Satō Tatsuya, "Rises and Falls in Clinical Psychology in Japan: A Perspective on the Status of Japanese Clinical Psychology," pp. 138–139.
83 Ihara Shigehiko, "Ichi Jisatsu Rei no Kōsatsu," *Shinkeigaku Zasshi*, 29, 1928, pp. 534–552.
84 Naka Shūzō, "Seishin Ryōhō no Gaiyō," *Gyōkei Eiseikai Zasshi*, 7, 1932, pp. 32–39.
85 Kusakari Haruitsu, "Jisatsu ni Tsuite," *Hoken Igaku Zasshi*, 29, 1930, pp. 247–259.
86 Sugita Naoki, "Jisatsu ni Tsuite," *Hoken Igaku Zasshi*, 28, 1929, pp. 228–250.
87 Hyōdō Akiko, *Seishinbyō no Nihon Kindai: Tsuku Shinshin Kara Yamu Shinshin he*, p. 226.
88 Ōto Tessei, "Kanjūsei no Gaibu Tōshi" [Outward Manifestation of Sensibility], *Hentai Shinri* [Abnormal Psychology] (Tokyo: Fuji Shuppan), 20, October-December 1922, pp. 432–446.
89 Miyagawa Mangyo, "Yushima Yawa" [Evening Tale of Yushima], pt. 9 in *Edo Jidai no Seiteki Hanzai, Hanzai Kagaku*, February 1931, pp. 63–72; Miyagawa Mangyo, "Nanshoku Adauchi Bidan" [The Story of a Homosexual Vendetta], *Hanzai Kōron*, October 1932, p. 164.
90 Asada Hajime, "Ero-guroteki Satsujin" [Erotic and Grotesque Homicide], *Chiryō Oyobi Shohō*, 147, 1932, pp. 714–715; Asada Hajime, "Muri-Jōshi – Okoto wa Misui, Onna wa Futari Korosaru" [Suicide-Homicide: A Man Kills Two Women and Disappears], *Chiryō Oyobi Shohō*, 136, 1931, pp. 1223–1226.
91 Yano Harutoshi, "Nihon no Ishi Hyaku-Nijū-Yon Rei ni Tsuite yo ga Hōigakuteki Kenkyū," [A Medical-Legal Study on 124 Cases of Suicide by Hanging in Japan], *Kokka Igaku Zasshi*, 410, 1921, pp. 109–124. For more details, see Akihito Suzuki, "Psychiatry in the Land of Suicide: Medicalization of Self-killing in Early Twentieth-Century Japan," *Nihon Ishigaku Zasshi*, 59, 2013, pp. 3–15, p. 7.
92 Kaneko was a graduate of Tokyo Imperial Medical School. He served early in his career as director of the Matsuzawa Hospital, which had become the country's premier mental institution. Holding an advisory position at the hygienic department of the Home Ministry's Tokyo Metropolitan Police Board from 1923 and occupying the newly established chair in criminal psychiatry at Keio University's Medical School from 1925, he was recognized as the leading authority on criminal psychiatry.
93 Kaneko Junji, "Jisatsu Mangen," pp. 95–96.
94 Kaneko contended that suicide was an unfailing index of a people's racial degeneration. For example, Kure noted the high suicide rate of the Taiwanese after their brutally quashed rebellion against Japanese rule in 1930, calling it a clear indication of their primitive nature and predicting their extinction. Kaneko also reported that military medical officers identified a high suicide rate as an ominous signal of the likelihood of a communist revolution. See Kaneko Junji, "Shakai Mondai to Shiteno Seishin Byōsha (1)" [Mental Patients as a Social Problem], *Nihon no Ikai*, 17(15), 1927, pp. 5–8; idem., "Jisatsu no Shinri" [Psychology of Suicide], *Nihon no Ikai*, 71, 1928; 72, 1928, pp. 5–7.
95 Kaneko Junji, *Hanzai to Seishin Ijō* [Crime and Mental Abnormalities] (Tokyo: Kōbunsha, 1929), p. 112.
96 In the mid-1920s, Kaneko responded enthusiastically to Gotō Ryūkichi's request to support the transformation of the Japan Society of Eugenics [*Nihon Yūsei Gakkai*] into a full-fledged research foundation, and in 1932 he was an active member at the International Congress of Eugenics held in New York. Later in his career, however, he was a loud voice contesting the National Eugenics Law issued in 1940. Janice Matsumura,

"Mental Health as Public Peace: Kaneko Junji and the Promotion of Psychiatry in Modern Japan," *Modern Asian Studies*, 38(4), 2004, pp. 899–930. See also Yōko Matsubara, "The Enactment of Japan's Sterilization Laws in the 1940s: A Prelude to Postwar Eugenic Policy," *Historia Scientiarum*, 8(2), 1998, pp. 187–201. Yōko Matsubara, "Senjika no Danshūhō Ronsō" [The Wartime Debates over Sterilization Law], *Gendai Shisō*, 26(2), 1998, pp. 286–303.

Bibliography

Suzuki Akihito, "A Brain Hospital in Tokyo and Its Private and Public Patients, 1926–45," *History of Psychiatry*, 14 (2003), pp. 337–360.

Suzuki Akihito, "Psychiatry in the Land of Suicide: Medicalization of Self-killing in Early Twentieth-Century Japan," *Nihon Ishigaku Zasshi*, 59 (2013), pp. 3–15.

Hyōdō Akiko, *Seishinbyō no Nihon Kindai: Tsuku Shinshin Kara Yamu Shinshin he* [Mental Disease and Japanese Modernity: From the Possessed Mind/Body to the Diseased Mind/Body] (Tokyo: Seikyūsha, 2008).

Anonymous, "Bungaku Jiji" [Literary Affairs], *Taiyō*, 2(18) (September 5, 1896), pp. 158–168.

Anonymous, "Seikatsunan to Jisatsu" [Life Difficulties and Suicide], *Taiyō*, 12(8) (June 1, 1906), pp. 28–34.

Alexander R. Bay, *Beriberi in Modern Japan: The Making of a National Disease* (Rochester, NY: University of Rochester Press, 2012).

Timothy Brook and André Schmid (eds.), *Nation Work: Asian Elites and National Identities* (Ann Arbor: University of Michigan Press, 2000).

Nina Cornyetz and Keith Vincent (eds.), *Perversion and Modern Japan: Experiments in Psychoanalysis* (London: Routledge, 2009).

Émile Durkheim, *Le Suicide: Étude de Sociologie* (Paris: F. Alcan, 1897).

Waltraud Ernst and Thomas Mueller (eds.), *Transnational Psychiatries, Social and Cultural Histories of Psychiatry in Comparative Perspective, c. 1800–2000* (Cambridge: Cambridge Scholars Publishing, 2010).

Jean-Étienne Dominique Esquirol, *Dictionnaire des Sciences Médicales* (Paris: C.L.F. Panchouch, 1812).

Joseph Fletcher, "Moral and Educational Statistics of England and Wales," *Journal of the Statistical Society of London*, 10 (1847), pp. 193–221.

André-Michel Guerry, *Essai sur la Statistique Morale de la France* (Paris: Crochard, 1833).

Asada Hajime, "Muri-jōshi – Okoto wa Misui, Onna wa Futari Korosaru" [Suicide-Homicide: A Man Kills Two Women and Disappears], *Chiryō Oyobi Shohō*, 136 (1931), pp. 1223–1226.

Asada Hajime, "Ero-Guroteki Satsujin" [Erotic and Grotesque Homicide], *Chiryō Oyobi Shohō*, 147 (1932), pp. 714–715.

Kusakari Haruitsu, "Jisatsu ni Tsuite," *Hoken Igaku Zasshi*, 29 (1930), pp. 247–259.

Akimoto Haruo, *Seishin'igaku to Hantai Seishin'igaku* [Psychiatry and Anti-psychiatry] (Tokyo: Kongō Shuppan, 1976).

Akimoto Haruo, *Meisai no Dohyo: Hyoden Nihon no Seishin Iryō* [Camouflaged Signs: A Critical Biography of Japanese Emotional Healing] (Tokyo: NOVA Shuppan, 1985).

Yano Harutoshi, "Nihon no Ishi Hyaku-Nijū-Yon Rei ni Tsuite yo ga Hōigakuteki Kenkyū" [A Medical-Legal Study on 124 Cases of Suicide by Hanging in Japan], *Kokka Igaku Zasshi*, 410 (1921), pp. 109–124.Ann Bowman Jannetta, *The Vaccinators: Smallpox,*

Medical Knowledge, and the Opening of Japan (Stanford, CA: Stanford University Press, 2007).

Wolfgang G. Jilek, "Emil Kraepelin and Comparative Sociocultural Psychiatry," *European Archives of Psychiatry and Clinical Neuroscience*, 245(4–5) (1995), pp. 213–238.

Matsumoto Junichirō, "Dyurkeemu no Shakaigakuron ni Tsuite" [Durkheimian Theories on Sociology], *Shakaigaku Zasshi* (December 10, 1925), pp. 25–60.

Kaneko Junji, "Shakai Mondai to Shiteno Seishin Byōsha (1)" [Mental Patients as a Social Problem], *Nihon no Ikai*, 17(15) (1927), pp. 5–8.

Kaneko Junji, "Jisatsu no Shinri" [Psychology of Suicide], *Nihon no Ikai*, 71(72) (1928), pp. 5–7.

Kaneko Junji, *Hanzai to Seishin Ijō* [Crime and Mental Abnormalities] (Tokyo: Kōbunsha, 1929).

Sawada Junjirō, "Jisatsu to Jisatsu Kishitsu" [Suicide and Disposition to Suicide], *Taiyō*, 19(16) (December 1, 1913), pp. 117–122.

Kitanaka Junko, *Depression in Japan* (Princeton, NJ: Princeton University Press, 2012).

Miyatake Kameshirō, "Shōnen Tetsugakusha wo chōsu" [Begrudging the Death of a Young Philosopher], *Yorozu Chōhō* (May 27, 1903).

Sugie Kaoru, "Jisatsu no Dōki to Hōhō" [Trends and Patterns on Suicide], *Fujin Kōron* (September 1921), pp. 35–38.

Ōhara Kenshirō, *Nihon no Jisatsu* [Suicide in Japan] (Tokyo: Seishin Shobō, 1965).

Hoi-Eun Kim, *Doctors of Empire: Medical and Cultural Encounters between Imperial Germany and Meiji Japan* (Toronto: University of Toronto Press, 2014).

Moriyama Kimio, *Gendai Seishin Igaku Kaitai no Ronri* [Criticism of Modern Psychiatry] (Tokyo: Iwasaki Gakushutsu Shuppansha, 1975).

Emil Kraepelin, *Lectures on Clinical Psychiatry* (New York: Wood, 1904).

Howard I. Kushner, *American Suicide: A Psychocultural Exploration* (New Brunswick, NJ: Rutgers University Press, 1991).

Asakura Kyōji, *Jisatsu no Shisō* [Thoughts on Suicide] (Tokyo: Ōta Shuppan, 2005).

Charles M. Leslie and Allan Young (eds.), *Paths to Asian Medical Knowledge* (Berkeley: University of California Press, 1992).

David Lester, *Suicide Prevention: Resources for the Millennium* (New York: Taylor and Francis, 2001).

Miyagawa Mangyo, "Yushima Yawa" [Evening Tale of Yushima], pt. 9 in *Edo Jidai no Seiteki Hanzai, Hanzai Kagaku*, February 1931, pp. 63–72.

Miyagawa Mangyo, "Nanshoku Adauchi Bidan" [The Story of a Homosexual Vendetta], *Hanzai Kōron*, October 1932.

Kōsaka Masaaki, *Nihonjin no Jisatsu* [Suicide of the Japanese] (Tokyo: Sōbunsha, 1966).

Matsushita Masaaki (ed.), *Rinshō Seishinigaku Kōza* [Clinical Psychiatry Course] (Tokyo: Nakayama Shoten, 1999).

Yōko Matsubara, "Senjika no Danshūhō Ronsō" [The Wartime Debates over Sterilization Law], *Gendai Shisō*, 26(2) (1998), pp. 286–303.

Yōko Matsubara, "The Enactment of Japan's Sterilization Laws in the 1940s: A Prelude to Postwar Eugenic Policy," *Historia Scientiarum*, 8(2) (1998), pp. 187–201.

Janice Matsumura, "Mental Health as Public Peace: Kaneko Junji and the Promotion of Psychiatry in Modern Japan," *Modern Asian Studies*, 38(4) (2004), pp. 899–930.

Théodore Millon and Seth Grossman, *Personality Disorders in Modern Life* (New York: John Wiley and Sons, 2004).

Ministry of Health, Labor and Welfare, *Dai 5 Kai Jisatsu Shibō Tōkei: Jinkō Dōtai Tōkei Tokuchō Hōkoku* [5th Statistics Concerning Suicide Deaths: Special Report on Demographic Statistics] (Tokyo: Ministry of Health, Labor and Welfare, 2005).

Enrico Morselli, *Il Suicidio: Saggio di Statistica Morale Comparata* (Milano: Dumolard, 1879).

Sugita Naoki, "Jidaibyō to Sono Ryōhō" [Illness of an Era and Its Treatment], *Ikai Jihō*, 1407 (1921), pp. 1429–1436.

Sugita Naoki, "Jisatsu ni Tsuite," *Hoken Igaku Zasshi*, 28 (1929), pp. 228–250.

Bessho Naoki, *Jisatsu no Bigaku* [The Aesthetics of Suicide] (Tokyo: Nichigei Shuppan, 1972).

Hasegawa Nyozekan, "Jisatsu no Kenkyū – Shakai Genshō Toshite no Jisatsu" [On Suicide: Suicide as a Social Phenomenon], *Fujin Kōron*, 9 (September, 1921), pp. 22–25.

David Pollack, "The Love Suicides at Shinagawa: A Sort of Love Story," *Monumenta Nipponica*, 57(1) (Spring, 2002), pp. 73–89.

Roy Porter and David Wright (eds.), *The Confinement of the Insane: International Perspectives 1800–1965* (Cambridge: Cambridge University Press, 2003).

Hoashi Riichirō, "Jisatsu no Rinriteki Igi" [The Ethical Significance of Suicide], *Fujin Kōron*, 9 (September, 1921), pp. 39–45.

Thomas Rimer (ed.), *Culture and Identity: Japanese Intellectuals during the Interwar Years* (Princeton, NJ: Princeton University Press, 1990).

Takayama Rinjirō, "Jiji Hyōron – Bukkyō no Kanka to Jōshi" [Essay on Contemporaneity – Buddhism and Lover Suicide], *Taiyō*, 5(6) (March 20, 1899), pp. 63–71.

Mita Sadanori, "Jisatsuron" [On Suicide], *Kokka Igaku Zasshi*, 343 (1915), pp. 1–31.

Ihara Shigehiko, "Ichi Jisatsu rei no Kōsatsu" [Considerations on a Suicide Case], *Shinkeigaku Zasshi*, 29 (1928), pp. 534–552.

Ōkuma Shigenobu, "Seishinbyō ni tai Suru" [Impressions on Mental Illness], *Shinkeigaku Zasshi*, 4(12) (1906), pp. 614–625.

Komine Shigeyuki, "Jōshi ni Taisuru Igakuteki Kōsatsu" [Medical Considerations on Lovers' Suicides], *Komine Kenkyūjo Kiyō*, 6 (1938), pp. 1–301.

Fukushima Shirō, *Fujinkai Sanjūgonen* [Thirty-five Years of a Woman's Life] (Tōkyō: Fuji Shuppan, 1984).

Michael Shiyung Liu, *Prescribing Colonization: The Role of Medical Practices and Policies in Japan-ruled Taiwan, 1895–1945* (Ann Arbor, MI: Association for Asian Studies, 2009).

Yamana Shōtarō, *Nihon Jisatsu Jōshiki* [Records on Japanese Suicide] (Tokyo: Shichō Bunken, 1928).

Tsubouchi Shōyō, "Jisatsu no Zehi" [Suicide Approval], *Taiyō*, 9(9) (1903), pp. 56–71.

Kagawa Shūtoku, "Ippondo Gyoyo Igen" [My Extra Medical Commentary], in Kure Shuzō, *Kureshi Iseido Sōsho* [Kure Collection of Great Physicians' Texts] (Tokyo: Shinbunkaku, 1970), pp. 579–601.

Naka Shūzō, "Seishin Ryōhō no Gaiyō," *Gyōkei Eiseikai Zasshi*, 7 (1932), pp. 32–39.

Kure Shūzō, "Seishinbyōsha no Jisatsushō ni Tsuite" [On Suicide in Mentally Ill Patients], in *Kure Shūzō Chōsakushū*, 2 vols. (Kyoto: Shibunkaku, 1982), vol. 2, pp. 255–301.

Kure Shūzō, *Seishinbyōgaku-shūyō* [Textbook of Psychiatry] (1894), 2nd ed. (Tokyo: Tohōdō, 1916).

Ōtsuka Sokō, "Jisatsu to Seinen" [Suicide and Teenagers], *Taiyō*, 9(8) (July 1, 1903), pp. 207–213.

Steven Stack, "Suicide: A Comparative Analysis," *Social Forces*, 57(2, Special Issue) (1978), pp. 644–645.

Miyanaga Takashi, *Meiji Taishō shōWa no Nihon Shakaigakushi* [Considerations on the Heredity of Sociology – Japanese Sociology in the Meiji, Taishō and Shōwa Period] (Tokyo: Kadokawa Gakugei Shuppan, 2007).

Yorimatsu Tamao, "Taishōki no Jitsuroku shōSetsu ni Kakareta Shinjū Jiken to hōTeki Mondai," *Hōshigaku Kenkyūkai Kaihō*, 8 (2003), pp. 55–58.

Satō Tatsuya, "Rises and Falls in Clinical Psychology in Japan: A Perspective on the Status of Japanese Clinical Psychology," *Ritsumeikan Jinbungaku Kenkyū* (2007), pp. 83–84.
Hasegawa Tenkei, "Jinsei Mondai no Kenkyū to Jisatsu" [Research on Problems of Living and Suicide], *Taiyō*, 9(9) (August 1, 1903), pp. 174–176.
Ōto Tessei, "Kanjūsei no Gaibu Tōshi" [Outward Manifestation of Sensibility], *Hentai Shinri* [Abnormal Psychology] (Tokyo: Fuji Shuppan), 20 (October-December, 1922), pp. 432–446.
Terada Torahiko, "Jisatsu ni Yoru Manzoku – Jisatsusha no Shinriteki Kōsatsu" [A Sense of Satisfaction from Suicide – Psychological Considerations of Suicide Victims], *Fujin Kōron*, 9 (September, 1921), pp. 26–34.
Etsuro Totsuka, "The History of Japanese Psychiatry and the Rights of Mental Patients," *Psychiatric Bulletin*, 14 (1990), pp. 193–200.
Ōmichi Waichi, *Jōshi no Kenkyū* [A Study on Lover Suicides] (Tokyo: Dobunkan, 1911).
Kataguchi Yasufumi, *Sakka no Shindan* [Analysis of Novelists] (Tokyo: Shibundo, 1966).
Hayami Yasutaka, *Tsukimono Mochi Meishin* [Superstition of Tsukimono Mochi] (Tokyo: Akashi Shoten, 1999).Ōtsuki Yasuyoshi, "Hyōi to Seishinka Rinshō" [Spirit Possession and Clinical Psychiatry], *Rinshō Seishingaku Kōza*, Vol. 23 (Tokyo: Nakayama Shoten, Tabunkakan Seishinigaku, 1998), pp. 335–356.

2 Culturalizing the meaning of suicide (1930s–1945)

Exonerating "virtuous suicides" from biological norms

It would be tempting to assume that the debate on suicide between the psychiatric discourse and the sociological, psychological, intellectual, and nationalistic narratives worked as a binary opposition – the discourse of modernization on the one hand, and the anti-modern ethos on the other. Nonetheless, the conceptualization of social relations and practices instead based itself on a hegemonic formation that involved a mutual contamination of identity and difference, an iterability that shaped and reshaped the internal logic of this conceptualization.

In the late 1930s, despite incessant efforts to standardize the nosology and clinical assessment of suicide, and despite acrimonious competition with other disciplines to establish itself as the dominant one, psychiatry slowly but increasingly abandoned any ambition to provide a monolithic and coherent theorization of voluntary death. For the first three decades of the twentieth century, the discipline proved to be rather static, even uncompromising at times. It showed a relatively consistent and solid theoretical apparatus, in the sense that it was exclusivist and centered on a set of core ideas about what constituted mental illness. Nonetheless, psychiatrists showed divergent tendencies in their interactions with other discourses. In their dialectic on suicide with psychologists, sociologists, and intellectuals, psychiatrists had demonstrated that they were capable of maintaining their authority in reconciling, controlling, or monopolizing the resistant discourses. In their dialectic with the nationalistic discourse that began to intensify in the 1930s, however, they demonstrated a rather compliant and conforming attitude.

The 1930s were a turbulent decade in Japanese history. The nation experienced a deep economic downturn, the military established almost complete control over the government, and imperial ambitions intensified, pushing the country to expand its borders in East Asia. Shōwa nationalism, the ideological component behind Japan's rise to world power status, was a complex phenomenon that permeated everyday behaviors and thoughts as well as the structured daily experience of the Japanese. It was *in primis* an indictment against foreign ideas and practices with the attitude that, if unrestrained, Western pollution might contaminate the very essence of indigenous culture. Furthermore, Shōwa nationalism emphasized

Japan's cultural distinctiveness in order to – using Kosaku Yoshino's words – regenerate the national community by creating, preserving, and strengthening the people's cultural identity.[1] It was under this ideology that the medical community, in service to the government's effort to envision an alternative international order, articulated eugenics as the scientific language of Japanese expansionism. For the government, it was imperative to maintain and develop national superiority [*kokumin no yūshūsei*] in order to carry out the great project of building the so-called Greater East Asia Co-Prosperity Sphere. This, the government believed, was achievable partly by improving the quality of the population through health and hygiene policies. Such interventionist policies were intensifying globally in the 1930s in all countries because of the Depression, and in Japan had initiated the transformation of the state into a modern welfare state. In 1934, one year after Germany's sterilization law was passed, the Japanese Race Hygiene Association [*Minzoku Eisei Gakkai*], tightly connected with the Japanese bureaucracy, drafted a National Eugenic Protection Bill [*Minzoku Yūsei Hogo Hōan*]. This was modeled on the German law that protected the 'fit' and purged the 'unfit' with the argument that this would build a stronger nation. The Japanese bill, which was the blueprint for the government's wartime population policy and was touted as a means of improving the national character, did not pass. It was resubmitted in 1937, and again in a watered-down version in 1940, when it was finally approved. The law's endorsement illustrated the way in which eugenics had by 1940 amalgamated effectively with the established elite ideology of the family-state and with the dictum that in all realms of life individuals must act for the good of the organic whole.

The co-optation of culture by the hegemonic nationalistic discourse was of central ideological and political importance; culture was used as a unifying feature, crucial to a cohesive nation-state. Sharing values, myths, and origins guaranteed a certain degree of homogeneity. Under this discourse, culture determined behavior, necessarily including behaviors such as suicide. But if suicide was determined by contextual factors like culture, should it then be framed within the realm of medicalization? Should certain 'character types' be criminalized? Should all 'rebellious deaths' – perceived or proclaimed – be subjected to the process of pathologization? These lingering questions urged psychiatrists to show a more accommodating attitude towards the nationalistic propaganda and to emerging new interpretations of suicide, even to the detriment of their theoretical coherence and standardization of practices.

Even before the nationalistic discourse overwhelmed the nation in 1937, the medical community had already abstained from pathologizing certain so-called traditional suicide patterns (by 'traditional' they meant those patterns commonly performed during the period before Westernization started, with the Meiji revolution serving as the most convenient demarcation point). These suicide patterns were said to express the 'values of the Japanese' (including *on* or indebtedness, *giri* or social obligation, *ninjō* or compassion, loyalty and obedience, and reciprocity). Psychiatrists excluded three traditional suicide patterns from any kind of biological investigation: Buddhist martyrdom; the practice of *seppuku*, animated by *bushidō* [the ethics of samurai]; and *shinjū* [double suicide]. Physicians made room for the acceptance of suicide when practiced for the sake of religious devotion or altruistic sacrifice; as a means to gain honor; or as a spectacle of immeasurable love. It can be hypothesized that when motivations were deemed adequate, suicide was absolved from the realm of pathology and reconceptualized as the incarnation of national values. But how could psychiatrists accept such exceptions from the universality of biological norms on suicide? What is evident is that room for such acceptance progressively increased under pressure from the rampant nationalistic discourse.

The first of the three suicide patterns that psychiatrists absolved from their biological scrutiny was Buddhist martyrdom. Psychiatrists considered the Buddhist canon to clearly permit certain forms of suicide, which incorporated ideals of altruistic sacrifice mixed with religious offering. Despite the fact that Buddhism does not explicitly condone suicide, the notion of Buddhism as a suicide-permitting religion was endorsed by the convergence of various factors, such as ambivalent Indian Buddhist doctrinal sources about self-mutilation and suicide, Japanese monastic traditions valorizing suicide for the purpose of attaining birth in the Pure Land, and traditional views of martyrdom based on Confucian values of warrior suicide.[2] While they decried the absence of a Buddhist prohibition against the taking of one's own life, Japanese psychiatrists in the first half of the twentieth century offered no commentary or inquiry on martyrdom. Psychiatrists accepted Buddhist suicide as an act of self-sacrifice in service to ideals that transcended the individual. In this way, suicide was seen as acceptable when it was committed based on internalization of sociocultural norms (honor, etc.); suicide was seen as pathological, and therefore unacceptable, when it was committed as an expression of individual will.[3]

The second suicide pattern exonerated from psychiatric examination was *seppuku* or *harakiri*. Allegedly *bushidō* inspired, this suicide pattern also included obligatory *junshi* (the samurai practice of following one's master to death – the most highly ritualized violent form of *seppuku*). *Seppuku* had been banned by the Tokugawa shogunate in 1663 and was rarely practiced after that. It was then officially abolished during the Meiji era, and in 1881 – in order to prevent suicide-homicide [*muri-shinjū*] – the government issued a further Imperial Edict stating, "Whoever invites, suggests, [or] forces anyone to commit suicide will face a punishment of over 6 months and less than 3 years in prison, with an additional fine."[4] Although *seppuku* had been outlawed since the Tokugawa period, in popular culture it remained a symbol of purity of motives whenever it was practiced. When forty military men committed *seppuku* in 1895 as a protest against the return of the Liaotung peninsula to China, for example, newspapers portrayed their act as a courageous mutiny against the tarnishing of Japan's victory over China. In 1899, Nitobe Inazō provided a philosophical basis for *seppuku* in his work in English titled *Bushido: The Soul of Japan*. In this foundational text about Japan's national identity, which explained the fundamental Japanese codes of ethics, Nitobe discussed *seppuku* as the noblest form of suicide, thus rediscovering and popularizing it.[5]

Despite having been made illegal, *seppuku* returned in the form of a new imperial faith with the act of General Nogi Maresuke, which catalyzed both cultural and medical attention. In 1912, General Nogi, hero of the Russo-Japanese War, committed *junshi*, and his wife committed *jigai* (suicide traditionally committed by a female belonging to a samurai family), shortly after Emperor Meiji's funeral cortege left the Imperial Palace. The event caused public astonishment because, as Carol Gluck explains, "In a nation in the midst of a solemn celebration of its modernity, its foremost soldier [. . .] had followed a custom that had been outlawed by the Tokugawa shogunate as antiquated in 1663."[6] National newspapers led the charge in support of *seppuku*, in order to demonstrate patriotism and support for the nation. Nogi and Shizuko's suicides were spiritualized, aestheticized, and sublimated as national symbols of "beauty and nobility."[7] Reporters extensively acclaimed the nobility in particular of Nogi's deed, and devoted much space to the proper bounds and expressions of his loyalty: "[Nogi's] voluntary death [*jishi*] teaches us the most solemn lesson in life."[8] They showered the anachronistic soldier with praise and admiration for his demonstration of the brilliance of the national character, as well as for the loyalty and devotion of the warrior's way that prompted self-sacrifice. The press portrayed his act as the height of patriotism, a virtue so unique to the Japanese that "[it] is impossible to explain to a foreigner."[9] Despite being a lawbreaker, Nogi became an incontestable example of Japanese tradition in popular culture. By reenacting an ancient suicide pattern and regenerating a forgotten tradition, Nogi achieved sublimation not only as the symbol of an unchanging and eternal past, but also as the emblem of the romantic rebirth of the pre-industrial era's ideals, in contrast to modernity's chaos.[10]

The press's exaltation of *seppuku* was perhaps to be expected. The neutral or even favorable position taken by some psychiatrists was more of a surprise. The previously mentioned cases, which occurred in the first half of the twentieth century, achieved extraordinary coverage in the media, thus stimulating commentary by the medical community. Psychiatrists did not uniformly respond with the same emphasis or intensity to these cases, but they generally acknowledged them to be 'traditional suicide.' Mita Sadanori, for example, in his long dissertation on suicide as the outcome of mental illness, maintained an impartial position vis-à-vis *seppuku*: "[S]uicide motivated through the spirits of loyalty and patriotism, which are unique to our country, are not relevant to my argument here."[11] In so doing, Mita removed particular suicide patterns from the realm of pathology and identified them instead as supporting national culture. Unlike Mita's neutral approach to traditional suicide patterns, Komine Shigeyuki, a practicing psychiatrist and specialist on suicide, wrote admiringly that *bushidō* "is the essence and the flower of the spirit of the nation. It is through the spirit of *bushidō* that the nation rules the world in eternal peace."[12] Clearly, Komine valued self-control and discipline as features crucial to the making of a healthy and loyal citizenry, and consequently to the making of a strong nation. In any case, whether sympathetic or neutral, the psychiatric response made no attempt to pathologize patterns of traditional suicide. In fact, psychiatrists refrained from suggesting that a *bushidō*-inspired suicide was the result of any internal abnormality. Largely influenced by the nation-building project of the rising totalitarian regime, medical experts confronting suicide seesawed between eager participation in a nationalistic patriarchy and a guarded awareness that their profession could exist only by engaging with the state.

Glorified by the media and absolved by psychiatrists, *seppuku* was largely romanticized by the totalitarian regime, as it epitomized the values of the indigenous culture.[13] Sympathetic images of glorious suicides increasingly became a defining characteristic of Japanese civilization and its accompanying lifestyle. *Harakiri* was framed and narrated by a new set of moral understandings and social circumstances, becoming part of a modernizing urban landscape. With the beginning of the war with China in 1937 and the US in 1941, the cult of traditional suicide engulfed the nation.[14] The militaristic suicide pattern was brought back into vogue when, with the coup d'état in February 1936, the Kodōha lieutenant Aoshima Kenkichi and his wife retraced Nogi's path and committed *junshi* and *jigai* respectively. From that point forward, a vigorous theorization of *seppuku* clearly and symbolically associated the act with loyalty to the nation. In 1937, the intellectual Saitō Kaname retraced the history of *bushidō* in his *Nihon bushidō no saiginmi* [Reconsiderations on Japanese *Bushidō*], concluding that because of ethnic characteristics of loyalty, honor, and empathy, the Japanese committed suicide in a unique, righteous way.[15] Later, in 1943, the intellectual Shibukawa Keiō, in his *Nihonteki Seishikan* [A Japanese View on Life and Death], asserted that the combination of national character, Buddhism, and *bushidō* molded the Japanese attitude toward life and men's readiness [*kokorogamae*] for death.[16] Between 1935 and 1945, roughly fifty publications discussed and commented upon Yamamoto Tsunetomo's *Hagakure* [In the Shadows of Leaves, 1716], invoking *bushidō*-inspired suicide as an ideology underpinning the national identity.[17] Intellectuals' efforts to reason about and extol *seppuku* proved particularly fruitful when, during the last years of war, the irrational and uncoordinated acts of Japanese 'death-defying warriors' were displayed as the ultimate expression of national devotion. In October 1944, the *tokkōtai*, or suicide squads, were 'encouraged' to sacrifice their lives for the Emperor and for the nation, and in 1945 the mass suicides of civilians in Saipan and Okinawa were romantically called *gyokusai* [literally 'jewels scattering'], defined as an honorable form of death and a nobler act than surrender to the enemy. The public discourse exalted this spectacle as the incarnation of loyalty and patriotism; the medical community remained silent – probably not indifferent, but neutral.

The third suicide pattern absolved by psychiatrists was double suicide or *shinjū*. Unlike Buddhist suicide and *seppuku*, *shinjū* began to be excepted from the realm of pathology starting only in the 1930s, under the pressures of Shōwa nationalism. *Shinjū* (literally 'oneness of hearts') originally meant a mutual suicide agreement by lovers to prove their genuine love for each other – an act also known as *jōshi*. Over time, the *shinjū* label grew to encompass other kinds of 'double suicides.' Records on *shinjū* dating back to the Kamakura period show that this suicide pattern was extremely ritualized and romanticized. In 1722, after the suicide epidemic triggered by Chikamatsu Monzaemon's *Sonezaki Shinjū* [Double Suicide at Sonezaki, 1722], the Bakufu punished lovers' suicides as immoral and forced wrongdoers who attempted it to endure public humiliation. The punishments usually took place at Nihonbashi or Sennichimae in Osaka and lasted three days. From that point on, double suicides for love were considered an act of violence, rebellion, and resistance and thus were banned, first by the Tokugawa government and then by Meiji leaders. Still, *shinjū* survived, surrounded by a romantic aura within the popular discourse, and pathologized by physicians. The psychiatrist Nakamura Kokyō, for example, an active proponent of psychological research and mental science as well as the editor of the journal *Hentai Shinri* and founder of the *Nippon Seishin Igakkai* [Society for Japanese Psychiatry], skewered the romanticism entailed in *jōshi*: "[*jōshi*] is not a death aiming to realize love, but rather to avoid life. Love comes second, and death is not immoral and impure. [. . .] Love is everything, but it is a foolish love. It makes [lovers] forget about everything, about duties and about logic."[18] Kaneko Junji further argued that the Genroku era (1688–1704) was an age of degeneration, a time when people were sexually aroused by bloodshed, and he argued that *shinjū* was the result of the slave-like status of prostitutes at that time.[19] Whereas Nakamura emphasized the element of escapism in lovers' suicides, thus lessening their romantic claims and reducing their act to a symptom of irrational feelings, Kaneko disparaged the values of potential victims of *shinjū* – women in particular – as resulting from diminished authority and independence.

In 1932, a lovers' suicide case known as the Sakata *shinjū* thoroughly catalyzed popular fascination, as well as medical attention, revealing the inherent contradictions within the psychiatric discourse. A young man and a young woman committed *shinjū* on a seaside hill in Kanagawa prefecture, not far from Tokyo. The young woman's parents had opposed the couple's marriage, so they decided to "aim for eternal love."[20] Their bodies were found lying on Sakata Mountain facing the sea. He was wearing his Keio University uniform; she was wearing a purple *yukata* and holding her lover with one hand. With the other hand, she gripped some grass, possibly a reaction to the pain she had gone through after swallowing poison. This lovers' suicide could hardly have been better planned to become a media sensation. Here was the tragic end of a thwarted passion between two youths from society's upper crust, with a picturesque locale as its backdrop. To add to the dramatic interest, an elderly man from a nearby town was suspected of engaging in necrophiliac behavior over the woman's dead body.[21] The common interpretation was that the two victims had taken their lives for the sake of a bond that was entirely private in nature, thereby denying their obligations to external authority. This rebellious attitude against social rules – characterized in the Tokugawa period as romantic escapism – was now welcomed by the media. In less than one month, the case was adapted as the basis for a film, *Tengoku ni musubu ai* [Love Consummated in Heaven, by Gosho Heinosuke]. Its title was taken from the name of the first article that had appeared about the *shinjū*, in *Tōkyō Nichinichi Shinbun*.[22] The double suicide and film predictably prompted dozens of imitation suicides. Within seven months of the first case, twenty couples had killed themselves on Sakata Mountain.[23]

Some historians and some sociologists fully embraced the Sakata case as an illustration of their long-standing claims that suicide was a cultural and social act and the outcome of environmental conditions. Based on almost no comparative statistical data, they argued that double suicides were much more numerous in Japan than in the West, implying the presence of something valuable in Japanese culture which lent nobility and distinctiveness to their national identity. Already in 1907, Takada Yasuma, an influential sociologist and economist, most widely known for his power theory of economics, had argued, "[*jōshi*] is a traditional artifact and a traditional institution that, thanks to Buddhist influence, crafted [our] spirit to sacrifice one's own life for duty [*giri*] and emotions [*ninjō*]."[24] In 1928, the sociologist Kobayashi Ryūnosuke reasserted the notion that *jōshi* was a phenomenon intrinsic and endemic to Japanese culture, claiming, "[foreigners] cannot understand the true meaning of *jōshi*, which for every Japanese represents the oasis of pure sentiments."[25] Mikami Sanji, professor of Japanese history at the Imperial University of Tokyo, who specialized in the Edo period and was chief editor of the monumental compilation of historical sources *Dai Nihon Shiryō*, argued, "The major reason we are prone to call Japan 'the lovers' Suicide Nation' is that love between man and woman in Japan is more passionate than in other countries."[26] Mikami suggested that Buddhism and *bushidō* had galvanized this noble and elevated sentiment during the Tokugawa period. Unfortunately, Mikami did not use reliable statistical data: in fact, the number of lovers' suicides had increased exponentially in more recent times. However, the number was indeed shown to be disproportionate to the sporadic cases occurring in the West. After the 1932 Sakata case, Takata Yasuma agreed with Mikami's argument that *jōshi* and *shinjū* were more numerous in Japan than in any other country in the world. He defined *jōshi* as an "unexplored field of study" and suggested that an analytical breakthrough on the topic would shed light on unique national features. To achieve this, though, Takata demanded that the government systematically collect data regarding *jōshi* and *shinjū* cases, in order to make a complete comparative analysis possible.[27] Then, in 1934, the sociologist Iguchi Takachika, an exceptional connoisseur of European sociological studies on suicide and a well-known advocate for the necessity of investigating the suicide phenomenon from a sociological perspective, reiterated the idea that Japan is a "*jōshi no kuni*" [a lovers' suicide nation], a country highly unique compared with Western countries.[28] The scholar was convinced that the elevated number of *jōshi* could be explained by the Japanese tendency to self-sacrifice for the sake of duty and love. Iguchi insisted on Buddhism's crucial role in differentiating Japan from China as well as from Western countries in terms of the norms and values regulating public life, and encouraged sociological studies to scientifically demonstrate Japanese singularity. Lovers' suicide was thus an important locus where historical and sociological enthusiasm vis-à-vis Japanese distinctiveness was vigorously catalyzed. The nationalistic propaganda of the era surely played a crucial role in making this happen.

Unexpectedly, some psychiatrists as well found the Sakata case redeeming for its romantic and aesthetic features; as a result, they refrained from trying to pathologize this particular act. For them, the victims in the Sakata case did not represent a social danger and did not match the typical characteristics of suicidal patients; on the contrary, physicians recognized in their act the 'uniqueness' of the Japanese. In 1937, Ōnishi Yoshie, a psychiatrist who specialized in suicide, mapped the historical development of suicide in Japan in three stages.[29] According to his model, the first stage came in the sixteenth century, when the unique form of suicide known as *seppuku* was elaborated as part of the *bushidō* ethics adopted by the samurai class. The second stage saw the development of *shinjū*, which was born from the urban and commercial refinements of the Genroku era in the early eighteenth century. During the third stage, in the 1920s and 1930s, dramatic socio-economic changes, which Ōnishi explained as the effect of Japan's rapid ascent to the status of world power, led to the phenomenon of family suicide [*ikka shinjū*].[30] Ōnishi claimed that these three suicide patterns were a distinctly Japanese contribution, "original" in world history.[31] The style of suicide represented by the Sakata *shinjū* exemplified Japan's uniqueness as a nation blessed with a creative gift for inventing remarkable forms of suicide.[32] In the late 1930s, when war with China broke out, the suicide rate dropped in Japan; Ōnishi didn't just note the reduction in suicides, but also trumpeted that this event 'improved the quality' of suicide in Japan. In his eyes, the war with China had brought back traditional suicide with pure motives, and reduced frivolous, rebellious, faddish, and egocentric suicides. Ōnishi identified the 'traditional patterns of suicide' of which he approved as ones that were committed for the sake of the nation, and according to customary values that included altruism, sacrifice, and passionate love. He rationalized that good suicides embodied the righteousness of Japanese national identity.

Without a doubt, the medical community diligently demonstrated their usefulness in serving political ends with their neutrality toward, and at times support for, the highly politicized nationalist discourse on traditional patterns of suicide. When the tension between culture and psychopathology could not be ignored, medical professionals refrained from constituting culture as the subject and domain of psychiatric practice. They positioned allegedly 'Japanese values' inside the range of normality and exonerated them from medicalization. Some exonerated *shinjū* – and the lovers' suicide on Sakata Mountain, for example – as the alleged quintessence of Japanese traditional values and as a pattern animated by respectable motivations (altruism, passionate love, etc.). In other words, psychiatrists selectively refrained from deploying the biological model, and even began to call it into question. Under the influence of the positivist sociological discourse, they increasingly adopted new tools of analysis and definitions as well as new therapeutic practices in order to reformulate their theories and to redeem 'good' suicides. Was this, then, the co-optation of culture by a hegemonic psychiatric discourse, creating confusion in the newly developed psychiatric theoretical apparatus? And were the inconsistencies truly negotiable, or even reconcilable, with the nationalist discourse? Such questions became salient in the 1930s for those psychiatrists who aimed to extend medicine beyond the bounded frameworks of state legitimation.

Synthesizing biological universality and cultural uniqueness

The rehabilitation of the samurai code that reestablished Japanese historical continuity, the reaffirmation of cultural uniqueness through the enshrining of old-fashioned altruistic suicide motivations, and the putative propensity of an entire society to *shinjū* all demanded that psychiatrists reformulate their theoretical apparatus on suicide. In essence, the nationalistic discourse required that particular suicide patterns be presented as cultural artifacts, that is, as products of social and historical forces situated outside the mental state of isolated individuals. Psychiatrists saw a need to reconcile the professed *de facto* evidence of suicide as a symptom of mental illness with the idea of Japan as a 'Suicide Nation' in which customary suicide types were resurging anew. In trying to perform this task, psychiatrists often deployed inconsistent and contested strategies and gave confused rationales to justify them.

Psychiatrists were concerned about the rising rate of suicide in Japan, a phenomenon that urged academia to elaborate a comprehensive theory to identify the norms and mechanisms animating it. After 1913, the suicide ratio remained consistently high, reaching a peak in 1936 at a rate of 22.0 per 100,000 people per year.[33] From 1936 until the end of World War II, the suicide rate was persistently low, a condition that contemporary scholars attribute to the fact that this period coincided with the era of militarization and the war.[34] In 1936, the *Yomiuri Shinbun* explained the increase in the suicide ratio as the outcome of economic constraints, mental illness, and more than anything else the "expression of our nationality" [*minzokusei*].[35] In 1942, the sociologist Koshida Hisamatsu analyzed suicide statistics between 1930 and 1938, hypothesizing that both the increased suicide rate through 1936 and the subsequent decrease were caused by the most problematic portion of Japanese society: males in the 20–29 age group (Koshida claimed that suicides by men dropped from 9,766 in 1936 to 7,585 in 1938 despite the fact that the population was growing – the total population was 70,114,000 in 1936 and 71,013,000 in 1938).[36] Koshida inferred that the war in China brought a great number of young men to the front, stemming a suicide epidemic. Along with mourning the lack of a young, healthy generation, Koshida also lamented the malaise of farmers, who – according to his statistics – accounted for 44 percent of the total number of male suicides. For Koshida, suicide was a symptom of a society at risk, dismembered by a dual economy; a society suffering the hidden costs of the unevenness of modernity; a society in agonizing response to industrialization and Westernization.

Apprehension regarding the increasing number of suicide cases pushed certain psychiatrists toward the slow but increasing incorporation of sociological, cultural, and psychological elements into their theoretical apparatus on suicide. By weaving the biological narrative together with these other narratives, on the one hand psychiatry merged with the nationalist discourse that held that suicide was an acceptable and even attractive 'feature' of the Japanese; on the other hand, it succeeded in temporarily expanding into the popular domain, before coming to a halt in 1937 as a result of wartime priorities.

Komine Shigeyuki was a psychiatrist who stood out from his colleagues in his strong desire to rationalize the medical response to traditional suicide patterns and to reconcile psychopathology with the vibrant nationalist discourse on suicide. He aimed to resolve the theoretical inconsistencies in the discourse on voluntary death; additionally, he sought to synthesize biological norms with proclaimed 'cultural features' by deploying a variety of methodological tools. He concluded that suicide was a psychiatric object of inquiry, assessment, and treatment that could only be understood in its entirety if it were both psychologically evaluated and culturally analyzed. Komine managed to absorb and integrate a variety of discourses in his theorization of suicide, overcoming the rifts among psychiatry, psychology, and sociology. His enterprise was encouraged by the nation's intensifying cultural discourse and was deeply influenced by eugenics and its revolutionary developments in biology and medicine. In the 1930s the medical community embraced genetic theories, although at the time little research had demonstrated links between mental illnesses and genes [*iden*]. Many physicians such as Komine worked in institutions affiliated with the emerging totalitarian state, and the preoccupation with the question of national identity played a crucial role in forging their positions in the debate on suicide. The newly favored discipline of eugenics promised a new cure not only for a wide range of diseases but also for social problems. This new biological theory of human improvement could be regarded as a social and cultural philosophy of individual and collective identity within the context of modernity. Physicians' and academics' interests shifted to social medicine and cultural medicine, and Komine was not immune to these changing perspectives.[37]

Komine wrote prolifically between 1919 and his death in 1942.[38] In his early years, he mainly engaged with questions of biological medical science; then in the late 1920s and early 1930s he was attracted by the clinical sides of psychiatry, such as its etiology, diagnostics, and therapeutics; throughout the 1930s he dedicated his attention to socio-medical issues; and in 1940 he published two eminent essays opposing sterilization, a thorny question that divided the Japanese medical world for years.[39] Komine explored a wide range of topics, from the history of psychiatry and psychology in Japan to the history of insanity and the psychiatric analysis of folklore. He dedicated important studies to the psychoanalysis of suicide as well, exploring diverse patterns and motivations, in particular aspects of love, sexual desire, and domestic affection. His analysis was based mainly on the Freudian theoretical framework, which was at that time still a novelty in Japanese psychiatry. Unfortunately, though, Komine's use of Freudian psychology went no further than the level of popular and rather crude explication of basic psychoanalytic ideas. Therefore, despite the diversity of the topics discussed, Komine's studies remain very basic and not well formulated.[40]

Komine proceeded systematically and thematically through a psychiatric exploration of suicide, examining each suicide pattern one by one within its historical context. This was a useful way to validate the cultural values standing behind the act without problematizing the process of pathologization put in motion by his former colleagues. He pioneered a number of studies on four *shinjū* patterns in particular – *jōshi*, *dōseiai shinjū* [homosexual suicide], *muri-shinjū* [suicide-homicide], and *oyako-shinjū* [parent-child suicide] – in four monographs that remain arguably unsurpassed as the most substantial historical works on the topics.

Komine argued that throughout Japanese history, *jōshi* had been prompted by the social and familial system, by the Buddhist promise of a better life, and by *bushidō* ethics.[41] These features of Japanese society exacerbated the condition of those who suffered from psychiatric abnormalities.[42] The number of *jōshi*, he added, increased exponentially in the early twentieth century because of poverty, a condition that further amplified historical and cultural motivations.[43] Komine argued that *jōshi* was the expression of a Japanese trait that was the antithesis of Western individualism or egotism: while Westerners focus on their own selves, the Japanese die for something to which they belong. This might be one's family, one's master, the Japanese nation, or the ties of romantic love between a couple. In other words, Komine reconciled culture and psychopathology by recognizing the validity of both the theory of character type and the uniqueness of national values. He suggested that their very synergy triggered the suicide phenomenon. However, he cleverly implied that part of this synergy (that is, psychiatric abnormalities) was 'treatable.'[44]

Komine did not restrict his investigation of love to heterosexual suicides but included homosexual ones as well, defining the pattern of homosexual double suicide as "typically Japanese."[45] He published an extensive work in 1938 that dealt with lovers' suicide among both male and female homosexual couples. In it, Komine gathered substantive data and carried out a comparative analysis between heterosexual double suicides and homosexual double suicides. He questionably concluded that whereas heterosexual couples who committed suicide tended to belong to disparate social classes, partners in homosexual suicides belonged to the same social status, class, or occupation. Furthermore, heterosexual double suicides were premeditated and often provoked by the impossibility of marrying, while homosexual double suicides were mostly motivated by trivial events such as fleeting jealousy or a bad day, especially in lesbian suicides.[46] In a later study, Komine gathered 8,800 cases of accomplished and attempted *dōseiai shinjū* recorded between 1873 and 1935, concluding that more than half of the cases were committed by women. He focused on 342 cases of female same-sex love suicide reported in the Japanese daily press and committed between 1925 and 1935.[47] The unusually high concentration of lesbian suicides in this decade constituted, according to Komine's analysis, 31 percent of all suicides reported in Japan.[48] Based on a thorough scrutiny of this sample, the psychiatrist concluded that women were psychologically weaker than men and that they usually committed suicide uniquely for the sake of love, sympathy, or compassion – as opposed to men, who resorted to suicide when they found themselves simultaneously in a storm of passion and in economic difficulties. Komine defended the cultural uniqueness and peculiarity of lesbian suicide in Japan, arguing that it was based on Buddhist precepts of searching for a better life. Further, he saw it as expressing the Japanese proclivity for escapism – that is, the tendency to abandon one's reality when it was marred by embarrassment, humiliation, or distress. Finally, Komine criticized the popular discourse on lesbianism and lesbian suicide for being remarkably homogenizing and injurious. He accused newspapers of portraying lesbians' voluntary deaths as acts of political dissent because they were promoting an alternative, threatening idea of womanhood. Komine bravely exposed the press's suppressive mechanisms toward minor and disturbing discourses, mechanisms that worked to reinforce the dominant narrative on suicide. Sadly, though, his work heavily relied on newspapers and on haphazardly collected, categorized, and interpreted suicide statistics, all of which call into question its methodological consistency.[49]

Komine's work on lovers' suicides walked a fine line between contradictions. On the one hand, with little or no comparative data, Komine argued that Japan had a record high rate of *dōseiai shinjū*; on the other hand, he agreed with the Italian criminologist Cesare Lombroso that homosexuality was based on a genetic character type visible from childhood or manifested during later development. Komine redeemed the exceptionality of the lovers' suicide pattern, which did not need to be cured, as it only mirrored the cultural practice of the nation.[50] Nonetheless, he simultaneously posited a 'curable' patient profile, enhancing his profession's potential for institutional and medical success.

The same contradictory conclusion was reached in Komine's argument regarding *muri-shinjū*, as well as his historical exploration of jealousy, which he was convinced was the triggering motive of *muri-shinjū*.[51] He explained the suicide pattern psychiatrically as the result of hysteria, psychologically as the expression of an overwhelming passion and destructive jealousy, and culturally as the outcome of *bushidō* and its values of virtue and chastity (a husband and wife needed to protect purity within their marriage).[52] In short, hysteria combined with what he called the peculiar excess of passion of Japanese men could ignite *muri-shinjū*. Thus, the psychiatric and psychological aspects were pathologized, and therefore 'treatable,' while at the same time the 'Japaneseness' of the act was exonerated from the process of medicalization.

Nevertheless, when it came to *oyako-shinjū*, Komine had a hard time reconciling psychiatric diagnosis and treatment with the nationalistic discourse on 'traditional values.' He examined parent-child suicide cases in Meiji, Taishō, and Shōwa Japan, maintaining that the rate had increased in the 1920s and the 1930s because it reflected the general poverty caused by modernization (Komine referred to poverty as *puroretariabyō*, or proletariat disease).[53] Although his data were questionable, his explanation was confirmed by Wada Muneki in his own 2005 study of newspaper articles on *oyako-shinjū* during the Meiji and the Taishō eras.[54] Wada reasoned that media coverage at the time was not inclined to compassion or even sympathy toward *oyako-shinjū*; on the contrary, *oyako-shinjū* was perceived to a certain extent as a child homicide, rather than a joint suicide. From his research, it also emerged that *oyako-shinjū* attracted more attention under certain circumstances: when committed by women, when committed in big cities (probably because modernization had irreversibly changed the family structure, leading to nuclear families that were more exposed to social imbalances and risks), and when brought about by disappointed love rather than by poverty and economic hardship.

In contrast to the unsympathetic narrative supported by the press, Komine defended the act of *oyako-shinjū*, advocating that it was an amalgam of *bushidō* ethics and the Japanese patriarchal code of behavior: "[Parent-child] suicide was a product of the *bushidō* spirits concerning loyalty to one's master and one's nation and of the patriarchal system of the feudal age. They did not give in to the enemy when defeated. Nor did the family suffer disgraceful separation. Rather, the family or the clan chose to kill themselves."[55] Commenting on a mother-child suicide a bit later, he asserted, "this is an example of how *bushidō* influenced a mother-child suicide in my country."[56] The mother who killed her children and then took her own life was – Komine argued – practicing the ethic of family solidarity, refusing to allow either herself or her children to go on living alone in this world.[57] Thus, the ethos behind the act of parent-child suicide was, paraphrasing Komine, unique to Japanese culture and absent in countries dominated by individualism, like those of the West.[58]

In 1936, in conformity with the official wartime pro-natalist policy, the government began to devote more attention to the issue of poverty and its impact on increased rates of *oyako-shinjū*. This concern led to the passage of the mother-child protection law, which provided relief for impoverished mothers and children as well as counseling for pregnant women.[59] Komine lauded the preventive policy of the government toward parent-child suicide cases and promptly took a step back from wholehearted defense of the act. In 1937, he wrote about mother-child suicide in a highly ambiguous way.[60] He explained that mothers who suffered from psychiatric problems committed 60–70 percent of *oyako-shinjū* cases and that women's proclivity to murder their children and commit suicide mirrored the desperate awareness they had of their economic hopelessness [*keizaiteki muryoku*].[61] In other words, Komine was stating that poverty exacerbated mental illnesses.

In essence, with Komine, the psychiatric theories that treated suicide as a symptom of an internalized pathology, and assigned very little weight to cultural and historical factors, were reformulated and rationalized. When the nationalistic discourse coerced all medical disciplines to contribute to the making of the Japanese race, Komine reasoned that suicide could be rooted in social and cultural conditions as much as it was in genetics and biology. With Komine the cultural orientation of those who committed suicide – and of the group to which they belonged – played a critical role in how illness was enacted, interpreted, explained, responded to, dealt with, and given meaning. Suicide defined as an illness was not supposed to contain such social and cultural parameters; however, Komine assigned these meanings via symbolic conventions.[62] Rather than identifying universal 'indicators' of suicide per se, Komine described the phenomenon by incorporating factors reflecting social reality. I argue that this process began with a slow re-incorporation of cultural and historical explanations of given suicide patterns (psychiatric studies were first enriched by studies of the history of psychiatry and psychology in Japan and then of the history of the nation). It proceeded with the assimilation of sociogenic explanations (given suicide patterns were caused by altruistic motives and/or by economic problems). Finally it arrived at the acknowledgment that suicide could be either curable (as in the case of Fujimura Misao) or incurable (as in the case of the lovers on Sakata Mountain).

Komine is a prime example of those psychiatrists who accommodated themselves to the current ideologies and values, rather than impose new views upon society. They assembled appealing bits and pieces from different disciplines and incorporated a kaleidoscope of elements into their scholarship, showing great adaptability. The variety of narratives had the potential to cultivate a 'biocultural' understanding of suicide; what had previously been explained by psychiatrists exclusively as a biological, and thus universal, pathology was now explained as an act that was also culturally and socially negotiated. After all, theories of illness are cultural, aiming at explaining and rationalizing the treatment of illness, theories based on a system of meanings that are highly socialized and politicized. Recognizing suicide as a 'biocultural' artifact meant that the view of suicide was to some extent ethnocentric. The idea of 'culture' was strongly attached to national identity; and nationality is not voluntary, but determined by birth. This meant that traditional patterns of suicide – which were inherited by the fact of being Japanese – would have an exclusivist nature. The fusion of medical and sociocultural perspectives empowered psychiatrists to diagnose and treat the diseases of a culture, but also transformed those diseases into a potential threat to the culture's very survival. The tension thus lay in the contradictions embodied within the concept of national identity, which was construed as both that which 'cures' and that which must be cured: national identity as illness, national identity as panacea. Was national identity in fact the altering pathogenic vector that had to be corrected in order to cure patients? Of course, raising such a question was not an option in 1930s Japan, but a careful reader can find it in Komine's late rearticulation of his overarching characterization of Japanese culture.

Desisting from culturalizing women's "blameful suicides"

Paradoxically, in seeking to transcend the dichotomy between biological and cultural explanations of voluntary death, Komine's theoretical enterprise unveiled a deep rift between the conceptualization of suicide committed by men and that committed by women. Traditional suicide patterns like *seppuku*, committed by valiant males, were essentially examined through cultural lenses, whereas women's suicides were scrutinized through their organic and physical dimensions, and thus viewed mainly as the expression of mental illness. The solidification of this divergent approach was probably not only the consequence of the reassertion of the uniqueness of Japanese patterns of suicide, which reaffirmed traditional gender constructions, but also the paradoxical effect of the biocultural narrative. In both cases, patterns and values were rearticulated that positioned men's and women's suicides differently in relation to the notion of normality.

Despite the fact that psychiatrists wanted to include the sociocultural sources of pathology in their analysis so as to accommodate the highly politicized nationalistic discourse, they tended to refrain from 'culturalizing' women's suicide. Or more accurately, they did not deny the role of the cultural environment in women's suicide: they accepted that many causes of suicide lay outside women themselves. However, they emphasized that the mechanism of activation was within female biology and tried to locate its manifestations within the female body. The result was a heightened concern on the part of medical experts regarding the allegedly problematic mental health of women, an attitude that reinforced the unsympathetic gaze toward women's suicide in popular culture.

In 1933, a fierce public debate over the suicide of a young girl at Mihara Mountain received widespread visibility throughout the archipelago, triggering an indefatigable determination in both the press and the medical community to construct a gendered notion of voluntary death. The lack of an unequivocal motivation not only stimulated a public thirst for news, but also encouraged both reporters and psychiatrists to speculate on the mechanisms that led the girl to kill herself. In February, the 19-year-old Matsumoto Kiyoko, a student at Jissen Women's University in Tokyo, committed suicide by throwing herself into the active volcano of Mihara. Five days before undertaking the journey toward Mihara Mountain, Kiyoko left a long suicide note for her father, which ended, "I want you to think of me when you see the ashes of Mihara Mountain."[63] Kiyoko's best friend, Chimoto Masako, escorted her to the island of Ōshima, some three hours' steamer ride from the capital: Masako had a return ticket in her hands, but Kiyoko had just a one-way ticket. Once on Mihara Mountain, Kiyoko turned to her friend, bowed, and jumped into the crater. The Japanese press extensively covered the suicide case; Kiyoko and Masako became instant national figures, and a wave of copycat suicides began. The death toll mounted quickly: by 1935, Mihara Mountain had swallowed up 350 suicides (143 in 1933, 167 in 1934), including young males as well as females, and had seen more than 1,380 suicide attempts. Local authorities eventually erected a fence around the base of the mountain to curb the number of suicides and banned the purchase of single-way tickets to the island.

The high incidence of suicides at Mihara Mountain was followed by an intensive debate among journalists and psychiatrists over the causes of the epidemic. The hypothesis of *dōseiai shinjū* – though it was soon eliminated from further consideration – as well as Kiyoko's father's reference to her 'difficulties in finding a husband' contributed to the sensationalizing of the case. The Yomiuri Newspaper referred to the copycat suicides on Mihara Mountain as "victims of suicide disease" [*jisatsubyō kanja*] and to the phenomenon as the "Mihara syndrome" [*Mihara kanjabyō*]. A reporter pointed out that the waterfalls in Nikkō or the Mountain Shinshū in Nagano had been famous locations for suicide, "but after the popular case of the young lady who committed suicide on Mihara Mountain, people prefer Ōshima. There is a particular point near the crater where azalea flowers profusely blossom; this spot surely has a certain appeal to irrational young girls."[64] If the Yomiuri Newspaper suggested discreetly that Kiyoko's suicide was an act of indulgence and thoughtlessness, the Asahi Newspaper's coverage took instead a romantic but aggressive tone. One journalist reported that Kiyoko had confessed to her school friend Masako that she was "bewildered to distraction by the perplexities of maturing womanhood" and went on to describe how Kiyoko "disappeared in the yellow light of the morning, and flew away like a cicada."[65] The yellow light may have been intended to symbolize Kiyoko's youth and immaturity. I further read the image of the cicada as an unsympathetic symbol embodying the tactic of using deception to escape danger, specifically by using decoys (leaving the old shell) to fool enemies. The Asahi Newspaper's coverage poetically portrayed the girl's suicide as an act of immature escapism, of 'moral deficiency,' and of emotional instability. Journalist, political activist, and feminist Hiratsuka Haru described the two girls as mild [*onwana*] and maternal, but too fond of reading Japanese novels, especially Kiyoko. Kiyoko had lost her mother when she was young, and from this fact Hiratsuka promptly constructed an image of a melancholic girl whom she harshly criticized. To paraphrase the journalist, Kiyoko was anything but the image of modern femininity; she was instead a girl who had led a sheltered life [*hakoiri musume*] and had never taken on responsibilities. Hiratsuka then observed: "The Mihara Mountain case is the outcome of exaggerated youthful passion and devotion to the construction of a petty self who denies the importance of society [*shakaisei*]."[66] After railing against the young woman's selfishness, this unforgiving critic then provided an even more bitter assessment. She admonished the irrational, fragile, unemancipated young lady with the observation that despite the fact that Kiyoko had invested heavily in a modern education, she ultimately chose an old-fashioned form of suicide more appropriate for a middle-aged woman [*hoken jidai no musume no yōna kanenna shinikata wo shimashita*]. For Hiratsuka, Kiyoko was irredeemable; the journalist portrayed the young woman as a vessel of modern alienation and egotism, and at the same time an executor of an anachronistic pattern. In other words, the Mihara Mountain suicide was represented as a case of female psychological maladjustment and emotional instability. Men too were involved in the copycat suicides that followed Kiyoko's death, but interestingly enough, they were inexplicably left out of newspaper critiques. The idea inherent in popular commentaries was that when it came to judging women's suicides, personal flaws and failings were more relevant than broad cultural causes.

The obsession with the Mihara Mountain case and the harsh criticism of a supposed personality flaw in young Japanese women encouraged the intervention of the medical community. Medical experts criticized the press's sensationalizing of the case. At the same time they less explicitly supported the underlying asymmetric gendered construction by assuming that medical techniques were justified in treating women and that cultural causes were less relevant to their suicides.

In an interview with the Asahi Newspaper, psychiatrists at the Aoyama Seishin Hospital warned that suicide could potentially be an epidemic, and thus journalists should not sensationalize or glamorize it as they had in the past with the Fujimura case.[67] The physicist and essayist Terada Torahiko objected to the newspapers' mania for the Miharayama incident, their impreciseness and greed for sensationalism, and their simplistic conjectures about "a very complex event."[68] Referring to a short article appearing in *Fujin Kōron* that claimed to reveal all the secrets related to Kiyoko's suicide, Terada commented that it was nothing but a highly speculative account of a conversation that Kiyoko and Masako might have had the day before Kiyoko's suicide, in which Masako likely failed to convince her friend not to kill herself.[69] Terada observed that such trivial articles appeared in newspapers and popular magazines at least once a month; the coverage probably occurred as a result of the Japanese desire for "eternality of 'stereotyped expressions'" [*'teikei' no eikyūsei*].[70] Remarking that the public appetite for news was beyond satisfied, he directed his plea toward the press that had unscrupulously interpreted the reasoning behind the young girl's suicide. Sarcastically, he advised journalists that if they wished to add a hint of freshness to their accounts, they ought to replace the despicable stories on Mihara Mountain with poems from *Genji Monogatari* or *Kojiki*.[71] Terada argued that this making of news was backward, using a strategy of sensationalism to attract public visibility, and oversimplifying complicated suicides. Such newspaper actions, in his opinion, were creating biased knowledge regarding women's voluntary death by molding it in patterns of inclusion and exclusion without any scientific evidence.

Interestingly, psychiatrists' views on men's and women's suicide echoed the conventional descriptions that had been appearing in newspapers since the press was established. Female constitutions were thought to be finer-nerved than those of men, and the female womb, in previous centuries, had been thought to be the source of disorder that needed regulating. Such views did not go entirely unchallenged, but their legacy was visible in both medical and popular literature. Women were often framed within the discourse of the finer-nerved sensibility that led to suicide, and psychiatrists' imagination persisted in a tendency to blame women's suicides on moral and physical deficiencies intrinsic to their gender. Reporters had extensively talked about hordes of beautiful but irrational young women giving up their lives at popular sites. They had also dedicated particular attention to professions identifiable with the female gender, such as café waitresses [*kissa gaaru*], which embodied modern decadence and alienation in the public imagination.[72] Motivations adduced to women's suicides ranged from emotionality to irrational rashness [*kokoro no yure*].[73] Of 146 descriptions of lesbian suicides that occurred in the first half of the twentieth century, for example, all were analogous:[74] the women all poisoned themselves with morphine and tied up their extremities [*shimatsu wo musunde*]. Allegedly these women committed suicide because of loneliness, boredom, and a desire for sympathy [*dōjō*], and it was unquestioned that they killed themselves because they were weak and ill. The novelist Hirabayashi Taiko explained the distinction between men's and women's motives for double suicides with a loved one. Women were described as showing signs of alienation, neurosis, and mental illness, whereas men were described as showing a proclivity to exhaustion due to overwork.[75] Women were thus thought to be affected by mental derangement [*seishin sakuran*] and were defined as weak and ill [*byōjaku*].[76] In fact, newspaper titles regarding approximately fifty suicides by women that occurred between 1900 and 1945 used the word *byōjaku*: women were described as being affected by neurasthenia, endlessly living in a melancholic and desperate state, and investing their last energies to purchase pills from drug stores in order to poison themselves.[77] When, for example, a 20-year-old nurse and her girlfriend committed *shinjū*, their suicide note stated "life is boring" [*jinsei ga tsumaranai*], which hinted at depression and a sense of estrangement as the causes of their act. Despite the note, one reporter commented that the only possible reason for the joint suicide was the sadness and melancholia inspired by a novel they were both reading (whose title was not mentioned, likely an intentional choice). Newspaper coverage thus adduced that the motivation triggering the two women's suicides was trivial, as ephemeral as the momentary effect of reading a romantic novel.[78] In another example, Yamakawa Kikue, an essayist on gender studies, scrutinized the assessment of the Ministry of Treasury [*Ōkurashō*] adducing "lack of peace in the family" [*katei no fuwa*] as the cause of a family suicide case [*ikka-shinjū*]. Yamakawa added that the reason behind the annihilation of this entire family originated in the decline of patriarchal society. He lamented that the powerful, assertive, and omnipotent figure of the husband was disappearing under the pressures of modernization and economic hardship, but sadly was not being replaced by a strong female figure.[79] Economically dependent, physically weak, and mentally fragile, Japanese women could not provide relief or consolation to a family in danger. Yamakawa assumed that the merits of past and present solid families were to be found in sturdy and healthy males. More subtly, he sympathized with men and did not believe that they were capable of such horror as the homicide of children, which tradition had legitimized as suicide in the case of *oyako-shinjū*. Yamakawa transformed the potential male 'murderer' into a victim, obfuscating his social and historical character and framing him in a timeless, nostalgic manner. Neither was the popular discourse inclined to show compassion toward women committing *oyako-shinjū*. On the contrary, when committed by a mother, *oyako-shinjū* was categorized as 'child-homicide,' while they were conventionally labeled 'joint suicide' when committed by the father. Reporters alienated readers' potential sympathy by describing mothers as mentally unstable and cruel [*muzan*] assassins of innocent [*mujaki*] children.[80]

In general, women were portrayed as passionate and beautiful, and at the same time inherently weak and foolish. Psychiatrists explained the latter observation biologically. By 1913, Sawada Junjirō had already drawn the defining characteristics of the suicide/criminal, arguing that women who showed such a disposition and such symptoms were more numerous than men.[81] In 1915, Mita Sadanori had posited that the deviations that led to suicide were located in the central nervous system in men and in the reproductive system in women. In 1917, Kure had attributed the increase in suicide rates among prostitutes to mental illness rather than economic hardships (as had originally been hypothesized by journalists). He was convinced that these women possessed "inherent mental abnormality," which would also explain why they were prostitutes in the first place.[82] Komine's asymmetric assessment of men's and women's suicide was evident in his analysis of parent-child suicide. Despite the fact that many women involved in *boshi-shinjū* [mother-child suicide] were divorced, separated, widowed, or unmarried mothers living with their children, or experiencing extreme economic hardship, Komine tended to emphasize their unstable mental and physical conditions rather than their economic troubles. He defined women as *byōjaku* and pictured them as sensitive to love affairs and emotional problems. Komine openly ascribed women's suicide to 'madness,' while contrarily interpreting father-child suicides as an act of men's responsibility that reincarnated the samurai ethos.

Needless to say, the praise of Japanese patriarchy and the careful but distinct endorsement of male suicide inspired by the samurai ethos were not shared by all, especially by feminists. Sasaki Shigetsu, sculptor, poet, and founder of the Buddhist Society of America, wrote in *Fujin Kōron* that in such a paternalistic society where women could not live their lives freely, it was somewhat normal for a woman to desire death. Sasaki even encouraged suicide in women, as they were sheer "slaves" or "an appendix" to their husbands. People commonly referred to women as *dokufu* [evil, wicked women], he argued, so what is better than buying poison and killing oneself? Sasaki offered strong sympathy for the plight of women in a patriarchal society and a perspective that claimed free agency for women as well as men. His provocative way of claiming this agency was to advocate suicide as a free choice, as an alternative to a life of misery, a life that he denounced and profoundly refused.[83] In the 1930s, a harsh judgment against Westernization as the cause of women's suicide was leveled by Yamada Waka, a Christian feminist and an activist in the maternalist movement. Yamada opined that the noxious influence of Western thought patterns had intensified women's sense of individualism and egotism while weakening their sense of engagement with family, society, and state. Isolated, less willing to sacrifice themselves, these women became psychologically unstable, and their condition was responsible for the levels of mother-child suicide. It is notable that Yamada, with no medical background, used the terms 'neurasthenia' and 'hysteria' to name this state.[84] Paradoxically, in introducing a critique of the West as the vector of infection, the feminist Yamada adopted the prevailing stereotype of femininity: women as custodians of morality and the repository of tolerance and understanding. She defended women's sovereignty by accusing external factors of causing a deterioration in women's traditional character, constraining their independence and contaminating their health.

By modeling gender distinctions in suicide, the psychiatric and the popular discourses were not only differentiating men and women, but also sanctioning heterosexual unions, and assessing how to be a well-functioning family – the smallest unit of the nation – that anchored itself to traditional gender divisions. Suicide in fact became an important site where evaluating the distinction between virtuous and blameful motivations enacted larger judgments on gender roles in a historically patriarchal society. When psychiatrists like Komine demarcated the difference between 'good' traditional suicide and frivolous, vain self-murder that incorporated modern alienation or individualism, they also gave an oblique endorsement to the proclaimed motivations (altruism, patriotism) of male suicides to the detriment of women's suicides.

If the beauty of women's suicide was idealized, women were at the same time put firmly in their place. The discourse on suicide revealed a deep mistrust of women who might live up to ideals of independence, or act as self-regulating individuals: such women were perceived as a menace to society and the nation, threatening the established order they were intended to uphold. This mistrust was manifested in medical treatment and in popular disdain. Psychiatrists denied the qualities of balance, motherhood, and tolerance in women, leaving the female patient a creature composed solely of an unstable nervous system combined with irrational passions and emotions. In this discourse, women were primarily governed by the influences of menstruation, pregnancy, and menopause, but hardly by cultural aspects. Descriptions of female suicidal behaviors were presented by male authors whose studies not only contained constructions of different patterns for females and males, but also attempted to place female behavior at the perimeter of male behavior, with women defined by, and dependent on, the male. Emancipation was argued to be the cause of the increased female suicide rates; that is, women's misuse of their bodies led to self-annihilation, or they were engaging in acts of rebellion against a patriarchal system. A countermodel was in fact Shizuko, General Nogi's wife. She incarnated the values of the past, and more precisely, she incarnated values whose moral rigor was directed against modernity and against the modern woman as the nursery of vice. Psychiatrists' analysis of women's suicide read like a condemnation of the existing image of woman rather than an assimilation of this image into their thought. Modern women's suicide, however fascinating it might be, was seen as decadent, and unpatriotic because it weakened the nation and deprived it of healthy sons and daughters. So, were psychiatrists misogynists? Were they holding to the nineteenth-century ideal of woman as a patient to treat relentlessly?

Scientific and popular interpretations of suicide certainly recognized different degrees of intentionality in those who killed themselves, ranging from an impulsive desire to escape from an unbearable reality (usually associated with women) to a fully premeditated act (commonly associated with traditional patterns and men's suicides). Such interpretations were quick to acquit the latter. 'Conscious suicides' actively created meaning, thanks to their own deaths, whether it was by demonstrating loyalty toward a master or toward the nation. However, physicians were concerned by irrational suicides and the supposedly weak female nervous system: they saw it as their duty to cure women, restoring their dignity and self-control. Thus the dichotomous interpretation of suicide tended to cleave to the lines of gender construction. On the one hand, scientific and popular interpretations of suicide revealed the need to frame 'good' suicides within a logic that made them acceptable, both socially and morally, even aestheticizing them at times as cultural acts. Doing so meant, to a considerable extent, exonerating the 'national culture' from psycho-biological scrutiny, and exonerating men as the repository of this culture. Other suicides, allegedly those committed by foolish and fragile women, were guided by forces, mainly biological, over which only psychiatrists could exert control. In this way, women's agency was removed. Women who killed themselves became, according to popular culture, victims to be pitied and patients to be treated by the medical community. By desisting from culturalizing women's suicide, psychiatrists safeguarded male-dominated structures and secured large-scale medicalization.

1937–1945: the temporary end of biological reductionism

By 1937, the compelling nationalistic propaganda was increasingly channeling the medical community's efforts toward the interests of a nation-state committed to imperial expansion, and the nation had successfully coerced all medical disciplines to devote themselves to the making of the Japanese race. Under the pressure of the chauvinistic rhetoric, the division between normal and pathological began to erode. Psychiatrists reasoned that suicide could be rooted in socialization as much as it was in genetics and biology, and it might be catalyzed by a particularly difficult time period or environment. Suicide came to be conceptualized less and less as a universal, static phenomenon and more as a collective, relational, and even historical act. Komine, as we have seen, committed to resolving seemingly contradictory conceptualizations. He sought to reconcile the debate between psychiatric and sociological theories of suicide that could be traced back to Esquirol and Durkheim, as well as the disagreement between the psychiatric and cultural discourses. Komine called for moderation and for conciliatory policies: he recognized the social character of suicide but also reduced the phenomenon to the aggregate of individual actions in a way that allowed physicians to discriminate against and victimize those found biologically abnormal or defective. Komine did not contest the nationalistic propaganda that lauded the power of Japanese cultural uniqueness. On the contrary, he went along with the nation's idea that society had established its superiority over the individual through historical traditions and customs, and conveyed the notion that shared historical and cultural factors determined the collective inclination of the Japanese to voluntary death in general and to 'traditional' suicide patterns in particular.

Although there was an apparent tension between the psychiatric pathologization of suicide and the national discourse that enhanced its historicity, both narratives shared the leitmotif of silencing the political meaning of voluntary death and the authoritative role of the individual in choosing it. Both discourses lessened the individual's independence and self-sovereignty, whether by reducing the act to a symptom of brain abnormalities or by rendering it as a conveyance of traditions, inherited culture, and historical continuity. In this ambivalent process, Japanese patients were unmistakably acknowledged as 'victims' of disease, and/or 'victims' of culture. While psychiatrists discriminated against, constrained, or excluded those found biologically abnormal or defective – thus diminishing responsibility for their actions – the act of suicide was at the same time depoliticized as an act of individual rebellion and reduced to a collective phenomenon.

After a brief but intense phase of attempts at conciliation with the national propaganda captained by Komine, physicians' efforts to negotiate in this way began to come to a halt in 1937, when the government pushed for full mobilization of the national spirit for the war effort. At this point the eugenics section – just included in the newly created Ministry of Health and Welfare – subsumed the medical community under war policies. Many physicians found themselves working in institutions affiliated with the emerging totalitarian state, and the national preoccupation with the question of national identity and the military needs of war played a crucial role in forging their voice in the debate on suicide.

The psychologists Matsumoto Matatarō, Watanabe Toru, Tanaka Kan'ichi, and Obonai Torao, for example, sent out questionnaires to their colleagues at the 12th meeting of the Japan Association of Applied Psychology in 1937, asking what psychologists should be involved in during a time of national mobilization. The psychologists at the gathering responded that they should "continue usual research." However, as the war deteriorated, the research priority soon shifted strictly to "papers directly useful for improving military service," and the discipline's efforts were quickly absorbed into the nation's war program.[85]

Psychiatrists were encouraged to contribute to the conceptualizing of the Japanese race. A vigorous debate and complex negotiations between those who supported and those who rejected the eugenic discourse on mental illness took place in 1940, immediately before the passing of the Eugenics Law on Sterilization.[86] However, once the National Eugenics Act was issued, the government galvanized the medical community into supporting the war using the national slogans "progress in efficiency" [*nōritsu zōshin*] and "soul care" [*kokoro no yōjō*]. At this point, psychiatrists began to show a certain degree of consensus with the national policies. They certainly saw advantages in the new governmental strategy, as they gained an increasingly large number of patients.[87] Uchimura Yūshi, chair of the psychiatric department of the Imperial University of Tokyo, at the inaugural ceremony of the Mental Welfare Association in 1943, declared, "The spirit of the citizens is healthy and this is because since 1937 we have halved the number of patients suffering from neurasthenia. However, we cannot be complacent when we are fighting against many nerve wars [*shinkeisen*]."[88] At a time when citizens were constantly being urged to strengthen their bodies and their souls, Uchimura was proudly advertising the success with which psychiatrists, working within the framework of hygiene, were taking medical and emotional care of the Japanese.

Extraordinarily, only a few psychiatrists kept carrying out research that aimed at demonstrating the universality of biological laws. The most relevant studies carried out during the war were those by Kure Keiki and Sugiyama Shigeteru. Between the nineteenth and the twentieth century, in their efforts to discover a consistent biological premise behind every suicide case, several German pathologists and biologists had pursued research regarding the relation between suicide, or mental illness in general, and pathological growth of the thymus gland.[89] Following these studies, first Kure Keiki conducted a postmortem analysis of suicide cases and found that several victims had pathological growth of the thymus gland. A year later, Sugiyama Shigeteru, professor of medicine at Kyoto University, confirmed the results in an article of his own with the exact same title as Kure's previously published research.[90] In 1890, in the first study of the association between mental illnesses and pathological growth of the thymus gland, the German biologist Pfeiffer had examined 595 suicide cases in Germany, concluding that the link between suicide and glandular abnormality, as well as cardiovascular problems, was undeniable. Pfeiffer also identified pregnancy and the menstrual cycle as being extremely deleterious for women's mental health, writing, "[Pregnancy and menstrual cycles] have a direct impact on suicide."[91] Sugiyama conducted his study on a much more limited sample, simply aiming to prove that Pfeiffer's results were valid for the Japanese too. Of 253 cases, he concluded that 8 cases (3.16 percent) showed clear enlargement of the gland, advocating to his colleagues that the biological basis of suicide should be investigated more extensively.

Despite the determination of a tiny group of psychiatrists and a handful of biological studies aiming to prove the genetic basis of suicide, the years between 1937 and 1945 were characterized by a general decline in studies articulating a psychiatric etiology of suicide and in the biological standardization of its patterns. As Akimoto Haruo has suggested, wartime Japan saw political priorities lead to psychiatry's shift from a dominant to a secondary discourse.[92] Pushing Akimoto's argument further, then, nationalistic interests determined the temporary end of biological reductionism. This also marked the termination of the process through which psychiatry proliferated into broader domains by popularizing the language and ideas of the psychiatric discipline.

While growing nationalism and the war's intensification domesticated the medical community, these factors also reinvigorated the glorification of so-called traditional suicide patterns in the popular discourse. Between 1937 and 1945, a conventional representation of voluntary death vigorously emerged in newspapers, fiction, and film. The protagonists of these suicide stories – whether *kamikaze*, lovers, or desperate couples or families annihilated by economic hardship – were animated by 'good' values largely shared by the Japanese, such as patriotism, altruism, and honor. *Ikka-shinjū*, for example, was essentially portrayed as an act of decency motivated by financial worries. Unfortunate parents in a suicidal state seemed to reason that it was somehow better for their children to die honorably with their parents than to endure what they believed was the hardest time of Japan's history.[93]

Interestingly, mental status and biological norms were no longer mentioned in the press. Suicide motivations, methods, and aesthetics turned by the late 1930s into a generalized representation of suicide as a mythologized expression of the past. Suicide patterns were subsumed within old paradigms, tending to 'normalize' and 'naturalize' a new Japanese historicity. Newspaper coverage portrayed suicide in traditional terms, seeking echoes of conventional aesthetics in an obstinate use of archaic terminology. It is worth noticing, for example, that the press suddenly began using old-fashioned terms like *jigai* and *jiketsu* (both terms mean 'suicide,' but they referred uniquely to suicides committed by *bushi*, thus carrying a rather strong nuance of violent self-annihilation). Unused since the early Meiji period, the terms *jigai* and *jiketsu* had achieved new popularity soon after Nogi's death. Nevertheless, these descriptors were no longer used in their original sense, to describe patriotic actions leading to honorable and heroic voluntary deaths, but instead became increasingly used to erroneously label those suicides resulting from disappointment in love. When the war in East Asia intensified in 1937, a refreshed use of the terms *jigai* and *jiketsu* by reporters demonstrated the fervent desire to create links to the romantic premodern era in order to reestablish a sense of aestheticized historical continuity and infuse characteristics of patriotism and loyalty into all manner of actions. When a young man committed *jiketsu* because he was ill and "unable to help his country by joining the army," one reporter emphasized his loyalty and lauded his deed as the demonstration of honor and manliness.[94] The nostalgia for the past in a rapidly changing world was also evident in the newspaper report of a man who decided to join the army after his father committed *jigai*. Here the journalist meticulously portrayed the outmoded death of the father and then described his son's act through the old-fashioned expression "*yumiya no michi he*" (literally meaning "to become a warrior," an expression largely used in premodern Japan).[95]

The intensification of the war unquestionably encouraged reporters to recharge the cult of youth and the cult of the beauty of voluntary death, along with associated stereotypes of masculinity. National newspapers poetically celebrated *seppuku* for its primitive strength and manliness, but ambiguously portrayed it as an act of voluntary death rather than as sacrifice. Its beauty was not new or unprecedented; on the contrary, it was a reinvigorated version of a national stereotype. Imaizumi Kotarō, professor of law at Keio University, defined *seppuku* as a symbol of a "total sense of responsibility" for Japanese: "*harakiri* is for my people an act of pride" and "an act of courage."[96] The resilient discourse asserting national pride and Japanese uniqueness was vigorously defended in academic works too. In 1943, the historian Wada Katsunori, author of *Harakiri no tetsugaku* [The Philosophy of *Harakiri*, 1927], wrote that the rapidly transformed international and domestic scenario did not change *bushidō* aesthetics but rather reasserted them: "loyalty, courage, and heroism are not simply characteristics of the Japanese, but a peculiarity of the Japanese."[97] Wada even reproached those Europeans who underevaluated the role that *bushidō* and *seppuku* played in Japanese society (specifying certain Russian historians who "forgot" to include *bushidō* and *seppuku* in their studies on Japanese characteristics).[98] He was convinced that the suicides committed for the sake of the Great War in Asia [*Dai tōa sensō*] were a manifestation of the Japanese sense of responsibility [*sekininkan*] and of morality [*dōgikan*].[99] To paraphrase his words, *seppuku* was a sacrifice that incarnated the Japaneseness of the nation.

In the last nine months of World War II, thousands of Japanese *kamikaze* pilots flew their bomb-laden planes on one-way flights to attempt to crash onto US battleships. Newspaper coverage mythologized the cases of these "death-defying warriors" and cleverly avoided the question of whether *kamikaze* should be framed within the realm of suicide or sacrifice. Reporters instead highlighted the extent to which such heroic deeds embodied cultural and historical continuities with premodern Japan, and turned the 'actors' into sites for nostalgic projection of a return to the Tokugawa ethos. As nationalistic propaganda engulfed the entire nation, *kamikaze* acquired nobility and social recognition thanks to its premodern symbolism and to the ambiguous concept of 'altruistic motivation.' As remarked by Kōsaka Masaaki, established philosopher of the School of Kyoto, in his last work on suicide, the association of *kamikaze* with suicide patterns performed during the Tokugawa period – that is, before Japan's encounter with the West – not only evoked historical continuity within Japan, but also emphasized the distance between the values behind the Japanese act and those of Western individualism and modernity.[100] Behind the apparent violence, *kamikaze* ethics were offered as a logic for national regeneration.

Kamikaze in World War II also epitomized the apex of a process that limited the subjectivity of the individual 'choosing' death voluntarily. This process had first been set in motion by psychiatrists, for whom the patient had no self-determination because suicide was regulated by biochemical rules. National propaganda further silenced the personal disruptive voice and limited the degree of individual subjectivity in its own way, interpreting suicide according to national and social priorities. The monological, private character of death was transformed into a public, dialogical event, turning a potential disturbance into a functional expression of social continuity. This tendency nostalgically recalled the notion that many so-called 'traditional suicides' fulfilled a dialogical function: examples included expressing gratitude, bidding farewell, or redeeming a serious offense that had shamed someone. The representation of suicide as a dialogical function pushed the private sphere further and further into the public one: individual autonomy was suppressed by a sense of collective solidarity, by responsibility for those dependent on one, and by the duty to respect the customs and the harmony of one's community. Thus the individual's personal death was transmuted into a 'public function' by society's efforts to socialize that death.

To conclude, for the first half of the twentieth century, suicide was a locus where the critical tension between a highly politicized nationalist discourse and the universality of the biopsychiatric assessment was enacted. During the 1910s and 1920s, in a climate of scientific optimism, the medical community aimed to acknowledge suicide as a symptom of an internalized pathology, in order to secure infrastructure for medical professionals and justify a paternalistic approach. This work owed itself to their adherence to a utilitarian apparatus (the Mental Hygiene Movement and the eugenics theories). By defining suicide as a pathology, they shifted people's attention away from the social conditions that may have given rise to it in the first place; this distancing from social conditions worked to establish their primacy over sociology and psychology. Psychiatrists thus established their domain as a moral enterprise, as formative of notions and practices of self-discipline, and as a guarantor of national health. But why were certain suicide patterns *not* seen as pathological while others were? Discourses on issues as diverse as nationalism, gender, and sexuality intersected and prescribed the ways in which, throughout the first half of the twentieth century, some narratives – or some representations of these narratives – became more influential than others.

The origins of Japan's reputation as a 'Suicide Nation' are traceable in the cultural narrative of those years. Psychiatrists initially confronted this set of discourses, which lacked any scientific support, by offering biological norms in opposition to them, explaining the universality of suicide, and labeling it as mental illness. They established their primacy over the cultural narrative thanks to their ability to popularize their own discourse, to control and monopolize resistant narratives, and to reconcile them. However, with the rise of a totalitarian regime, psychiatrists showed a tendency to reconceptualize suicide less as a disease and more as a historical act, to the detriment of their theoretical coherence and standardization of practices.[101] When sociocultural elements were incorporated into the psychiatric discourse, so as to reconcile the idea of suicide as pathology with the cult of voluntary death that was engulfing the nation, psychiatrists like Komine conferred authority on the idea that there was something unique in the Japanese way of killing oneself, that Japan was indeed a 'Suicide Nation.' Accepting multiple explanations for suicide meant relativizing the romanticized cultural argument to the detriment of psychiatric genetic determinism, paving the way to wider acceptance of the suicide-sacrifice performed during World War II.

Fervent nationalism thus solicited physicians and writers to serve government ideology and the imperative of national sovereignty. By the early 1940s, the argument of Japanese uniqueness had reached a large consensus among historians and sociologists, as well as amongst the medical community. Not all members followed the guidelines outlined by the Shōwa regime; however, the dissenting voices remained unheard and the questions they raised did not receive much attention from their contemporaries. Furukawa Tetsushi, for example, a very prolific student even before he obtained his PhD in ethics from Kyoto University under the supervision of professor Watsuji Tetsurō, raised fairly interesting questions regarding the nationalistic discourse and the proclaimed Japanese peculiarities. Renowned as a connoisseur of the work on *bushidō* carried out by the philosopher Kaneko Takezō and by his supervisor Watsuji,[102] Furukawa raised two fundamental questions. The first was whether it was useful to categorize voluntary death patterns as diverse as *seppuku*, *jōshi*, and *shinjū* together under the label 'suicide.' The second was why Japan was perceived domestically and abroad as a 'Suicide Nation.'[103] To the first question, Furukawa, writing in two separate articles, responded by offering a distinction between suicide and sacrifice.[104] A person who commits suicide, by his definition, was someone who has not sacrificed his/her own life, who has not ended his/her life over an ideological matter but who has chosen to kill him/herself as an act of free will (ergo, someone who could have decided to keep living). According to these principles, Furukawa labeled *seppuku* as sacrifice and *jōshi* and *shinjū* as suicide. In response to the second question, Furukawa showed evidence contradicting the assumption that suicide was more frequent in Japan compared with Western nations, or that it was historically a peculiarly Japanese phenomenon.[105] He then answered the question 'Why is Japan known as the Suicide Nation?' by claiming that the stereotyped image of samurai *seppuku* established by A. B. Mitford's *Tales of Old Japan* of 1871 had created this myth in Western countries.[106] Furthermore, Furukawa suggested that the immense interest in suicide aesthetics on the part of the Japanese bestowed great visibility, both domestically and internationally, on the phenomenon, thus constructing a false reputation as a 'Suicide Nation.' Furukawa's unconventional interpretation not only questioned the then-incoherent and fragmented conceptualization of suicide, but also sought to find a logical rationalization. However, his ideas never gained visibility.

The debate on voluntary death that at the beginning of the twentieth century had opened up a series of philosophical questions concerning the nature of the relationship between thoughts and events, psychology and politics, the individual and society, and concerning the socio-economic evaluation of life and death receded under the intensification of the nationalistic discourse. This promising confrontation encountered a temporary end between 1937 and 1945, under the pressure of national mobilization. Very few authors dared to confront the chauvinistic discourse on race and the uniqueness of the Japanese, and their voices were systematically quieted. It was not until the postwar period that it became possible to witness the blooming of a newly reinvigorated debate on suicide, when the absence of the nationalistic narrative permitted its emergence.

Notes

1 Kosaku Yoshino, *Cultural Nationalism in Contemporary Japan: A Sociological Enquiry* (London: Routledge, 1992), p. 1.

2 Mark Blum, "Collective Suicide at the Funeral of Jitsunyo: Mimesis or Solidarity?" in Jacqueline Stone and Walter Mariko Namba (eds.), *Death and the Afterlife in Japanese Buddhism* (Honolulu: University of Hawai'i Press, 2009), pp. 137–174; Max Moerman, "Passage to Fudaraku. Suicide and Salvation in Premodern Japanese Buddhism," in Bryan Cuevas and Jacqueline Stone (eds.), *The Buddhist Dead* (Honolulu: University of Hawai'i Press, 2007), pp. 277–296; Koike Kiyoyuki, "The Philosophical Argument against the Right to Die, from a Buddhist Viewpoint," *Journal of Philosophy and Ethics in Health Care and Medicine*, 1, July 2006, pp. 27–42.

3 This is the same confusion between sacrifice or self-sacrifice and suicide found in Durkheim's definition of altruistic suicide: that is, the act committed by individuals who are so integrated into social interests that they are even willing to sacrifice their own lives. See Émile Durkheim, *Le Suicide*, pp. 110–121. With the usefulness of the distinction between suicide and sacrifice disregarded, the tension embedded in the complicated relationship between the role of suicide motivations and suicide medicalization remained unresolved until the late 1960s. At that stage, several researches on Durkheim and his study on suicide highlighted the ambiguity of the concept of 'altruistic suicide' and the need to draw a distinction between suicide and sacrifice, as well as the need for sound research to clarify the roles of motivations and intentions in order to better understand suicide and attempted suicide. A debate emerged between those who recognized the usefulness of the distinction between suicide and sacrifice and those who rejected the distinction. In this book, suicide and sacrifice are acknowledged as two different categories: the first is motivated by a set of reasons internal to the individual; the second by factors external to the individual (duty, social obligations, etc.). See Christie Davies and Mark Neal, "Durkheim's Altruistic and Fatalistic Suicide," in W.S.F. Pickering and Geoffrey Walford (eds.), *Durkheim's Suicide: A Century of Research and Debate* (New York: Routledge, 2000), pp. 38–39; Steve Taylor, *Durkheim and the Study of Suicide* (New York: The Macmillan Press, 1982), pp. 132–136; Steve Taylor, "Suicide, Durkheim, and Sociology," in David Lester (ed.), *Current Concepts of Suicide* (Philadelphia: The Charles Press Publishers, 1990), pp. 195–200.

4 Cited in: Komine Shigeyuki, *Meiji Taishō Shōwa Nenkan ni Okeru Oyako Shinjū no Igakuteki Kōsatsu* [Medical Analysis of Parent-Child Suicide in the Meiji, Taishō and Shōwa Era] (Tokyo: Kyūzansha, 1998; reprint of original 1937).

5 George M. Oshiro, "Nitobe and Japanese Nationalism," in Roy Starrs (ed.), *Japanese Cultural Nationalism* (Kent: Global Oriental Ltd., 2004), p. 65.

6 Carol Gluck, *Japan's Modern Myths* (Princeton, NJ: Princeton University Press, 1987), p. 221.

7 *Yomiuri Shinbun*, "Kono Otto Kono Tsuma" [What a Husband, What a Wife], September 18, 1912.

8 *Yomiuri Shinbun*, "Genshukunaru Mondai" [A Matter of Solemnity], September 22, 1912.

9 *Yomiuri Shinbun*, "Kyōretsuna Sekininkan" [An Intense Sense of Responsibility], September 22, 1912.

10 For a thorough exploration of Nogi Maresuke and Shizuko's death, see Doris Bargen, *Suicidal Honor: General Nogi and the Writings of Mori Ōgai and Natsume Sōseki* (Honolulu: University of Hawai'i Press, 1996).

11 Mita Sadanori, "Jisatsuron" [On Suicide], *Kokka Igaku Zasshi*, 343, 1915, pp. 1–31, p. 1.

12 Komine Shigeyuki, "Koga Oyobi Ukiyo-e ni Kakaretaru Shitto no Yōkai Genshō ni Tsuite" [Desire and Jealousy in Ukiyo-e], *Iji Kōron*, 1389, 1939, pp. 709–712; 1391, 1939, pp. 899–900; 1392, 1939, pp. 977–980 and p. 711.

13 Between Nogi's suicide and the beginning of the war in 1937, a fairly extensive number of *junshi* had received news coverage. However, a deeper analysis of newspaper coverage shows that apart from a handful of cases, the term *junshi* was improperly used – or more accurately, it was used to romantically evoke Shizuko's passionate act, and thus employed to describe wives following their husbands in death after their partners' long illness, or disenchanted lovers killing themselves one after the other. See *Yomiuri Shinbun*, "Junshi no Keiro" [The Path to *Junshi*], March 25, 1914; *Yomiuri Shinbun*, "Rojo Junshi wo Tamotsu" [An Old Woman's Plan to Commit *Junshi*], May 27, 1914; *Yomiuri Shinbun*, "Otto no Kōchō ni Junshi su" [A Woman Commits *Junshi* after Her Husband, Dean of a High School], July 27, 1920.

14 Ōhara Kenshirō, *Jisatsu wo Kangaeru* [About Suicide] (Tokyo: Keizai Ōraisha, 1971), p. 106.

15 Saitō Kaname, *Nihon Bushidō no Saiginmi* [Reconsiderations on the Japanese *Bushidō*], 1937.

16 Shibukawa Keiō, *Nihonteki Seishikan* [A Japanese View on Life and Death] (Kyōto: Kōkyō Shoin, 1943).

17 The *Hagakure* was a practical and spiritual guide for warriors, drawn from a collection of commentaries by the samurai Yamamoto Tsunetomo and his conversations with Tsuramoto Tashiro from 1709 to 1716. The *Hagakure* was not a popular text until Nitobe and Inoue transformed it into a practical guide, using it to explain Japan's military victories over the Chinese and Russians. In the 1930s and 1940s, as imperial victories required increasing sacrifices, *bushidō* rhetoric became more macabre, and the *Hagakure* increasingly emerged as a central topic in the discourse, displacing the upbeat, ever-victorious *bushidō* Inoue championed. An early text signaling the new prominence of the *Hagakure* was Nagayoshi Jirō's *Nippon Bushidō Shi* [History of Japanese *Bushidō*], published in 1932, but the number of publications intensified as the war became increasingly harsh. One of those editions of *Hagakure* was avidly read by Mishima Yukio, who later published his own commentary on the work in 1967 and committed suicide by *harakiri* three years later. See Kathryn Spalding, trans., *The Way of the Samurai: Yukio Mishima on Hagakure in Modern Life* (New York: Basic Books, 1977); John Allen Tucker, "Tokugawa Intellectual History and Prewar Ideology: The Case of Inoue Tetsujirō, Yamaga Sokō, and the Forty-Seven Rōnin," http://chinajapan.org/articles/14/14.35-70tucker.pdf (accessed April 2015).

18 Nakamura Kokyō, *Jisatsu Oyobi Jōshi no Kenkyū* [Studies on Suicide and Double Suicide] (Tokyo: Nihon Seishin Igakkai, 1923), p. 51.

19 Kaneko Junji, "Shinjū no Seishinbyōgakuteki Kenkyū" [Psychological Research on *Shinjū*], *Tokyo Iji Shinshi*, 2613, 1929.

20 *Asahi Shinbun*, "Shinjū Meisho ha Tasukaranu to – Sakata Shinjūchū" [We Have to Save the Famous Locations for Suicide – The Sakata *Shinjū* Case], June 25, 1932.

21 *Yomiuri Shinbun*, "Sakatayama Shinjū Isshūki – Jisatsu Kanja 10yonin ni Oyobu" [The Anniversary of the Sakata *Shinjū* Case Triggers 10 More Suicide Victims], May 8, 1933.

22 *Tokyo Nichinichi Shinbun*, "Tengoku ni Musubu ai" [Love Consummated in Heaven], May 13, 1932.
23 *Yomiuri Shinbun*, "Sakatayama Shinjū Isshūki – Jisatsu Kanja 10yonin ni Oyobu"; *Asahi Shinbun*, "Nigumi no Fūfu ga Sakata Shinjūchū Hitori ha Zetsumei, Nimei Kiki" [Two Couples Involved in the Sakata *Shinjū* case, One Is Dead, One Is Critical], February 16, 1937.
24 Takata Yasuma, "Jōshi no Shinkenkyū" [New Research on Lovers' Suicide], *Chūō Kōron*, 4, 1907.
25 Kobayashi Ryūnosuke, *Jōshikō* [On *Jōshi*] (Tokyo: Bungei Shiryō Kenkyūkai Henshūbu, 1928), p. 35.
26 Mikami Sanji, "Rekishijō Yori Mitaru Jisatsu Toku ni Jōshi" [A Historical Perspective on Suicide and Lovers' Suicide in Particular], *Meiji Shi Ronshū*, 78, December 1909, reprint in 1976, pp. 181–192, p. 183. See also his later work: Mikami Sanji, "Fukanzen Naru Suikō" [An Incomplete Accomplishment], *Chūō Kōron*, 1931.
27 Takata Yasuma, "Jōshi Shinkenkyū."
28 Iguchi Takachika, *Jisatsu no Shakaigakutekina Kenkyū* [Research on Social Suicide] (Tokyo: Seiwa Shoten, 1934), p. 105. Iguchi worked as a journalist for *Asahi Shinbun*, as a consultant at the Japanese Ministry of Foreign Affairs, and as a professor at the Imperial University of Kyūshū. Referring to Takata's research, Iguchi added that in the late nineteenth century, in some European urban centers (such as Paris), *jōshi* cases reaching levels as high as 60 percent of the number of cases in Japan had been recorded. However, Iguchi promptly remarked that the loose categorization of the European authorities might have included all suicide patterns involving two or more people, regardless of the motivation behind the act. Iguchi Takachika, *Jisatsu no Shakaigakutekina Kenkyū*, pp. 185–190.
29 See also Akihito Suzuki's analysis of Ōnishi Yoshie's theory: Akihito Suzuki, "Psychiatry in the Land of Suicide: Medicalization of Self-killing in Early Twentieth-Century Japan," *Nihon Ishigaku Zasshi*, 59, 2013, pp. 3–15, p. 12.
30 Ōnishi Yoshie, "Kako Nijūnenkan ni Kagawa Kenka de Okonawareshi Jisatsusha ni Tsuite no Tenbō" [Considerations on Patients Involved in Suicides in the Last Decades], *Kansai Iji*, 326, 1937, pp. 8–10; 327, 1937, pp. 6–7; 328, 1937, pp. 5–7.
31 Ōnishi Yoshie, "Oyako Shinjū ni Tsuite" [On Parent-Child Suicides], *Nihon Iji Shinpō*, 758, 1937, pp. 954–957.
32 Ōnishi Yoshie, "Kako Nijūnenkan ni Kagawa Kenka de Okonawareshi Jisatsusha ni Tsuite no Tenbō," pp. 5–7.
33 Ministry of Health, Labor and Welfare, *Dai 5 Kai Jisatsu Shibō Tōkei: Jinkō Dōtai Tōkei Tokuchō Hōkoku* [5th Statistics Concerning Suicide Deaths: Special Report on Demographic Statistics] (Tokyo: Ministry of Health, Labor and Welfare, 2005), p. 42.
34 It is a widely accepted theory that suicide is less frequent during wartime and more frequent in periods of economic depression. Durkheim's explanation of the effect of war on the suicide rate was subjected to empirical scrutiny and has been broadly accepted by many sociologists. He explained the mechanism underlying war's effect on suicide as an example of political integration that works in the following way: during such political crises as wars, individuals think less of themselves as individuals and more of themselves as members of social groups. War and other national crises arouse popular enthusiasm for a common purpose, centralizing people's attention in a way that keeps their minds off their own troubles and allows them to escape for a time from personal miseries. "As [the struggles] force them to close ranks and confront the common danger, the individual thinks less of himself and more of the common cause." War, in other words, increases political integration, and political integration lowers the suicide rate. Furthermore, it is noteworthy that the sex ratios in suicide during war differ minimally compared with the periods before and soon after the war: during war, women's tendency toward suicide equals that of men. David Lester carried out a detailed scrutiny of Durkheim's political integration theory about suicide during

wartime. He compared analyses of different forms of violence (suicide and homicide) in various historical periods (wartime, peacetime, economic crises, and so forth) and demonstrated a certain degree of acceptance for Durkheim's integration theories. As a reference to this theoretical issue, see David Lester, *Patterns of Suicide and Homicide in the World* (Commack, NY: Nova Science Publishers, 1996), pp. 116–119; David Lester and Bijou Yang, *Suicide and Homicide in the Twentieth Century: Changes over Time* (Commack, NY: Nova Science Publishers, 1998), pp. 79–81; Émile Durkheim, *Suicide: A Study in Sociology* (New York: The Free Press Corporation, 1951), p. 208; James R. Marshall, "Political Integration and the Effect of War on Suicide: United States, 1933–76," *Social Forces*, 59(3), March 1981, pp. 771–785.

35 *Yomiuri Shinbun*, "Kokkateki Fukō no Hitotsu – Jisatsu Shinjū no Hinshutsu" [One of Our National Misfortunes – the Frequency of Suicide and *Shinjū*], April 21, 1936.

36 Koshida Hisamatsu, "Tōkeigaku Yori Mitaru Jisatsukō" [Thoughts on Suicide Based on Statistics], *Shakai Hōken Jihō*, 16(6), June 1942, pp. 36–49. Koshida's statistics are not given in terms of the number of cases per 100,000 inhabitants, but as an absolute number of suicide cases, which is unfortunately not a scientific method for explaining suicide trends.

37 The main goals of eugenics in Japan were health control, population growth, identification of hereditary diseases, and the establishment of a sterilization law for mentally handicapped people and those with hereditary diseases. Physicians' efforts came to a halt in 1937 when the government pushed for the full mobilization of national spirit and the eugenics section – just included in the newly created Ministry of Health and Welfare – subsumed the medical community under war policies. These policies meant that the medical community was no longer autonomous and now had to operate following rules that supported the war efforts.

38 For more information on Komine's stature and impact within the field, see Akihito Suzuki, "A Brain Hospital in Tokyo and Its Private and Public Patients, 1926–45," *History of Psychiatry*, 14, 2003, pp. 337–360.

39 Yōko Matsubara, "The Enactment of Japan's Sterilization Laws in the 1940s: A Prelude to Postwar Eugenic Policy," *Historia Scientiarum*, 8(2), 1998, pp. 187–201. Yōko Matsubara, "Senjika no Danshūhō Ronsō" [The Wartime Debates over Sterilization Law], *Gendai Shisō*, 26(2), 1998, pp. 286–303.

40 Komine's interest in Freudianism might have been forged as a result of his connection with Tōhoku University, where he received his medical degree. Tōhoku University was one of the few universities whose psychiatry department showed an early and ongoing interest in Freudian analysis.

41 Komine Shigeyuki, "Jisatsu Kōi wo Aeteseru Mōsōsei Yokuutsu Jōtai no Seishinbunseki Rei" [Psychological Analysis of Delusional Depression in Suicide Cases], *Shinkeigaku Zasshi*, 27, 1927, pp. 605–609.

42 Komine Shigeyuki, "Jōshi ni Taisuru Igakuteki Kōsatsu" [Medical Considerations on Lovers' Suicides], *Komine Kenkyūjo Kiyō*, 6, 1938, pp. 1–301, pp. 1–2.

43 Komine Shigeyuki, "Jōshi ni Taisuru Igakuteki Kōsatsu," p. 121.

44 Ibid., pp. 289–290.

45 Ibid., pp. 299–301.

46 Ibid.

47 See also other works on lesbianism and lesbian suicides occurring during the 1920s and 1930s: Sabine Fruhstuck, "Managing the Truth of Sex in Imperial Japan," *Journal of Asian Studies*, 59, May 2000, pp. 332–359; Jennifer Robertson, "Dying to Tell: Sexuality and Suicide in Imperial Japan," *Signs*, 25(1), Autumn 1999; Reynen Scott, "Exclusive Liberation and Lesbian Suicide in Interwar Japan," *Honors Projects*, Paper 8, 2002. http://digitalcommons.iwu.edu/history_honproj/8 (accessed April 2015).

48 Shigeyuki Komine, *Dōseiai to Dōseiai Shinji no Kenkyū* [A Study of Homosexuality and Homosexual Double Suicide] (Tokyo: Makino Shuppan, 1985), pp. 174–175.

49 Komine Shigeyuki, *Dōseiai to Dōseiai Shinjū no Kenkyū* [A Study of Homosexuality and Homosexual Double Suicide] (Tokyo: Komine Kenkyūjo, 1985), pp. 197–198 and pp. 232–233; Komine Shigeyuki, "Jōshi ni Taisuru Igakuteki Kōsatsu," p. 118.
50 Komine Shigeyuki, *Dōseiai to Dōseiai Shinjū no Kenkyū*, p. 59.
51 Komine Shigeyuki, "Seishingakujō Yori Mitaru Ukiyo-e no Yōkai ni Tsuite" [Ukiyo-e and Desire Observed from a Psychiatric Laboratory], *Iji Kōron*, 1313, 1937, pp. 37–39. See also Komine Shigeyuki, "Koga Oyobi Ukiyo-e ni Kakaretaru Shitto no Yōkai Genshō ni Tsuite," pp. 977–980. Komine Shigeyuki, "Muri Jōshi no Igakuteki Kōsatsu" [Medical Considerations on Suicide-Homicide Cases], *Komine Kenkyūjo Kiyō* (Tokyo: Komine Kenkyūjo Kiyō, 1938), pp. 1–420.
52 Komine Shigeyuki, "Muri Jōshi no Igakuteki Kōsatsu," pp. 14–15 and pp. 418–420.
53 Komine Shigeyuki, *Meiji Taishō Shōwa Nenkan ni Okeru Oyako Shinjū no Igakuteki Kōsatsu*, p. 35.
54 The methodological apparatus of Wada Muneki's study is also problematic. Wada interchanges statistical data with newspaper articles, building a heterogeneous statistical dataset, which is unreliable in its ability to support his argument. Wada Muneki, "Meiji Taishō-ki no Oyako Shinjū no 'Zōka' ni Kan Suru Kōsatsu" [Some Thoughts on the 'Increase' in Parent-Child Suicide during the Meiji and Taishō Period], *Shakaigaku Kenkyūka Kiyō*, 60, 2005, pp. 15–28.
55 Komine Shigeyuki, "Oyako Shinjū no Seiin ni Tsuite no Kōsatsu" [Considerations on Parent-Child Suicides], *Seishin Shinkeigaku Zasshi*, 42, 1937, pp. 210–226, p. 210.
56 Komine Shigeyuki, *Meiji Taishō Shōwa Nenkan ni Okeru Oyako Shinjū no Igakuteki Kōsatsu*, p. 19.
57 Ibid., pp. 7–15.
58 Komine Shigeyuki, "Seishingakujō Yori Mitaru Ukiyo-e no Yōkai ni Tsuite," pp. 37–39; Komine Shigeyuki, "Oyako Shinjū no Seiin ni Tsuite no Kōsatsu," p. 226.
59 Komine Shigeyuki, *Meiji Taishō Shōwa Nenkan ni Okeru Oyako Shinjū no Igakuteki Kōsatsu*, p. 2.
60 Komine Shigeyuki, "Oyako Shinjū no Seiin ni Tsuite no Kōsatsu," p. 226.
61 Komine stated that cases of *bōshi-shinjū* (mother-child suicide) were three times more numerous than *fushi-shinjū* (father–child suicide), which was explained by the greater number of females suffering from mental diseases. Komine Shigeyuki, *Meiji Taishō Shōwa Nenkan ni Okeru Oyako Shinjū no Igakuteki Kōsatsu*, p. 144. Komine Shigeyuki, "Oyako Shinjū no Seiin ni Tsuite no Kōsatsu," p. 224.
62 Horacio Fabrega, "Culture and Psychiatric Illness," in Anthony Marsella and Geoffrey White (eds.), *Cultural Conceptions of Mental Health and Therapy* (London: Reidel Publishing Company, 1982), p. 42.
63 *Asahi Shinbun*, "Hi wo Fuku Miharayamachō" [The Crater in Mihara Mountain That Is Boiling], February 15, 1933.
64 *Yomiuri Shinbun*, "Ōshima ni Sattō Suru Jisatsubyō Kanja" [Victims of Suicide Disease Aim at Ōshima], April 22, 1933.
65 *Asahi Shinbun*, "Ai Naki Katei ha Kanashi, Hitori Nayande Taezu, Reijō Tsuini Shi wo Erabu" [Sad for Not Having a Family and in a Rush of Thoughts, She Eventually Chooses to Commit Suicide], February 17, 1933. See also Asakura Kyōji, *Jisatsu no Shisō* [Thoughts on Suicide] (Tokyo: Ōta Shuppan, 2005), pp. 97–98.
66 Hiratsuka Haru, "Jōsei no Tame no Hihan – Nyūsu Kara Mondai wo Hirotte / Yowakatta Nireijō 'Hakoiri Musume' no Ooi Koto Yo" [Criticisms of Young Women – Problems Emerging from the News / Too Many Weak Young Women Living a Sheltered Life], *Asahi Katei*, February 20, 1933.
67 *Asahi Katei*, "Miharayamabyō Kanja no Tōshin Shinri no Shindan" [Psychological Analysis of Who Suffers the Mihara Mountain Syndrome], May 10, 1933.
68 Terada Torahiko, "Jaanarizumu Zakkan" [Miscellaneous on Journalism], *Chūō Kōron*, April 1934, pp. 127–138. On p. 128, Terada further argues, "Articles have the power, along with portraying a differentiated world, to produce the illusion of a

multitude of different forms and patterns, and to support the propagation of the image they created."

69 Shimada Masako, "Miharayama Jiken no Manajiri: Goshinka no Himitsu wo Abaku" [A Close-up on the Miharayama Incident: Everything about the Mystery of Magma], *Fujin Kōron*, 18(5), May 1933, pp. 120–134.

70 Terada Torahiko, "Jaanarizumu Zakkan," p. 133.

71 Ibid.

72 *Yomiuri Shinbun*, "Jōshi to Satsujin – Gen'in to Hōhō no Henshitsu" [*Jōshi* and Homicide – Evolutions in Motives and Means], February 9, 1937; *Yomiuri Shinbun*, "Jōshi to Satsujin – Motto Mo Ooi Kissa Gaaru no Shi" [*Jōshi* and Homicide – An Incredible Number of Deaths among Café Waitresses], February 10, 1937; *Yomiuri Shinbun*, "Jōshi to Satsujin – Yotsu no Kidō" [*Jōshi* and Homicide – Four Motivations], February 12, 1937.

73 *Yomiuri Shinbun*, "Osoroshii Dōseiai" [A Scary Same-Sex Suicide Case], July 31, 1911.

74 Between the end of the Meiji period and the end of World War II, 146 articles on lesbian suicides appeared in the Yomiuri Newspaper, but most of these appeared in 1932, 1933, and 1934. It is unclear whether the concentration of articles reflected the actual situation or was rather the effect of a biased editorial selection.

75 Hirabayashi Taiko, " 'Onna no Tachiba Kara' Gendai to Jōshi" [Contemporary *Jōshi*: From Women's Point of View], *Yomiuri Shinbun*, August 12, 1937.

76 *Yomiuri Shinbun*, "Yotsuya no Hashishika ni Onna no Mizushitai – Seishin Sakuran to Hanmei" [The Drowned Body of a Woman Found under Yotsuya Bridge – Mental Derangement and Identification], November 20, 1900; *Yomiuri Shinbun*, "Musuko to Kōron Shi Jisatsu Hakaru" [She Has an Argument with Her Son and Kills Herself], January 6, 1901.

77 *Yomiuri Shinbun*, "Byō wo Ku Ni Shite Onna Futari Ga Dōseiai Shinjū" [Two Ill Women's Suicides], October 9, 1925; *Yomiuri Shinbun*, "Shisanka no Musume To Otetsudau no Dōseiai Shinjū" [A Wealthy Girl's Joint Suicide with Her Cleaning Lady], April 5, 1926; *Yomiuri Shinbun*, "Dōseiai ni ochiru" [Falling in Love with Someone of the Same Sex], May 8, 1926.

78 *Yomiuri Shinbun*, "Nikkō de Kangōfu no Dōseiai Shinjū" [Two Nurses Commit Suicide Together in Nikkō], March 7, 1922.

79 Yamakawa Kikue, "Kazoku Shinjū no Ryūkō" [Trends in Family Suicides], *Taiyō*, 33(5), May 1927, pp. 55–65.

80 Wada Muneki, "Meiji Taishō-ki no Oyako Shinjū no 'Zōka' ni Kan Suru Kōsatsu," pp. 15–28.

81 Sawada Junjirō, "Jisatsu to Jisatsu Kishitsu" [Suicide and Disposition to Suicide], *Taiyō*, 19(16), December 1913, pp. 117–122.

82 Kure Shūzō, "Jōshi Kenkyū, Shōgi ni Shinjū no Ōi Riyū" [Study of the Love Pact: Why So Many Prostitutes Commit Dual Suicide], *Yomiuri Shinbun*, July 19, 1917.

83 Sasaki Shigetsu, "Jisatsu ni Soto ha Nai" [There Is Nothing but Suicide], *Fujin Kōron*, 1, January 1922, pp. 106–109.

84 Yamada Waka, "Jisatsu wo Bōshi Suru Hōhō ha Nanika" [How to Prevent Suicide], *Shakai Jigyō*, 11, 1927, pp. 667–672. See also her agitation for a law for the protection of maternity in Yamada Waka, "Bosei Hogo Undō to Boshi Fujohō" [Maternalist Movement and the Law to Assist Mothers and Children], *Shakai Jigyō*, 20, 1937, pp. 65–67. A diagnosis of hysteria or neurasthenia given to a mother who committed parent-child suicide was common. See, for example, Ōnishi Yoshie, "Ichi boshi shinjū ni tsuite no kōsatsu" [Considerations on Mother-Child Suicide], *Nō*, 11(4), 1937, pp. 15–21.

85 Sato Tatsuya, "Prewar and Wartime Japanese Psychology – Involvement with Eugenics, Military Affairs and Education," *Collected Papers for Human Services Research*, March 2010, pp. 17–38.

86 According to Matsubara Yōko, sterilization was performed on 454 Japanese under this law between 1940 and 1945. According to the law, sterilization could be enforced on criminals "with genetic predisposition to commit crime," patients with genetic mental illness [*idensei seishinbyō*], and those who were genetically weak-minded [*idensei seishin hakujaku*]. Yōko Matsubara, "The Enactment of Japan's Sterilization Laws in the 1940s: A Prelude to Postwar Eugenic Policy," pp. 116, 187–201. Yōko Matsubara, "Senjika no danshūhō ronsō," pp. 286–303.

87 For further references, see Nagai Junko, *Sensō to Yūsei no Jidai ni Okeru Seishinbyōsha* [Mentally Ill Patients during the War and the Era of Eugenics] (Tokyo: Asahi Shinbunsha, 2007), pp. 111–142; Tsukasa Kobayashi, "Nihon no Shinsei Eisei Undō to ha Nan Deatta No Ka?" [What Was the Mental Hygiene Movement in Japan?], *Kokoro to Shakai*, 3(3–4), 1972, pp. 93–134, 113–116.

88 Uchimura Yūshi, "Seishin Kōseikai Hakkaishiki Kōen" [Lecture at the Inauguration of the Mental Welfare Association], *Seishin Shinkeigaku Zasshi*, 47(11), 1943, p. 527.

89 The first was Paltauf in 1890, followed by Pfeiffer in 1912, Beneke in 1916, and Groll and Neste in 1919.

90 Kure Keiki, Son Kyojutsu, and Nishida Seiko, "Jisatsusha to Kyōsen Rinpasei Taishitsu" [Suicide and the Thymus Gland], *Kyōto Igaku Zasshi*, 38, 1941, pp. 219–235; Sugiyama Shigeteru, "Jisatsusha to Kyōsen Rinpasei Taishitsu" [Suicide and the Thymus Gland], *Byōrigaku Zasshi*, 1, 1942, pp. 186–195.

91 Sugiyama, "Jisatsusha to Kyōsen Rinpasei Taishitsu", p. 187.

92 Akimoto Haruo, *Seishin'igaku to Hantai Seishin'igaku* [Psychiatry and Anti-psychiatry] (Tokyo: Kongō Shuppan, 1976), pp. 179–187.

93 *Asahi Shinbun*, "5 Mei wo Sasshō" [A Family of Five Wounded and Killed] (March 15, 1939); *Yomiuri Shinbun*, "Saichi no Zansatsu – Shitsugyōku no Ikka Shinjū" [Wife and Child Cruel Suicide – Family Suicide for Economic Hardships], March 22, 1939; *Asahi Shinbun*, "Ikka 3 nin no Dokushi" [A Family of Three Poisoned to Death], March 25, 1941); *Yomiuri Shinbun*, "Saichi Michizure Tōshin" [Wife Drags Her Child to Suicide by Jumping], October 3, 1942.

94 *Yomiuri Shinbun*, "Miyagi de Jiketsu – Okuni no Yaku ni Tatanu wo Hikan" [Pessimistic about Not Being Able to Help His Country, He Kills Himself], September 2, 1937.

95 *Asahi Shinbun*, "Jigai Shita Chichi no Ronshi, Boku Mo 'Yumiya no Michi He' Hōsō Ooshii" [Explaining His Father's Suicide, He Manfully Enrolled as a Soldier], March 29, 1942.

96 Imaizumi Kotarō, "Bujin no Waribara wo Tatau" [Admiring Warrior Disembowelment], *Yomiuri Shinbun*, December 6, 1943.

97 Wada Katsunori, *Seppuku* (Tokyo: Aoba Shoten, 1943), p. 21.

98 Ibid., pp. 13–14.

99 Ibid., pp. 265, 278.

100 Kōsaka Masaaki, *Nihonjin no Jisatsu* [Japanese Suicide] (Tokyo: Sōbunsha, 1966), pp. 356–357.

101 Moriyama Kimio argued that the failure to identify a standardized treatment for mental illness in the 1930s was due to a lack of rationalization in the nosology of psychiatric illnesses, such as a lack of customized treatments for different personality disorders. For further information, see Kimio Moriyama, *Gendai Seishin Igaku Kaitai no Ronri* (Tokyo: Iwasaki Gakujutsu Shuppansha, 1975), pp. 29–30. Kitanaka instead explained the lack of standardized practices among psychiatrists as a result of their tendency to work more as researchers than as clinicians. This resulted in an insufficient evaluation of standardized practices. Kitanaka Junko, *Depression in Japan* (Princeton, NJ: Princeton University Press, 2012), pp. 46–47.

102 Furukawa Tetsushi was deeply influenced by his supervisor Watsuji Tetsurō, whose ethical theories claimed the superiority of Japanese approaches to and understanding of human nature and ethics, and argued for the negation of self. Watsuji provided

support for certain nationalistic, military factions – a fact which, after the war, he said that he regretted.

103 Furukawa Tetsushi, "Jisatsu no Nihonteki Seikaku" [The Japanese Character of Suicide], *Shisō*, 206, July 1939, pp. 40–53.

104 Furukawa Tetsushi, "Gendai Furansu ni Okeru Jisatsuron No Hōkō" [Advances on Theories of Suicide in Contemporary France], *Shisō*, September 1937. Furukawa Tetsushi, "Jisatsu no nihonteki seikaku," pp. 40–53.

105 Furukawa Tetsushi highlighted the lack of a comparative statistical apparatus on suicide; he then compiled a do-it-yourself graph, gathering statistical data from psychiatrists' works around Europe and East Asia (14 countries in total), and deduced that in such a scenario Japan would shift to somewhere between the third and fifth positions in rank.

106 A. B. Mitford's stories focused on a selection of Japanese rituals, ranging from *seppuku* and marriage to sermons. His stories, in particular the widely known tale of samurai revenge, "Forty-Seven *Rōnin*," had a lasting influence, according to Furukawa, on the Western perception of Japanese history, culture, and society.

Bibliography

Doris Bargen, *Suicidal Honor: General Nogi and the Writings of Mori Ōgai and Natsume Sōseki* (Honolulu: University of Hawai'i Press, 1996).

Bryan Cuevas and Jacqueline Stone (eds.), *The Buddhist Dead* (Honolulu: University of Hawai'i Press, 2007).

Émile Durkheim, *Suicide: A Study in Sociology* (New York: The Free Press Corporation, 1951).

Sabine Fruhstuck, "Managing the Truth of Sex in Imperial Japan," *Journal of Asian Studies*, 59 (May, 2000), pp. 332–359.

Carol Gluck, *Japan's Modern Myths* (Princeton, NJ: Princeton University Press, 1987).

Hiratsuka Haru, "Jōsei no Tame no Hihan – Nyūsu Kara Mondai wo Hirotte / Yowakatta Nireijō 'Hakoiri Musume' no Ooi Koto Yo" [Criticisms of Young Women – Problems Emerging from the News / Too Many Weak Young Women Living a Sheltered Life], *Asahi Katei* (February 20, 1933).

Akimoto Haruo, *Seishin'igaku to Hantai Seishin'igaku* [Psychiatry and Anti-psychiatry] (Tokyo: Kongō Shuppan, 1976).

Koshida Hisamatsu, "Tōkeigaku Yori Mitaru Jisatsukō" [Thoughts on Suicide Based on Statistics], *Shakai Hōken Jihō*, 16(6) (June, 1942), pp. 36–49.

Kaneko Junji, "Shinjū no Seishinbyōgakuteki Kenkyū" [Psychological Research on *Shinjū*], *Tokyo Iji Shinshi*, 2613 (1929).

Sawada Junjirō, "Jisatsu to Jisatsu Kishitsu" [Suicide and Disposition to Suicide], *Taiyō*, 19(16) (December 1, 1913), pp. 117–122.

Kitanaka Junko, *Depression in Japan* (Princeton, NJ: Princeton University Press, 2012).

Nagai Junko, *Sensō to Yūsei no Jidai ni Okeru Seishinbyōsha* [Mentally Ill Patients during the War and the Era of Eugenics] (Tokyo: Asahi Shinbunsha, 2007).

Saitō Kaname, *Nihon Bushidō no Saiginmi* [Reconsiderations on the Japanese *Bushidō*] (Tokyo: Daitō Shuppansha, 1937).

Wada Katsunori, *Seppuku* (Tokyo: Aoba Shoten, 1943).

Kure Keiki, Son Kyojutsu, Nishida Seiko, "Jisatsusha to Kyōsen Rinpasei Taishitsu" [Suicide and the Thymus Gland], *Kyōto Igaku Zasshi*, 38 (1941), pp. 219–235.

Shibukawa Keiō, *Nihonteki Seishikan* [A Japanese View on Life and Death] (Kyōto: Kōkyō Shoin, 1943).

Ōhara Kenshirō, *Jisatsu wo Kangaeru* [About Suicide] (Tokyo: Keizai Ōraisha, 1971).
Yamakawa Kikue, "Kazoku Shinjū no Ryūkō" [Trends in Family Suicides], *Taiyō*, 33(5) (May 1, 1927), pp. 55–65.
Koike Kiyoyuki, "The Philosophical Argument against the Right to Die, from a Buddhist Viewpoint," *Journal of Philosophy and Ethics in Health Care and Medicine*, 1 (July, 2006), pp. 27–42.
Nakamura Kokyō, *Jisatsu Oyobi Jōshi no Kenkyū* [Studies on Suicide and Double Suicide] (Tokyo: Nihon Seishin Igakkai, 1923).
Shigeyuki Komine, *Dōseiai to Dōseiai Shinji no Kenkyū* [A Study of Homosexuality and Homosexual Double Suicide] (Tokyo: Makino Shuppan, 1985).
Asakura Kyōji, *Jisatsu no Shisō* [Thoughts on Suicide] (Tokyo: Ōta Shuppan, 2005).
David Lester (ed.), *Current Concepts of Suicide* (Philadelphia: The Charles Press Publishers, 1990).
David Lester, *Patterns of Suicide and Homicide in the World* (Commack, NY: Nova Science Publishers, 1996).
David Lester and Bijou Yang, *Suicide and Homicide in the Twentieth Century: Changes over Time* (Commack, NY: Nova Science Publishers, 1998).
Anthony Marsella and Geoffrey White (eds.), *Cultural Conceptions of Mental Health and Therapy* (London: Reidel Publishing Company, 1982).
James R. Marshall, "Political Integration and the Effect of War on Suicide: United States, 1933–76," *Social Forces*, 59(3) (March, 1981), pp. 771–785.
Kōsaka Masaaki, *Nihonjin no Jisatsu* [Japanese Suicide] (Tokyo: Sōbunsha, 1966).
Shimada Masako, "Miharayama Jiken no Manajiri: Goshinka no Himitsu wo Abaku" [A Close-up on the Miharayama Incident: Everything about the Mystery of Magma], *Fujin Kōron*, 18(5) (May, 1933), pp. 120–134.
Yōko Matsubara, "Senjika no Danshūhō Ronsō" [The Wartime Debates over Sterilization Law], *Gendai Shisō*, 26(2) (1998), pp. 286–303.
Yōko Matsubara, "The Enactment of Japan's Sterilization Laws in the 1940s: A Prelude to Postwar Eugenic Policy," *Historia Scientiarum*, 8(2) (1998), pp. 187–201.
Ministry of Health, Labor and Welfare, *Dai 5 Kai Jisatsu Shibō Tōkei: Jinkō Dōtai Tōkei Tokuchō Hōkoku* [5th Statistics Concerning Suicide Deaths: Special Report on Demographic Statistics] (Tokyo: Ministry of Health, Labor and Welfare, 2005).
Kimio Moriyama, *Gendai Seishin Igaku Kaitai no Ronri* (Tokyo: Iwasaki Gakujutsu Shuppansha: 1975).
Wada Muneki, "Meiji Taishō-ki no Oyako Shinjū no 'Zōka' ni Kan Suru Kōsatsu" [Some Thoughts on the 'Increase' in Parent-Child Suicide during the Meiji and Taishō Period], *Shakaigaku Kenkyūka Kiyō*, 60 (2005), pp. 15–28.
W.S.F. Pickering and Geoffrey Walford (eds.), *Durkheim's Suicide: A Century of Research and Debate* (New York: Routledge, 2000).
Jennifer Robertson, "Dying to Tell: Sexuality and Suicide in Imperial Japan," *Signs*, 25(1) (Autumn, 1999), pp. 1–35.
Kobayashi Ryūnosuke, *Jōshikō* [On *Jōshi*] (Tokyo: Bungei Shiryō Kenkyūkai Henshūbu, 1928).
Mita Sadanori, "Jisatsuron" [On Suicide], *Kokka Igaku Zasshi*, 343 (1915), pp. 1–31.
Mikami Sanji, "Rekishijō Yori Mitaru Jisatsu Toku ni Jōshi" [A Historical Perspective on Suicide and Lovers' Suicide in Particular], *Meiji Shi Ronshū*, 78 (December 1909, reprint in 1976), pp. 181–192.
Reynen Scott, "Exclusive Liberation and Lesbian Suicide in Interwar Japan," *Honors Projects*, Paper 8, 2002, http://digitalcommons.iwu.edu/history_honproj/8 (accessed April 2015).

Sugiyama Shigeteru, "Jisatsusha to Kyōsen Rinpasei Taishitsu" [Suicide and the Thymus Gland], *Byōrigaku Zasshi*, 1 (1942), pp. 186–195.
Sasaki Shigetsu, "Jisatsu ni Soto ha Nai" [There Is Nothing but Suicide], *Fujin Kōron*, 1 (January, 1922), pp. 106–109.
Komine Shigeyuki, "Jisatsu Kōi wo Aeteseru Mōsōsei Yokuutsu Jōtai no Seishinbunseki Rei" [Psychological Analysis of Delusional Depression in Suicide Cases], *Shinkeigaku Zasshi*, 27 (1927), pp. 605–609.
Komine Shigeyuki, "Oyako Shinjū no Seiin ni Tsuite no Kōsatsu" [Considerations on Parent-Child Suicides], *Seishin Shinkeigaku Zasshi*, 42 (1937), pp. 210–226.
Komine Shigeyuki, "Seishingakujō Yori Mitaru Ukiyo-e no Yōkai ni Tsuite" [Ukiyo-e and Desire Observed from a Psychiatric Laboratory], *Iji Kōron*, 1313 (1937), pp. 37–39.
Komine Shigeyuki, *Meiji Taishō Shōwa Nenkan ni Okeru Oyako Shinjū no Igakuteki Kōsatsu* [Medical Analysis of Parent-Child Suicide in the Meiji, Taishō, and Shōwa Era] (Tokyo: Kyūzansha, 1998; reprint of original 1937).
Komine Shigeyuki, "Muri Jōshi no Igakuteki Kōsatsu" [Medical Considerations on Suicide-Homicide Cases], *Komine Kenkyūjo Kiyō* (Tokyo: Komine Kenkyūjo Kiyō, 1938), pp. 1–420.
Komine Shigeyuki, "Jōshi ni Taisuru Igakuteki Kōsatsu" [Medical Considerations on Lovers' Suicides], *Komine Kenkyūjo Kiyō*, 6 (1938), pp. 1–301.
Komine Shigeyuki, "Koga Oyobi Ukiyo-e ni Kakaretaru Shitto no Yōkai Genshō ni Tsuite" [Desire and Jealousy in Ukiyo-e], *Iji Kōron*, 1389 (1939), pp. 709–712; 1391 (1939), pp. 899–900; 1392 (1939), pp. 977–980.
Komine Shigeyuki, *Dōseiai to Dōseiai Shinjū no Kenkyū* [A Study of Homosexuality and Homosexual Double Suicide] (Tokyo: Komine Kenkyūjo, 1985).
Kure Shūzō, "Jōshi Kenkyū, Shōgi ni Shinjū no ōi Riyū" [Study of the Love Pact: Why So Many Prostitutes Commit Dual Suicide], *Yomiuri Shinbun* (July 19, 1917).
Kathryn Spalding (trans.), *The Way of the Samurai: Yukio Mishima on Hagakure in Modern Life* (New York: Basic Books, 1977).
Roy Starrs (ed.), *Japanese Cultural Nationalism* (Kent: Global Oriental Ltd., 2004).
Jaqueline Stone and Walter Mariko Namba (eds.), *Death and the Afterlife in Japanese Buddhism* (Honolulu: University of Hawai'i Press, 2009).
Akihito Suzuki, "A Brain Hospital in Tokyo and Its Private and Public Patients, 1926–45," *History of Psychiatry*, 14 (2003), pp. 337–360.
Akihito Suzuki, "Psychiatry in the Land of Suicide: Medicalization of Self-killing in Early Twentieth-Century Japan," *Nihon Ishigaku Zasshi*, 59 (2013), pp. 3–15.
Iguchi Takachika, *Jisatsu no Shakaigakutekina Kenkyū* [Research on Social Suicide] (Tokyo: Seiwa Shoten, 1934).
Sato Tatsuya, "Prewar and Wartime Japanese Psychology – Involvement with Eugenics, Military Affairs and Education," *Collected Papers for Human Services Research* (March, 2010), pp. 17–38. www.ritsumeihuman.com/hsrc/resource/20/20_17_38.pdf (accessed November 17, 2015).
Steve Taylor, *Durkheim and the Study of Suicide* (New York: The Macmillan Press, 1982).
Furukawa Tetsushi, "Gendai Furansu ni Okeru Jisatsuron no Hōkō" [Advances on Theories of Suicide in Contemporary France], *Shisō*, 176 (January, 1937), pp. 89–99).
Furukawa Tetsushi, "Jisatsu no Nihonteki Seikaku" [The Japanese Character of Suicide], *Shisō*, 206 (July, 1939), pp. 40–53.
Terada Torahiko, "Jaanarizumu Zakkan" [Miscellaneous on Journalism], *Chūō Kōron* (April, 1934), pp. 127–138.
Kobayashi Tsukasa, "Nihon no Shinsei Eisei Undō to ha nan Deatta no ka?" [What Was the Mental Hygiene Movement in Japan?], *Kokoro to Shakai*, 3(3–4), pp. 93–134.

John Allen Tucker, "Tokugawa Intellectual History and Prewar Ideology: The Case of Inoue Tetsujirō, Yamaga Sokō, and the Forty-Seven Rōnin," http://chinajapan.org/articles/14/14.35–70tucker.pdf (accessed April 2015).

Yamada Waka, "Jisatsu wo Bōshi Suru Hōhō ha Nanika" [How to Prevent Suicide], *Shakai Jigyō*, 11 (1927), pp. 667–672.

Yamada Waka, "Bosei Hogo Undō to Boshi Fujohō" [Maternalist Movement and the Law to Assist Mothers and Children], *Shakai Jigyō*, 20 (1937), pp. 65–67.

Takata Yasuma, "Jōshi no Shinkenkyū" [New Research on Lovers' Suicide], *Chūō Kōron*, 4 (1907).

Ōnishi Yoshie, "Ichi Boshi Shinjū ni Tsuite no Kōsatsu" [Considerations on Mother-Child Suicide], 11(4) (1937), pp. 15–21.

Ōnishi Yoshie, "Kako Nijūnenkan ni Kagawa Kenka de Okonawareshi Jisatsusha ni Tsuite no Tenbō" [Considerations on Patients Involved in Suicides in the Last Decades], *Kansai Iji*, 326 (1937), pp. 8–10; 327 (1937), pp. 6–7; 328 (1937), pp. 5–7.

Ōnishi Yoshie, "Oyako Shinjū ni Tsuite" [On Parent-Child Suicides], *Nihon Iji Shinpō*, 758 (1937), pp. 954–957.

Kosaku Yoshino, *Cultural Nationalism in Contemporary Japan: A Sociological Enquiry* (London: Routledge, 1992).

Uchimura Yūshi, "Seishin Kōseikai Hakkaishiki Kōen" [Lecture at the Inauguration of the Mental Welfare Association], *Seishin Shinkeigaku Zasshi*, 47(11), 1943, p. 527.

Part II

3 Humanizing the meaning of suicide (1945–1960)

A personal experience: psychoanalyzing suicide

During the traumatic years immediately after the war, Japan faced the socio-economic costs of a long conflict; sanitary and environmental conditions remained devastated. The earliest initiatives of the American occupation enforced the systematic purging from public office and punishment of all Japanese leadership, as well as the methodical dismissal of many professionals, particularly those from the medical community. It was only in the late 1940s that the public health system was rebuilt, financed mainly by the Japanese government and the Allied Forces. Preventive medicine [*yobō igaku*] and public hygiene [*kōshū eisei*] were at the core of the restructured health program. Part of this effort was led by the Public Health and Welfare Section of the US Occupation of Japan; this body's fundamental objective was to protect the health of the population by preventing or limiting the incidence of acute and chronic medical problems. Despite the conventional emphasis on American agency and Japanese passivity, though, recent historiography has proven that public health was a field in which Japan showed initiative. Akihito Suzuki and Christopher Aldous point out that rather than presiding over a revolution in public health, the Public Health and Welfare Section of the US Occupation of Japan recommended methods of epidemic disease control and prevention that were already established in Japan and were not the innovations that they were often claimed to be.[1]

The American occupation not only oversaw the nation's restoration of public health institutions, but also aimed at establishing a professional medical education system that made it possible to address pressing postwar health issues. The Japanese Welfare Ministry recognized the importance of uniformity and standardization on a national level in medical practice, and by the end of the occupation it had implemented a scheme that ensured national guidelines for uniform standards in the prefectural model health centers that were now training health officers. The American influence that had firmly taken root in many aspects of Japanese society under the occupation had a direct impact on this new medical practice and training. The field of psychiatry was no exception.

During the prewar period, academics had been the only Japanese drawn into Western learning; but after 1945 the dramatic expansion of the whole education system meant that Western learning was now potentially available to the entire population. This change was reflected in the spread of Western knowledge in every academic field. American psychiatry – or more accurately, 'American psychoanalytic psychiatry' – was the discipline that reorganized Japanese knowledge of mental illness immediately after the war. This field established its predominance over neurobiology and dominated Japanese medical institutions until the end of the American occupation in 1952. Deeply rooted in sociological and psychoanalytic thinking, the American model of mental health asserted the validity of a psychodynamic approach and saw psychoanalysis as the foundation of medical psychiatry. Grounded in this cooperative relationship between psychology and psychiatry, American psychoanalytic psychiatry reinvigorated research into concepts related to mental illness and their diffusion in the international arena. The experience of the war had suggested that a *humanistic* psychoanalytical model rather than a *mechanistic* biological one offered a more compelling consideration of environmental stress, which was thought to be a more reasonable explanation for mental disorders than was personality. Additionally, the unjustifiable cruelty of the world conflict brought about unprecedented dedication by the international community to an understanding of 'the irrational' in human behavior, which reawakened interest in the potential and originality of psychoanalytic studies. Finally, rapid developments in psychotherapeutic techniques conferred credibility on the discipline and quickly convinced psychiatrists to take on a psychoanalytic approach.

During the occupation years, this take on psychiatry was disseminated in Japan through the newly established psychoanalytically oriented departments of Japanese academia and promptly directed the guidelines and policies of the National Institute of Mental Health [*Seishin Hoken Kenkyūjo*], with little resistance from 'orthodox' Japanese psychiatrists. As a matter of fact, the decline in interest in biopsychiatry during the years after the war created a vacuum that psychology and psychoanalysis would grow into. With the nation being punished for war crimes once thought 'scientifically' justified, biopsychiatry, with its biological roots, was now understandably seen as anachronistic and became unpopular. The ever-shrinking interest in biological study in psychiatry during the years of the American occupation was manifested in poor turnout at meetings and conferences on neurobiology. In 1950, for example, only 35 neuropathologists and neuroanatomists attended the first meeting on histopathology, a branch of the 47th Japanese Annual Conference of Neuropsychiatry organized in Kyoto by Tadashi Inose, physician at the Matsuzaka Mental Hospital, and by Shikō Takeya, professor at the University of Kyushu. Barely twenty papers were presented, mainly on the neuropathology of schizophrenia and on interpretation of neuropathological findings. This minimal interest in the discipline was observed not only in Japan, but also internationally. When a few Japanese psychiatrists attended the first international conference of neuropathology in Rome in 1952, for instance, they found themselves surrounded by little more than 100 attendees, a rather limited number for a worldwide gathering.

Although the medical community had lost confidence in neurobiology, one individual worked against the tide: Kaneko Junji, who had championed biopsychiatry during the prewar period. His effort to once again reinvigorate the discipline was a brief but meaningful parenthesis in the history of medicine in postwar Japan. Kaneko engaged in a tireless crusade that aimed at strengthening the foundations of psychiatric institutions. Beginning in 1947 and culminating in 1949, he worked to establish the first psychiatric association, the Japanese Psychiatric Hospitals Association [*Nihon Seishinbyōin Kyōkai*], which initially included 82 private hospitals. Also with his indefatigable support, the Japanese Nurses Association [*Zen'nihon Kangōnin Kyōkai*], founded in 1947 and initially limited to the Tokyo area, grew to the point that it included the rest of the nation in 1949. Ultimately, Kaneko pushed for the passage of a new mental hygiene act that prohibited domestic confinement. Thanks to his efforts, the proposition reached the Ministry of Health and Welfare [*Kōseishō*], and the Mental Hygiene Act [*Seishin Eisei Hō*] passed in 1950, encouraging access to institutional medical care.[2] Kaneko not only supported institutional psychiatry, but was also convinced of the conceptual validity of neurobiology and biological mechanisms as the primary object of psychiatric investigation. As a result, he was reluctant to accept the environment as a significant influence on psychiatric conditions. However, Japan was not yet ready to embrace the rehabilitation of biopsychiatry.

With the exception of the brief parenthesis created by Kaneko's advocacy, the occupation years witnessed a dramatic surge in interest in psychoanalysis. Fascinated by the American model and encouraged by contemporary developments, a new generation of young Japanese psychologists studied in the United States, or in Japan under the supervision of Kosawa Heisaku, the clinical psychologist who laid the foundations of psychoanalysis there. Okonogi Keigo from Kyoto University, Doi Takeo from the University of Tokyo, and Takeda Makoto, Maeda Shigeharu, and Nishizono Masahisa from Kyushu University all became members of the so-called Kosawa School; they were, in Okonogi's words, 'the second generation of Japanese psychoanalysts' (the first generation being those of the prewar period) who made psychoanalysis 'mainstream' in Japan.[3] This school was centered on training students to become future psychotherapists and on the idea of formalizing their psychoanalytical orientation by promoting institutional change as quickly as possible. One step toward this goal occurred in 1953 when Marui Kiyoyasu, psychiatrist at Sendai University and pioneer psychoanalyst among Japanese psychiatrists, instituted the training-focused organization known as the Japan Psychoanalytical Society [*Nihon Seishin Bunseki Kyōhai*]. Then, in 1955, Kosawa Heisaku founded the Japan Psychoanalytical Association [*Nihon Seishin Bunseki Gakkai*].[4] Both Marui and Kosawa tried to Japanize and objectivize psychoanalysis at the same time – they believed that a simple identification with the West would not work to spread the discipline's popularity. Instead, they thought, a synthesis of Western rationalism and the "natural mentality of the Japanese" would achieve better results in rooting the discipline in the country, and in finding a new Japanese ego.[5] Kosawa in particular strove to maintain his distance from an insensitive and excessively scientific American orientation, seeking to join religious and cultural values to psychoanalysis. Regrettably, despite the promising start and the astonishing efforts that led to the founding of the Japan

Psychoanalytical Association and the Japan Psychoanalytical Society, the dissolution of American psychoanalytic psychiatry as an influence in Japan had already been set in motion. Although long-lived, the two institutions never achieved their anticipated influence.

While academic psychologists worked to establish their disciplinary predominance through the development of institutions, clinical psychologists began to expand their power by engaging in surveys and systematic applications of psychoanalysis. In the immediate postwar period, funding for research was limited, and the majority of medical departments could not support new research. As a consequence, research came to be more narrowly concentrated either on topics that could demonstrate a significant economic turnaround within the pharmaceutical field, or on observational surveys. A great number of patients were now observed regularly, and suicidal patients were further scrutinized, with a renewed focus on the purpose, meaning, and volition behind their act. Suicide was no longer seen merely as a by-product of mechanistic events. Psychologists were convinced that through close surveillance of suicidal patients, they could decipher and cure the 'greed for death,' the undeniable narcissism [*kyoshoku*] that victims often paraded in suicide notes, and the 'desire to display' [*engeki-sei mo kore ni takai*] evident in certain suicide patterns.[6] They insisted that they could diagnose and treat the irrational and instinctual components of the human being.[7] In other words, psychologists believed that the suicide phenomenon could not be conceptualized without an understanding of the patient as a whole person possessing individual and societal values, beliefs, and a worldview, as well as an acknowledgment of the irrational aspects that he or she possessed. Failure on the part of the clinician to capture all relevant issues could threaten the effectiveness of evidence-based interventions and prevent afflicted individuals from achieving recovery and well-being.

By closely monitoring and observing patients, some clinical psychologists identified as early as the late 1940s the seeds of a frightening potential inclination of the Japanese, and the young in particular, toward suicide (an insight that was actually borne out in an exponentially high suicide rate during the following decade). Sonohara Tarō, Segawa Yoshiro, and Satō Yoshiharu all noticed, in the aftermath of the war, a higher youth suicide rate in Japan than in other industrialized countries.[8] In noteworthy observational analyses of suicidal patients, Sonohara and Segawa hypothesized that the phenomenon could be explained by the combination of the widespread sense of hopelessness about the future instilled by defeat in the war along with the peculiar personality [*paasonariti*] of Japanese youth. They were thus convinced that it was essential to scrutinize the ecological dimension (that is, the depressed historical interlude the nation was experiencing) with respect to its intrapsychic re-elaboration by individuals. As a result, Sonohara Tarō followed 22 suicidal cases in therapeutic sessions and subjected 48 university students (31 females and 17 males) to surveys that probed their drive to kill themselves.[9] Sonohara determined that Japanese students were not scared of death but were instead irrational and unmindful, and a large majority reported having troubled relationships with their families. Accordingly, he wrote, "the cause [of such a high suicide rate] is to be found in the chaos that follows a war in which many young people lost their lives, and in the sense of nothingness and cluelessness that [. . .] pushes youth to end their lives with their own hands."[10] According to the researcher, such "emptiness of the spirit" [*seishin no kūdō*] needed to be explored, brought to the surface, and healed by therapists who could lead patients through the dark paths of their souls.[11] Notwithstanding the limited body of empirical evidence, Sonohara's study was the first attempt by psychologists to gather statistical data upon which a theory on suicide could be formulated. Sonohara's research was compact and elegant in scientific terms. In supporting a more humane approach to the patient, the researcher found that emotional pain was common among the Japanese youth demographic, and predicted that this would soon lead to a suicide rate that would increase over time.

A few years later, while he was a researcher at the department of psychology of Iwate University, Segawa Yoshiro repeated a similar survey, but on a larger sample (910 students between the ages of 13 and 22). Segawa drew the same conclusion: 34 percent of students showed a proclivity to suicide. The motivations behind this inclination could be found in the sentiments of hopelessness and negativity generated by the turbulent times and in the students' unsettled familial and academic settings, which were abruptly shifting under pressure from the American occupation.[12] Convinced that comprehending the precise first-person narrative was fundamental to understanding the contemporary suicide phenomenon, Segawa called for further investigations on psychological states such as frustration, loneliness, lack of self-esteem, and sexual drive in the Freudian sense, arguing that this knowledge would allow clinical psychologists to accurately diagnose and treat their patients. Segawa revealed how the ecological state intersected with the psychological one to shape a problematic generation; he perceptively predicted trends in suicide statistics and argued that it was advisable to approach those Japanese youth who demonstrated a proclivity to suicide with extreme care and long-term, solid psychoanalytic treatment. By claiming that a growing number of Japanese youth were having similar experiences of psychological distress, Segawa implied that all those young subjects were good candidates for psychoanalysis.

Clinical psychologists began to see disciplines such as sociology and statistical demography as useful to their work toward formulating an overarching theory on the suicide phenomenon. While they recognized a high level of sophistication in the psychiatric theories on suicide that had been articulated over the past several decades, which were solidly supported by data analysis, clinical psychologists reckoned that the integration of psychiatric theories of mental illness with the psychological ones offered no better explanation for voluntary death. Psychologists like Sonohara and Segawa chose not to incorporate psychiatric data on suicide into their surveys because such data failed to consider the "profound emotional harshness" that overwhelmed most of their patients.[13] However, sociology and statistical demography might be able to shed light on the impact of situational and social influences on individuals. Minami Hiroshi was the first to claim that the crucial task of contemporary psychologists was to unite statistical, sociological, and individual data on voluntary death in order to draw an identikit of the Japanese suicide.[14] A professor emeritus at the state-run Hitotsubashi University who was known for his contribution to the introduction and expansion of social psychology in Japan, Minami collated statistics on suicide. These were data that had been collected by the Ministry of Health and Welfare office from the Meiji period until 1950. Minami then examined the dataset within its socio-environmental context, cataloging suicide cases according to historical periods, weather, seasons, hours of the day, and so forth.[15] He concluded that in Japan voluntary death could be divided into two categories: institutional/organizational suicide in "traditional Japan" (as he referred to prewar Japan), and individual suicide in the postwar period. The first type was a direct result of social pressure, and Minami argued that it was "a natural phenomenon in particular societies."[16] On the other hand, individual suicide, seen as an act that exemplified postwar Japan, was committed because the "individual is independent and detached from institutional values."[17] In Durkheimian terms, Minami was referring respectively to altruistic suicide and anomic suicide, differentiating prewar from postwar suicide patterns according to this socio-psychological trope. In contextualizing and historicizing voluntary death, Minami stressed the impact of environmental contingencies and the centrality of the individual experience.[18] In other words, by scrutinizing the statistics using a sociological lens, Minami dismissed the neurobiological and cultural components of suicide. In so doing, he sought to rescue the notion of voluntary death and to remove any associated discomfort or embarrassment in order to open up a space where suicide could be discussed without immediately evoking its perceived symbolism as an act of Japanese patriotism. In a deteriorated society and a time in which the country's institutions were controlled by the occupation, psychoanalysis not only was a means to destigmatize and reexamine Japanese suicides, but also became a cultural tool that could be used to defend the Japanese against the onslaught of international criticism and the scrutinizing gaze of the occupiers.

During the American occupation, *the* object of study and contemplation within the growing fields of psychology, psychotherapy, and psychoanalysis was the suicidal patient and his or her inward gaze. Individuals were scrutinized for their values, beliefs, and conduct within the profound universe of the self. Their inner states were thus placed directly before the gaze of others. For psychologists, this delving into the universe of the self was dyadic in character – that is, the relationship with the therapist was central to interpreting the patient's 'cry for help.' Intellectuals, however, reframed the individual as a completely autonomous agent and the act of suicide as purely private. Despite their differences, these narratives converged when it came to the necessity of ethically reframing voluntary death and controlled dying, in order to defend the individual right to die.

The Japanese discussion on suicide and euthanasia was influenced by increasing international debates. Between 1945 and 1950, when the World Medical Association voted to recommend that euthanasia be systematically condemned by all national medical associations, debates on the right to die appeared unceasingly in medical and popular journals throughout the world. As early as 1938, the British Parliament had debated a bill to legalize euthanasia. Additionally, the Euthanasia

Society of America was founded in 1938, and proposals similar to the British one were introduced in state legislatures in the United States in subsequent years, including New York State in 1947. Yamana Shōtarō, who wrote extensively on suicide and euthanasia for the Asahi Newspaper beginning in the 1930s, rebuked Japanese intellectuals for being sheer spectators in this international debate on euthanasia. The writings of the German euthanasia advocate Karl Binding had already been translated and distributed in Japan, and were well known to Japanese criminal lawyers.[19] However, Yamana urged intellectuals and the medical community to more actively consider the ethical and moral questions involved in the debate about assisted suicide in order to be able to move with the times, asking: "Is it acceptable to kill incurable patients?" [*Fuchi no byōjin ha koroshite yoi ka?*][20] Togawa Yukio, a clinical psychologist and professor emeritus at Waseda University, followed the same logic, advocating that "suicide is a free choice of the individual [who], differently from animals, has a will and can decide to kill himself/herself."[21] Togawa, who wrote extensively on Japanese cultural psychology, encouraged his colleagues to dedicate more research to suicide as a legal right. He further reprimanded national newspapers for being superficial and trivial in hypothesizing victims' motives: simply owning a pistol does not make someone suicidal, Togawa claimed. Every individual has a strong will, and whoever "successfully commits suicide has even stronger will power."[22] He provocatively concluded his disquisition by suggesting that anyone contemplating suicide should "drink two grams of mescaline" for immediate, pain-free, and inexpensive results.[23] Saitō Shō, professor emeritus in philosophy at Tōyō University and Meiji University, advocated that suicide is a free choice, and thus should be denuded of the sociocultural attributes that had been deposited in it by history (suicide for the sake of responsibility, for the nation, and so forth). Saitō, who extensively researched life and death as well as voluntary death, was convinced that suicide was a form of human freedom and a right. He further argued that human beings should be legally protected if they chose to commit suicide: "If human beings did not have a certain degree of freedom, they would not be able to commit suicide. This is the proof that suicide is a right [. . .], regrettably not guaranteed by the Constitution."[24]

Japanese novelists too raised their voices to defend what the critic and essayist Hayashida Shigeo defined as "the right to freedom," or "the special right of human beings" [*ningen no tokken*].[25] They described voluntary death as a way out of a corrupt, degenerate, and immoral society, an individual decision not to bear such degradation. Contrary to the assumption that the desire to commit suicide was a passive submission to conditions external to one's will – whether this be society or a weak neurological system – novelists and intellectuals in the immediate postwar period defended the agency of the individual and saw such an action as a kind of freedom. An unambiguous example of such discourse is seen in the popular novel *No Longer Human* [*Ningen Shikkaku*, 1948] by Dazai Osamu, who was part of a double suicide the same year the novel was published. *No Longer Human* employs unsentimental, autobiographical language, describing a protagonist trapped between the traditions of an aristocratic Japanese family and Western culture. Three chapters describe the man's life, revealing his path toward self-destruction in the guise of alcohol abuse, indulgence in prostitutes, and suicide attempts, motivated by an awareness that suicide offers the only path to freedom. Toward the end, the protagonist brings the girl with whom he plans to commit suicide to buy one of their last meals. "She got up and looked inside my wallet. 'Is that all you have?' [. . .] This was a humiliation more strange than any I had tasted before, a humiliation I could not live with. I suppose I had still not managed to extricate myself from the part of the rich man's son. It was then I myself determined, this time as a reality, to kill myself."[26] Dazai interpreted suicide as an act of freedom, where freedom is seen as self-ownership over one's own life and body. The right to end one's own life was thus advocated as the most basic right of all.

In the tragic bitterness of the war's aftermath, in a context of desperation and disillusionment, novelists allegorically portrayed suicide as the final death of values and principles, most of which they saw as having already been buried under the ashes of the Allied Forces' bombings. Hakuchō Masamune, in *The Agonies of the War Victims* [*Sensaisha no Kanashimi*, 1946] and *The Victory of Death* [*Shi no Shōri*, 1949], raised the question of the 'appropriate death,' defining a death relatively acceptable to the dying person as the proper way to end a life. The novelist suggested that self-annihilation is a noble death in that it can triumph over one's sense of political and social malaise, historical decadence, and social deterioration. For writers such as him, voluntary death was a private, emphatic denial of the will to live. Therefore, it could be understood as a fleeing from life's sufferings, but also from its pleasures; that is, suicide was professed as the ultimate human freedom, a moral freedom.

Thus, in this historical period, intellectuals as well as psychologists shared a major concern about the quality of life, and the limits on life quality that an individual could bear. Certain psychologists, however, thought it indispensable that medical intervention be provided to help the individual adjust to environmental difficulties, while intellectuals tended to see such intervention as paternalistic and unviable; to them, suicide was an individual choice. Their discourse on suicide inherently valorized the intentions of a person who chooses to kill himself, and implicitly criticized the infantilization and dehumanization of the suicidal person in the medical discourse. In other words, such novelists viewed someone who aimed to prevent another's suicide as depriving the suicidal individual of a worthwhile aspiration.

In sum, the emotional trauma of the war had radically influenced the way the medical community perceived, comprehended, and conceptualized voluntary death. At the same time, American psychoanalytic psychiatry influenced the Japanese mental health community to reject the notion that the suicidal patient or the suicidal victim was a merely biological creature, divorced from the contingencies of existence. Clinical psychologists explored the inner self of suicidal patients, identifying a communal emotional pain in the Japanese; they embraced the socio-ecological context as a way of helping to comprehend the phenomenon and they incorporated statistical data to identify and predict trends. Psychological treatments were designed to cure the assumed proclivity of the Japanese to suicide, but more importantly to cure the psychic wounds that the war had inflicted. Traditionally reluctant to acknowledge suicide as a symptom of mental illness, intellectuals too opened up a space for psychological introspection about suicide. Thus, both intellectuals and psychologists reclassified the suicide phenomenon, initially interpreting it as a response to the natural order of biology and later seeing it as something that was embedded in the social and environmental contingencies of the human condition. Such interest in social forces, also mirrored in the psychological vocabulary absorbed by popular magazines, promulgated the belief that all people were potentially at risk of suicide, which was triggered as much as by environmental factors as by the individual's psychological makeup. The distinction between endogenously and exogenously motivated suicides began to dim.

A collective experience: suicide as a social by-product

Although much effort was directed toward understanding the mental states of suicidal patients, regrettably psychologists failed to translate individual stories, diagnoses, and treatments into a comprehensive theoretical apparatus. Furthermore, the departure of the American occupiers, advocates of American psychoanalytic psychiatry, left psychologists unprotected against the revival of the biological model and with no time to further consolidate their achievements.

As rightly suggested by Okada Yasuo, eminent psychiatrist-historian and prolific researcher and writer, when the American occupation ended, a new phase began in the history of medicine in Japan.[27] Between 1952 and 1960, the nation's vibrant, autochthonous biopsychiatric movement came to the fore, defending the validity of the discipline of psychiatry and warding off further American psychoanalytic influence and intrusion into psychiatric practice. Large institutions, with their growing influence on the medical field, had a major effect on this renewed enthusiasm. This dramatic change did not, though, happen overnight, and the retreat of the occupying forces does not entirely explain why psychiatrists managed to reestablish the predominance of neurobiology as the model of mental illness within academic and clinical walls.

Firstly, on the academic front, several intellectual leaders of psychiatry began to express skepticism about American psychoanalytic psychiatry. In particular, psychiatrists affiliated with Tokyo University soon mobilized to critique psychoanalysis and to reinstate Kraepelinian neurobiology as the official paradigm of Japanese psychiatry. In 1952, the Public Mental Hygiene Research Lab [*Kokuritsu Seishin Eisei Kenkyūjo*] was founded, reestablishing neurobiology as the supreme model of experimentation. Later, new academic journals were published aiming to rebuild biopsychiatry's credibility. In 1959, for example, *Seishin Igaku* [Clinical Psychiatry], an elite academic journal comparable to *Seishin Shinkeigaku Zasshi* [Psychiatria et Neurologia Japonica], issued its first volume. Furthermore, psychiatric associations and symposia recorded a progressively higher number of attendees. Beginning in 1960, the Japanese Annual Conference of Neuropsychiatry, later incorporated into the Annual Conference of Neuropathology, had large numbers of participants; it gradually became a vibrant intellectual arena for medical professionals interested in biopsychiatry and neurobiology.

Secondly, postwar economic policies aimed at reconstructing the domestic market gradually transformed medical care, inaugurating a prosperous time for clinical psychiatrists. The initial steps toward socio-economic recovery fueled massive migrations from rural areas to larger metropolitan areas, as individuals sought better jobs and education. The result was not only the beginning of a process of urbanization, but also the inauguration of mass consumption, which soon led to an increased interest in broader access to medical care. As demand for medical and mental health services increased, the number of hospitals and providers grew. Demand was also bolstered by the collapse of the *ie* system [family system] under the new Civil Law of 1947 and the outlawing of private detention under the 1950 Mental Hygiene Act.[28] Both of these policy changes reinforced the idea of hospitals as the new loci of confinement. The number of psychiatric hospitals as well as the number of beds dedicated to psychiatric patients skyrocketed.[29] Furthermore, in 1958 the National Health Insurance Act [*Kokumin Kenkō Hōken Hō*] was passed, creating the legal basis for health insurance for all. This system consisted of both private and public medical institutions paying for medical services under a point system, and ultimately it caused both private practitioners and private medical providers to rapidly become more prosperous. Private psychiatrists accounted for more than 80 percent of the provided psychiatric service, becoming a booming profession and dominating any competition from psychologists, social workers, and other nonmedical counselors.[30]

Thirdly, the changing direction of Japanese psychiatry was deeply influenced by rapid advances in neuroscience and pharmacology, which enabled exponential growth in the pharmaceutical industry in the decades following World War II. The Japanese pharmaceutical industry was almost nonexistent to begin with, but government economic policies pushed for its development through financial support, attempting to boost the domestic market and protect Japanese manufacturers from international competition. The emergence and further expansion of the pharmaceutical industry was central to neurochemistry research within Japan, but more importantly it established the dependence of private medical care on the goodwill of political authorities; this gradually led to the politicization of medicine. In 1955, for example, the introduction into Japan of chlorpromazine – a first-generation anti-psychotic used to treat several mental disorders, in particular schizophrenia – reinforced the connections among neuroscientists, psychiatrists, and the pharmaceutical industry, bringing into existence a new economically oriented medical ethic.

At the same time, a counter-trend mitigated the dominance of biopsychiatry. Starting in the early 1950s, the suicide rate in Japan suddenly increased, peaking in 1958. The phenomenon gradually pushed psychiatrists to consider reframing the biomedical approach to voluntary death within a more individual-centered, humanized schema, though one that differed from the psychoanalytical approach. According to the suicide rates provided by Japan's Ministry of Health and Welfare, between 1955 and 1958 Japan experienced a statistical wave of increased suicide (in total 25.7 suicides per 100,000 inhabitants; 30.7 for men and 20.8 for women).[31] That year, the nation recorded the highest suicide rate in the world for all age groups, and suicide became the single most common source of death for individuals under 30 in Japan.[32] Suicide, as a matter of fact, had long been the second-ranking cause, but with the radical decline in the death rate from tuberculosis it became the single highest.[33] The rate was so high that the late 50s were renamed "the era of suicide heaven" by national newspapers.[34] The 1958 suicide peak was mainly generated by an increase in suicide among those who were 20–24 years old.[35] This cohort was represented by young people who had been born in the 1930s, grew up in wartime, and became teenagers during the postwar crisis.[36] In other words, their childhoods spanned the unstable chaos of the 'dark valley' [*kurai tanima*], and as teenagers they experienced the unsettling changes common to a society in transition.[37] Whereas the statistical peak of the suicide rate was recorded in 1958, the narrativization of the phenomenon began to intensify in the mid-1950s, peaking in 1960 in terms of the number of articles published in academic journals and the popular press. The recurrent association of the words 'suicide' and 'youth' became the locus upon which the debate on contemporary social problems concentrated.

The suicide boom raised the question of why so many young people who had just survived a devastating war were being driven to kill themselves, and demanded immediate intervention. As the suicide rate continued to rise, a certain group of psychiatrists increasingly became persuaded that a monodisciplinary approach to the phenomenon was undesirable. The neurobiological approach was shown to be myopic in regard to existential anxiety, and indifferent toward the identification of suicidal individuals. These psychiatrists thus started questioning whether the emotional experience of the individual should remain secondary to the neurobiological approach, and increasingly began to engage more closely with the existential experiences of those who attempted suicide. If the ultimate goal of psychiatry was to alleviate the pain and suffering associated with the experience of mental illness, this could not be done without an understanding of what mental suffering meant to individuals, how it affected their lives, how it contributed to their personal stories, and what it would mean to liberate patients from mental suffering. Psychiatrists pursued this objective by embracing a 'humanistic' stance and by closely observing patients' experiences. This was the beginning of what the psychiatrist Kaketa Katsumi called the era of social psychiatry, which he defined as "a field involved in the reflection on the social nature of several concepts in clinical psychiatry [and] of various social pathological phenomena (including delinquency, crime, suicide, and prostitution)."[38] Kaketa's theorization of social psychiatry as a comprehensive human behavioral science clearly captured those changes in the psychiatric movement that throughout the 1950s slowly incorporated a humanistic dimension and an attention to the collective social body into its discipline. This was one of the most important conceptual shifts in Japanese psychiatry of the postwar period: psychiatrists promoted the pursuit of mental well-being through 'social control' – that is, engaging with the social order and attempting to make individuals more fit to exist within it.

Exploring the life experience of D-san, a 15-year-old student of the Soregashi High School in Tokyo who killed himself in 1950 by jumping from a high building, Kobayashi Akio, professor of psychiatry at Tokyo University of Education, became immersed in a sort of 'detective story.' D-san was a professional baseball player and an obsessive reader of Japanese and Russian literature, "which made him more eager to read novels than to go out with friends."[39] Despite his pronounced passion for literature and composition, D-san did not leave a suicide note for his friends or family, and Kobayashi deduced that D-san was most probably an "asocial boy."[40] Applying Kraepelin's categories of character types and focusing in particular on the so-called morbid personalities, those whom Kraepelin judged as tending toward criminality and other dissolute activities, Kobayashi described D-san as having an affective personality; he concluded that the cause of a healthy young boy committing suicide was lack of guidance [*gaidansu*].[41] That is, it was possible that D-san, an exemplar of his generation, suffered without a solidly structured family and educational system, and in an even broader sense without the support of his nation, whose values and beliefs had faded under the ashes of the war. In his article, Kobayashi described his earlier application of the observational model to other suicides by young college students. In the earlier study he had categorized them according to personality types and reached the very same conclusions: those with a morbid personality were sensitive to lack of 'guidance.' Kobayashi's model aimed at demonstrating that the exploration of the patient's narrative could provide a meaningful way for psychiatrists to conceptualize mental illness and rebuild a relationship with patients – thereby resulting in more effective therapy. However, the sketchy technique and the single observation of the existential experience of D-san proved inadequate to corroborate his hypothesis.

Three years after Kobayashi's hands-on survey, three young psychiatrists confirmed his hypothesis: the motives for youth suicide are to be found within a distressed family and educational system, rather than genes. Katō Masaaki, who went on to become a leading social psychiatrist contributing to the field's progress, development, and dissemination, along with Kosaka Hideyo and Mori Saburō at the National Center for Global Health and Medicine in Tokyo [*Kokuritsu Kokusai Iryō Kenkyū Sentaa*], examined a sample of 74 young people in their 20s who had attempted suicide. Katō, Kosaka, and Mori reckoned that 39 of them were mentally ill (schizophrenic or neurotic) and excluded them from their investigation; the remaining 35 patients' stories were explored in depth. By taking into account only those 35 patients, the psychiatrists cast their research within the socio-psychiatric framework, to evaluate its validity and set the stage for later discussions of the existential and humanistic perspectives on suicide. Katō, Kosaka, and Mori recognized the centrality of sociocultural and historical contingencies as suicide triggers: they supported the idea that the environment, as much as mental illness, rushed the patient into 'an incomprehensible act' or pushed the victim to stage a spectacular death. However, despite the fact that the three researchers overtly proclaimed that psychiatrists should dismiss prewar biological determinism as the sole tool of analysis and should be "cautious in stressing the genetic cause," they never undermined the biomedical approach. In excluding 39 patients from their sample, they implicitly asserted that although some suicidal patients were not mentally ill, many others were. Consequently, despite the interest aroused by the American psychodynamic orientation in alternative forms of environmental therapy capable of application in institutional and community settings, Katō, Kosaka, and Mori asserted that psychiatric treatments and prevention plans should still be applied 'in an orthodox manner.'

Katō completed a wider survey in 1955. In the previous 5 years and 8 months, attempted suicides had been monitored in several Japanese cities and towns, with observations that included more than 110,000 inhabitants. During this period, 392 attempted suicides were reported and examined for this survey population.[42] The majority occurred in urban areas, among people who were in their 20s or in their 70s, as well as in individuals who had never married or were housewives. Social alienation and anxiety, according to Katō, were the strongest predictors of suicide, and these conditions could be observed extensively in this historical period: the defeat and the disruption of the family system had a significant impact among "elderly men with a pre-modern personality [*zenkindaiteki seikaku*] and young urban housewives."[43] Drawing upon Durkheim's theory of anomic suicide, Katō claimed that his model proved the way in which social disengagement and social stressors exposed those who had no employment to the risk of voluntary death.[44] Once again, despite the remarkably large sample, Katō's research never truly let his sociological approach undermine the dominance of psychiatric practice. He advocated that the suicide rate was a sensitive barometer of a deeper and hidden social anxiety that came to the fore when weak individuals were positioned in an unaccommodating social environment.[45] The suicide rate was the sign that disruptions and social anxiety had been metabolized as mental illnesses and that these at some point could become visible through suicide.[46] In insisting on the social nature of living conditions along with genetic features, Katō reestablished the dominance of neurobiology in a new humanized guise and assigned it a decisive role in the diagnosis and treatment of suicidal patients. He explored the 'determinants' of suicide, and the pathological conditions within the social structure; he attempted to demonstrate the power of social data to explain psychiatric disorders, and recognized the sociogenic model of suicide. Katō, however, firmly believed that the environment could not be adjusted, and as a result, treatment would have to be directed at adjusting the individual to the environment; changing society might be impossible, but its members could certainly be treated.

The trend of social psychiatry continued, firstly, to move the focus of interest from the asylum to the larger community, and secondly, to subordinate the patient's intimate subjectivity to an attention to the suffering shared by the entire collective. If social stressors were responsible for triggering suicide, those stressors then had an impact on all of Japanese society. Consequently, psychiatrists had to extend their vigilance and their active medical intervention to the collective unconscious. This process slowly led medical professionals to demystify suicide and went a long way toward fighting the stigma associated with seeking treatment. Ultimately this humanistic stance would allow social psychiatry to establish its unique role as a bridge between the mind and the body, the mental and the physical, the philosophical and the scientific.

Suicide as an image of poverty

As a reflection of the increasing medical attention focused on social stressors, the popular discourse too embraced sociogenic hypotheses in the narrativization of voluntary death. Media and fiction explored the role of social factors such as poverty, modernization, urbanization, and so forth, as well as their relationship to the generalized troubled 'collectivity.' During the American occupation, the so-called condition of despair [*kyodatsu jōtai*] was perceived as the major social force that was responsible for the physical and emotional suffering of the Japanese. Newspapers speculated on the cumulative effect of poverty on the mental health of the nation. Suicide became the symptom and the expression of a society suffering the costs of defeat. As the sociologist Sasaki Yōsei argued, suicide represented a warning about the precariousness of Japanese people's physical and psychological health: "In order to prevent suicide and the feeling of being 'losers,' we must be aware that since the defeat in the war, the hearts of the Japanese are full of greed, rivalry, unfairness, and regret. We must be aware of these feelings because, in any culture and in any society, whatever the individual's creativity produces is constructed upon [such feelings]."[47] Suicide was thus a figurative currency used as a marker of historical harm; it was acknowledged as the pathological symptom of a material poverty that degraded moral values, and to a further extent it was narrated as the embodiment of civilization's degeneration.

Between 1945 and 1949, no official statistical data on suicide were compiled, and very few articles on voluntary death were published by national dailies. Reports were extremely concise: their telegraphic style did not convey much information about the method, any suicide note that might have been left behind, or motivation. The protagonists of these reports were people of their time: prostitutes, hopeless workers in the black market, and *hibakusha* – victims of poverty and of social taboos. It was only in the early 1950s that a growing awareness of voluntary death as a symptom of social stress became visible and a remarkable change was observed in the editorial approach. Headlines began to report the profession of the victims, and articles became detailed and explanatory; suicide cases were increasingly described in terms of problematic social issues such as education, welfare, economy, politics, crime, gender, and youth culture and supplemented with quotations from the victims' suicide notes. Yoshimura Toshiko, an expert in media studies who devoted much of his work to the way newspapers sensationalized suicide stories, collected reports on voluntary death from the Tokyo edition of *Asahi Shinbun* between 1940 and 1973.[48] Yoshimura confirmed that the common point of the articles on suicide published during the American occupation was simplicity: reports were concise and informative and blindly associated with poverty, unemployment, and living difficulties [*seikatsu-ku*].[49] According to Yoshimura, this trend was probably due to the editorial board's concern with poverty as a powerful risk factor in the development of mental illness. The individual who chose to commit suicide was thus depicted as a 'potentially functional' element of society and someone who was a member of a family and/or institutions. Unemployment, however, meant that the individual suffered from a lack of self-esteem and social meaning, and these were perceived as plausible reasons that led to the act.[50] In other words, suicide was a rhetorical trope through which the economic losses brought about by the war defeat were endlessly evoked.

The popular discourse on voluntary death slowly acquired an isomorphism with the discourse on poverty, in which assertions about suicide were correlated one-to-one with poverty. *Kazoku shinjū* [family suicide] and *oyako-shinjū* [parent-child suicide] cases were portrayed as the ultimate exemplification of this correlation. Even during the first years of the American occupation, for example, Yamana Shōtarō extensively wrote about the destitution that compelled a family to commit suicide.[51] In 1948 an old couple with no children committed *shinjū* after having a rough time trying to put a bowl of rice on the table every day. In response, Yamana commented, "Isn't it better that such people kill themselves as they wish [instead of being a burden for their neighbors or families]?"[52] A suicide committed after enduring 15 continuous years of war and deprivation was – according to Yamana – far more understandable than a destitute life.[53] In Yamana's words, the dark historical period was responsible for such losses, rather than individual or philosophical reasons. In this regard, Yamana recalled the popular suicide case of Fujimura Misao and claimed, "Fujimura had no fault. History is at fault" [*Fujimura ni ha tsumi nashi. Jidai ni ha tsumi ari*].[54]

The Japanese press between the late 1940s and the early 1950s also arbitrarily identified poverty as the trigger for mother-child suicides and father-child suicides. In two representative reports, the young mothers in question were portrayed as psychologically weak, suffering from nervous breakdowns, and for this reason unable to keep a job and forced to live in misery with their families. The headlines of these accounts read: "Unemployed mother kills herself and her three children"[55] and "Jobless mother commits mother-child suicide."[56] Father-child suicides, on the other hand, were described as being caused by the gap between the overwhelming expenses of a large family and the father's very low income. One father-child suicide case that appeared in *Asahi Shinbun* was entitled "Dad, let us live a human life, a decent life." In the article, the long suicide note left by the child before being killed by his father was included.[57] The boy narrated the misery and starvation his family had been suffering, and the reporter used it to comment on the disastrous economic situation facing the country. The report, rather than being simply a suicide story, reported on a cross-section of Japanese society, followed by a harsh critique of "the unequal economic system generated after the defeat that made this man live in deprivation until he decided to allow his pride to end his meager existence."[58] In lieu of allowing the suicide notes to speak for those who had killed themselves, the media transformed family suicide cases into powerful visual and rhetorical symbols that were boldly associated with the defeat-related distresses of the entire society.

Voluntary death was clearly a crucial event in the narrative of the disrupted nation. The popular discourse depicted it as symptomatic of the struggle for

Japanese survival and of the impossibility of living at then-current wage levels. Contemporary Japanese likely found it extremely difficult to consider suicide as a mirror that might reflect parts of the national self that were uncomfortable to look at, particularly at a time in which Japan faced harsh distrust and intense scrutiny of its war crimes from the international community. It was far easier to use the image of poverty, an undeniable condition of hardship and victimhood, as a lens. The image of material poverty served firstly to internalize war trauma, and secondly to avoid resolving the tensions between the cultural notion of suicide as a unique feature of the Japanese and the biomedical presumption of the universal nature of suicide. The constant association of an action that might potentially have indicated illness (suicide) with a non-illness condition (poverty) permitted the popular discourse to ignore a number of sociocultural and psychopathological causes behind the act of suicide. In dismissing its biomedical and cultural components, the popular discourse was de-romanticizing and de-politicizing voluntary death, denuding it of its conceptual layers, freeing it from the weight of being identified as the repository of a despicable past. In the Japanese press, suicides were portrayed as merely 'victims' of the times, which conceptualized voluntary death as an indicator of a shared collective stress.

Suicide as an image of social maladjustment

As soon as the American occupation ended, the Japanese became increasingly convinced that their society had become dysfunctional, and there appeared a growing consciousness that voluntary death might be a reflection of deeper Japanese social maladjustment. Durkheim's theories had significant and pervasive impact on Japanese sociologists and psychiatrists, leading to widespread agreement within academia that the increase in the suicide rate was an expression of social anomie. The popular discourse portrayed suicide as a socio-pathological phenomenon and as a disease of adaptation, similar to homicide and other crimes, that reflected one's inability to survive in a particular ecological setting.[59] Meanwhile, Japan's remarkable economic recovery following the American occupation diverted the media from relegating suicide to being an expression of poverty, instead transforming suicide in newspaper reports into a reflection of social maladjustment.

In 1953, a reporter from *Asahi Shinbun* lamented the state of confusion into which Japanese people had plunged after "the defeat had deprived them of social, religious, and cultural regulating forces, leaving them without values." The vacuum left by the annihilation of the system of moral instruction (Shintō, the Emperor, national symbols, and so forth) and by the demonization of Japanese 'tradition' was filled by the formulation of a new system, one that could coexist with postwar democracy. However, "the violent substitution of autochthonous models with the unfit Western ones, and the passive and bungling attitude towards extreme postwar modernization, provoked a loss of identity."[60] Suicide was acknowledged as the by-product of such disruption, which was deep-rooted in the Japanese soul. In academic terms, Mita Munesuke, the most influential sociologist exploring anomie in Japanese postwar society, interpreted the contemporary maladjustment of the Japanese as the outcome of alienation and a feeling of purposelessness in the face of urbanization and machine civilization.[61] Mita believed that anomie was common in postwar Japan because society had undergone significant changes in its economic fortunes, and there was a significant discrepancy between the ideological values commonly professed – which pushed for the rebuilding of a strong nation – and what was actually achievable in everyday life.[62] As a result, the individual would suffer from anomie, as he/she was unable to legitimately attain those objectives given the structural limitations in society. Mita drew upon the evolution of social psychology in modern consciousness studies in Japan from the Meiji era up until the 1960s, and his persuasive view on modernity and anomie deeply influenced Japanese sociology throughout the postwar period in its treatment of disparate areas such as suicide and consumerist lifestyle. Along similar lines, the sociologists Kōsaku Masaaki and Usui Jishō described the anomie and the increasing number of suicides of postwar Japan as "the outcome of the emergence of democracy that created a widespread awareness of what people's rights are."[63] In other words, Kōsaku and Usui suspected that the recognition of democratic principles which remained unfulfilled in postwar Japan created a high level of frustration that in turn triggered an increase in the suicide rate. Kōsaku, professor at the department of medicine first at Kyoto University and later at Tokyo Gakugei University, hosted several workshops and meetings with colleagues in the psychology and medicine departments to explore the reasons behind the increasing suicide rate that peaked in 1958.[64] Along with Usui, professor at Kyoto University since 1932, pioneer of interpretative sociology in Japan and president of the Japanese Association for Social Studies [*Nihon Shakaika Kyōiku Gakkai*], Kōsaku assembled the proceedings of the academic gatherings and concluded that a thorough examination of Japanese 'culture' was fundamental to understanding the suicide phenomenon.[65] That is, although the anomic condition of the nation resembled that of other Western industrialized countries, it would have been too hard to explain why Japan presented an unusually high rate of suicide without inquiring into the nation's historical and cultural past. The amalgam of modern anomie and indigenous culture, argued Kōsaku and Usui, was responsible for the increasing rate of suicide, a high social cost that their country was facing.

A lightning rod for public concern about maladaptation as the trigger for suicide was provided by the case of Akada Haruo. Akada was an 8-year-old boy who killed himself by jumping in front of a train on the Tōkaidō Main Line on his way back home from school on July 5, 1955 in Kobe. While playing hide and seek with his classmates, Akada had playfully hidden one of his peers' belongings. Unfortunately, when his teacher caught him with someone else's property, he was reprimanded in front of the class, being told, "[If you are a thief,] go to thief school!" [*Dorobō gakkō he ike!*]. His classmates teased him for the rest of the school day and, on his way back home, Akada jumped in front of the train. The young age of the victim and the apparent lack of a rational motive offered fertile ground for debate. Newspapers promptly criticized the inhumane severity of Japanese schools that emphasized discipline over 'education,' and the teacher's lack of sensitivity, labeling Akada's case "a suicide caused by teacher punishment."[66]

Other reporters such as Yoshimura Toshiko interpreted Akada's case as a metaphor for the chaos into which the Japanese educational system had fallen after the war defeat, which had had "a terrible impact on the soul of students."[67] Various intellectuals, though, summoned three issues in particular to scrutinize Akada's act: the disruption of the Japanese family system, the inadequately developed modernization of the country, and the vacuum of values left by the defeat.

The inquiry into Akada's suicide catalyzed a spirited discussion on the disruption of the family system, and problematized the relationship between traditional family values in postwar Japan and youth suicide. Hayashida Shigeo, for instance, was convinced that the solitude and the fear the boy must have felt within his family were the motives standing behind his act. A critic and essayist who wrote extensively on postwar lifestyle and suicide, Hayashida asked readers to rethink the dynamics of the incident. Akada decided to kill himself on his way home, so presumably it must have been his family he was too ashamed to face. In this regard, Hayashida reminded the reader, "It is difficult for a Japanese family to move away from a long-standing history of education based on 'punishment' [*shitsuke*] as a form of guidance for children."[68] The critic thus blamed the failure of the traditional family educational system to leave space for the development of individual freedom. In Hayashida's perception, Akada claimed that freedom: his suicide was the desperate choice of a young boy who would have liked to live if he could continue to be satisfied with himself. Unfortunately, he could not assert his will against the power of circumstances because those circumstances were too strong.[69] Inaoka Junno, with theoretical sophistication, made a similar argument. An expert in religious studies, Inaoka correlated the increasing rate of youth suicide with the intricate interaction between the collapse of the family system, immature modernism, and the lack of religious deterrence, all of which created a "confusion in which the everyday life of the Japanese plummets."[70] Referring to Akada's case specifically, Inaoka claimed that his act "indicated how immaturely the Japanese embraced modernity."[71] He severely criticized Japanese children and teens for allowing themselves to be terribly dependent on a traditional family system that dissuaded them from becoming independent and instead incited them to embrace the community's goals. He defined their generation as "a transient world filled with hardship" [*aranami tatsu ukiyo*].[72] Inaoka relentlessly continued by stating that the country too was responsible because, although it had embraced modernization, "[t]raditional aspects had remained deeply buried within the society," permitting an asynchronous coexistence of the modern and non-modern social strata.[73] This argument was pushed even further by Isomura Eichi, a professor of sociology, specialist in urban sociology in Japan, and member of the Japanese Society of Health and Medical Sociology. Isomura claimed that "the very poor relationships with the other [referring to the family]" that the Japanese were experiencing in conjunction with their disastrous economic problems created the "condition," rather than the "motive," for suicide.[74] Entirely embracing Durkheim's paradigms, Isomura further explained that if both the deterrent and the trigger for suicide were social forces, then an individual who was immersed in satisfying relationships would be less attracted to death. However, when "the nation cannot guarantee" healthy interpersonal relationships, the result is an increase in the suicide rate, the logical consequence of a degenerated social stratum.[75] The disintegrated self that chose suicide was thus a metaphor for the disrupted family, which in turn was a trope evoking a nation adrift.

Akada's case might be explored as a lens through which the postwar vacuum of values was examined. The fading of the prewar era's 'imagined monolithic community' was thought to coincide with a dramatic loss of values (loyalty, reciprocity, altruism, and so forth) that, after the defeat, left the individual unprotected and at the mercy of loneliness. For Okazaki Ayanori, an economist, statistician, and demographer who wrote extensively on suicide between 1958 and 1960, Akada's suicide was an example of the individualistic act of a solipsistic, alienated urban child.[76] Akada, claimed Okazaki, had no backbone; he had no knowledge of his own race [*minzokusei*] and no one had taught him Buddhist precepts or Confucian traditions, history, and common sense [*jinseikan*]. In other words, no valuable lessons from the past were traceable in Akada, but only some remnants of an anachronistic "traditional system that ignored people's own personality, feelings, and preferences, and psychologically pushed them to carry the burden of responsibility [for the community]."[77] A young boy like Akada was thus stuck between an atemporal present and a demonized past, between a dismissive and assumedly 'modern' family and the melancholic reminiscences of a warm 'traditional' community. Analogously, Yamashita Hajime, a professor in the department of Humanities and specialist in German literature at Tokyo University, expressed his concerns regarding the contemporary generation of youth. In a special issue on suicide in *Fujin Kōron*, Yamashita wrote three lengthy articles on youth suicide and on Akada's case.[78] He argued that psychologically speaking, "suicide hides a feeling of defeat and shows a desire to perform. However, contemporary suicides do not show that desire any more, but rather a proclivity to succumb to the 'victory of death.'"[79] Akada, Yamashita explained, like many of his contemporary peers, showed a lack of vitality. He further added, "For a generation that entirely lives on ideals," such as children and teenagers, that sense of hopelessness is "extremely troublesome."[80] In this regard, an anonymous writer raised the provocative question of why this young generation was "so looking forward to dying," and hypothesized, "The examples of young people revolting against the morals of the old generation and the aged habits of their families are many. [. . .] For the new generation, psychological problems, rather than economic ones, are the true difficulty. [. . .] Youth suicides seem to be the tragic outcome of a period of transition that has generated a new morality."[81] Galvanized by the case of the 8-year-old boy, intellectuals and the popular press overtly stated that suicide was nothing but a by-product of the crisis of the moral and educational system. As expressed by Katō Hidetoshi later in 1977, "[the new morality of the 1950s] seemed to indicate a shift away from values of altruistic empathy, self-sacrifice and asceticism and toward individual-centered, liberated, joyful egocentrism. [. . .] There seems to be a tendency toward 'privatization,' towards more concern for one's private self than for social commitments and reforms."[82] As suggested by Katō, the disruption of kinship institutions such as the family and the school left the individual displaced among the inconsistencies and paradoxes generated by an empty new morality. Suicide cases were not portrayed as the affirmation of the individual's autonomy over the group, but rather as acts triggered by the dizziness felt by individuals who lacked a sense of collective solidarity.

However, the old pattern of interpretation was reproduced by problematizing the boy's own maladjustment and assuming that the social spectrum was the condition that triggered youth suicide. Many tended to neglect the personal motivations that might stand behind the act of a weak, uneducated youth wandering in an atemporal space, assuming instead that the community at risk that produced such individuals deserved greater attention. As Sasaki Kiichi, essayist and critic of Japanese literature, said tauntingly, "Someone who commits suicide is stupid [*baka*] and weak. [. . .] How should we perceive him/her? As a loser committing a heroic act? As the protagonist of a tearjerker theatrical piece? Or as a comedian who should be laughed at?" He then continued, "Nowadays, suicide is no longer an issue investigated within the realm of psychology, but instead within sociology. It is society that generates suicide. And many people of our society are weak."[83] Therefore, what might seem to be an individualistic act, determined solely by the actor's personal desires, was instead perceived as the product of sociocultural laws or forces outside the individual. Sasaki thus portrayed suicide as an indicator of social illness, which suggested a unitary understanding of the population. This assumed that the 'stressor,' or the socio-environmental situation or condition, carried more weight than the person's response to it. In defining and examining details regarding central problems of modern existence (poverty, social maladjustment, etc.), the popular discourse was acknowledging suicide as sociogenic. That is, it was necessary to treat the collective, or to tackle the ills of society, rather than to deal with the illness on an individual level.

A perspective in which suicide was the by-product of the cultural system's crisis and of the devastating chaos of values undoubtedly called for the application of a Durkheimian view of society. Similar to their biological counterparts who aimed at guaranteeing equilibrium among bodily organs, those who took the Durkheimian approach had the crucial goal of preventing suicide and curing the conditions that led to it in order to maintain an equilibrium between the competitive interests of individuals and groups within the society. In Durkheimian terms, the majority of the suicides scrutinized throughout the late 1940s and the 1950s in the popular discourse were labeled as anomic: social disengagement was the motive behind the act. Regarding the threatening increase in youth suicide, for instance, a reporter wrote, "Students are the new generation of the postwar era, the ones who suffer the most, as they are caught between the idea that there must be some sort of freedom in their lives and the other part of society, constituted by the generation of their fathers and elder siblings, who simply survive."[84] In so writing, the journalist illustrated an emotional pain that extended to an entire generation, and denounced the disconnect between the past and the future. In other words, suicide was not portrayed as the act of an autonomous liberal self, but rather as a phenomenon of a social body that was understood through and in contrast to a larger healthy collective. The notion of suicide thus embodied a paradox: the individual was at once damaged by society and maladjusted to it. Although contradictory, it was this assigning of social responsibility to the state of health of the population on the one hand and to the strength or vulnerability of the individual on the other that rendered the notion of suicide powerful. The emphasis on the collective, though, did not negate the exploration of individual experiences, but rather encouraged a focus on the social element of the self. Psychologists and psychiatrists too, despite their introspective and humanizing efforts, highlighted social stressors as triggers for suicide, thus reducing all Japanese to potential patients, and diminishing the person's responsibility for his or her own actions.

The point that this strand of the popular discourse shared with the medical discourse in their conceptualizations of suicide between 1945 and 1960 was that both deprived the phenomenon of its biocultural component. The idea of suicide was formulated in terms of a collective phenomenon, not because a common identity was ascribed to the Japanese race, but because of the challenging environmental conditions in which the Japanese were living. Such an understanding intrinsically excluded science from the realm of the conceptualization of suicide following the debacle of the prewar period's eugenic enthusiasm, and raised the question of responsibility: these ideas about suicide actively promoted a distinct vision of civic responsibility and of patient surveillance. If suicide was a symptom of social disruption, this implied that the individual should not be the ultimate subject of public attention. Excluding the few who remained reverent toward the individual's agency and advocated suicide as an act of freedom, both the medical and the popular discourses played a critical role in the construction of 'society' as an entity that could be scrutinized – and ultimately regulated – by medical professionals or social experts.

A cultural by-product: historicizing suicide

As the medical and popular discourses began to take into account the complexity of the relationship between individuals and social conditions, many intellectuals and novelists during the 1950s continued to romanticize and glorify suicide as a peculiar feature of the Japanese. The association between suicide and Japaneseness resisted the war and raised a voice seeking to rehabilitate the past and to revitalize the historical continuity of Japanese values and traditions.

The times were not sufficiently mature to embrace a renovated national pride in the uniqueness of the Japanese culture. The discrediting of the nationalistic discourse and the scrutinizing gaze of the international community had a moderating effect on the chauvinist enthusiasm of many. Nonetheless, several intellectuals and novelists praised, with reservations, the distinctive suicide patterns of what in 1958 an anonymous writer once again defined as *jisatsu no kuni* [Suicide Nation].[85] Although many intellectuals and novelists envisioned suicide as a sociogenic phenomenon (thus aligning themselves with the scientific trends of the times), others spontaneously romanticized 'traditional patterns,' nostalgically evoking prewar suicide cases. The intellectual Hayashida Shigeo, for example, in calling Japan "the first country in the world for suicide," glorified the sophisticated aestheticism of the unique motives and patterns of Japanese suicide. He wrote further, "Suicide is the last freedom, and freedom essentially contrasts with a lack of freedom. Thus, suicide [in Japan] is infused with beauty."[86] Inaoka Junno reestablished the association between suicide and the Japanese, offering a genetic explanation: "the proclivity to suicide of the Japanese lies in their race [*jinshuteki*]. In other words, I suspect that the inclination toward voluntary death is in our blood."[87] After providing an overarching perspective on the suicide phenomenon throughout history, from both biological and sociological perspectives, and comparing Japanese suicides to those in other industrialized countries, Yamana Shōtarō concluded that "the Japanese are culturally attracted to death."[88] Along the same lines, the demographer Okazaki Ayanori explained the proclivity to suicide in Japanese culture by the fact that Buddhism offered no strong deterrence against voluntary death, and this lack in turn promoted both aesthetic legitimation and social appreciation of the act. He wrote, "[In our society/culture] we learn so many religious and secular concepts that we cannot ignore their impact on the suicide phenomenon."[89] Other intellectuals highlighted the peculiarities of Japanese patterns of suicide. For instance, the sociologist Isomura Eichi claimed that Japan was renowned throughout the world as "the country where children are killed [*satsujikoku*]."[90] Okazaki Ayanori claimed – though regrettably without any statistical reference to support his conclusion – that Japan's rate of *oyako-shinjū* was the highest in the world: 49 out of 189 cases of suicide were parent-child suicides, an overwhelming number that provided an example of the uniqueness of the Japanese suicide phenomenon. Intellectuals also noticed a strong difference between suicide patterns in Japan and in the rest of the world when they considered rural Japan. Maeda Shinjirō, a law professor at Kindai University in Osaka who wrote extensively on crime and urbanization and dedicated some of his works to suicide, compared Japanese and Western patterns of suicide in urban and rural areas. He concluded that Japan presented a counter-trend: rural areas showed higher suicide rates than urban areas, especially among the elderly, contrary to the usual pattern in other industrialized countries.[91] This trend was probably due to the fact that the elderly in Japan may feel themselves to be a burden on the family and thus magnanimously choose to end their lives.

The suicide pattern recognized as the most representative of Japanese uniqueness was *shinjū*. This was particularly noticeable in the popular press, where *shinjū* became identified as the repository of Japan's distinctiveness, noble principles, and superior aesthetics. The total number of articles published by the *Asahi Shinbun* and *Yomiuri Shinbun* on *shinjū* between 1950 and 1960 was an average of 250 a year, a striking number compared with the prewar period, although it is important to note that 40 percent of the reported cases were about attempted rather than actual suicides.[92] In recounting these cases of lovers' suicide, journalists evoked a nostalgic and chronologically vague sense of an uncontaminated past. Most of the articles described the suicides of lovers who acted in response to their families' opposition to their marriage. "We kill ourselves together because we cannot marry"[93] was the poignant message of one of the innumerable suicide notes reported in newspapers that embodied the legacy of prewar patterns and language. Furthermore, titles like "*Shinjū* in the White Snow," a metonymy for romantic suicides set in romantic locations, became a clichéd title for love suicides, narrated as exemplars of unforgettable beauty.[94] Detailed descriptions of red blood standing out against the pureness of the snow epitomized a suffering generation squeezed between the traditional habit of arranged marriages [*omiai*], which considered marriage as more a merging of households than individuals, and the ideals of marriages based on romantic love [*ren'ai*]. Other reports exalted *shinjū* committed by lovers as virtuous acts that destroyed dishonorable relationships.[95] The article "*Shinjū* of 5 people in Hakone. Mother brings her 3 children with her in order to clear off her extramarital relationship," for instance, described the foolish gesture of a wife who had betrayed her husband and sought to wash away her own sins by eliminating her entire family.[96] Interestingly, the foolish gesture was seen as being not the suicide-homicide of her family, but the original betrayal itself. Once the betrayal was discovered, nothing could be done apart from cleansing the sin through death. The conventional terms *seisan* [to clear off, to break up a relationship] and *jaren* [illegitimate love, a troublesome, socially disturbing love relationship] embodied the 'attachment' to an old vocabulary that verbalized the silent ethical duties that lovers had toward their families and their society.[97] The sentimental narrative and the sanctity of immemorial customs were embodied in suicide stories that recounted the past and treated the present as a part of a timeless and cherished tradition. A linguistic strategy of the cultural narrative was the rigid use of old-fashioned terms. The terms *jigai* and *jiketsu*, for example, were once again, as during the prewar period, revived and extensively employed in the 1950s. These terms were now used to depict the suicides of indefatigable male workers or of responsible lovers.[98] The conventional use of suicide terminology hearkened to a constructed nostalgia for bygone suicide aesthetics, which ascribed certain motivations to the actors, and reasserted historical continuity.

The strongest representation of voluntary death as a cultural artifact of romanticized beauty was the traditional suicide staged by the heroine of *The Tower of the Waves* [*Nami no tō*, 1957]. This novel by Matsumoto Seichō, one of the most popular tales of suicide of all time in Japan, giving rise to more subsequent stagings and dramatizations than any other, featured a woman who killed herself in the Jukai Forest, in Aokigahara, Yamanashi prefecture.[99] After a long and troubled love affair, Yoriko decides to forget her lover forever and rushes into the Jukai forest, one of the most aesthetically stunning settings in Japan: "Although bird and insect noises can occasionally be distinguished during the day, the Jukai forest is more reminiscent of a dock at night. The blue lights reflect infinitely in the endless sea of trees. It is an immense space with no boundaries, a blue ocean under the moonlight."[100] It is here that Yoriko kills herself. The act is depicted in the novel as extraordinarily beautiful:

> I will die, because in this way I will obtain the proof of my love – The young woman stood on the tower on which the waves were breaking so harshly. She felt swallowed up by those same waves and jumped. – Thinking of you, I will leave this world alone. I will step into the path that goes nowhere. [. . .] Love is not eternal. One can obtain it only by cutting it off.[101]

Dispensing with formulaic plot devices, in *The Tower of the Waves* Matsumoto depicts an entire society and its thought through his detailed narration of crimes and memorable portraits of black marketers, prostitutes, and unscrupulous businessmen. In his effort to draw closer to the reality of human society, Matsumoto lets the reader perceive that the closer he/she gets, the nastier human beings are. In *The Tower of the Waves*, postwar Japanese society is identified as responsible for both troublesome romantic passions and inhuman crimes. However, an act of stunning beauty is able to legitimize the heroine's life and redeem her from the contemporary pragmatic skepticism that is so deeply rooted in postwar life. Yoriko's suicide, or better, *performance*, revives the past and its memories by claiming her separation from the present. Yoriko immerses herself in an instantaneous act that echoes a revitalizing past, one with a historical, nostalgic dimension.

During such a destabilizing historical moment for the nation, when the future was not even envisioned as 'one of the possibilities,' reviving images of age-old suicide patterns acted as a way to 'normalize' and 'naturalize' a renewed Japanese universality. The notion of the Japanese people's proclivity to suicide, the reaffirmation of old gender stereotypes, and the co-opting of traditional linguistic terminology were a rejection of the narrativization of suicide in new, contemporary forms or patterns. Though the resonance of this strand of the popular discourse was limited at the time, it made a grand gesture that resisted modernity. It reinvigorated old suicide patterns through sensational accounts of determined male workers who sacrificed themselves so that their country could be reconstructed, and women who killed themselves to resolve triangular love affairs. This search for symbols that could be traced from premodern suicide paradigms to the present was a manifestation in the popular discourse of the universal inner quest for a historical continuum. By reestablishing the legitimacy of old suicide patterns, the cultural discourse sought to reconstruct identity systems that could restore the ruptured continuity of the culture.

The proclivity of Japanese novelists to kill themselves was also summoned by the cultural narrative to reinforce the notion of the uniqueness of Japanese suicide. The novelist Togawa Yukio, who also largely romanticized Nogi Maresuke's *seppuku*, claimed that Japanese authors' suicides occur because writers have a restless temperament, like youth, and thus, "[T]hey can do it in a quite lighthearted way.[102] They can easily choose to kill themselves, to become criminals or commit kamikaze [*tokkōtai*]. They invest their time in love relationships and when love is not there anymore, they fill the void by fighting for justice or acting in a criminal way. [. . .] This is who they are."[103] Some explained the suicides of several middle-aged Japanese novelists as a response to intense feelings about the degradation of society and its underlying anxiety. For this reason, Umeda Haruo, novelist, essayist, playwright, and expert in French literature, argued that these writers were living in "a state of 'estrangement'" that often led them to commit suicide.[104] Similarly, the critic Haniya Yutaka claimed that Japanese artists breathed in the nihilism of the era and then translated it into a destructive act. In fact, they aestheticized their lives to the point that their suicides could be seen as an individual work of art.[105] As a result, argued Haniya, it is useless to speculate on the mental instability of novelists such as Hara Tamiki and Tanaka Hidemitsu[106] or to attempt to rationalize their suicides; they simply had the freedom to transform the disquiet of an entire nation into a silent, noble act.[107] Others closely scrutinized novelists' works and lives in search of shared characteristics. Referring to the suicides of Dazai Osamu, Arishima Takeo, and Akutagawa Ryunosuke, literary critic and novelist Shibukawa Gyō claimed, "I have finally understood that the reasons for [Japanese novelists' suicides] are related to their psychological being."[108] Shibukawa identified the lack of a life goal [*sonzai no riyū wo ushinatte*] as a motivation for voluntary death.[109] Such malaise was nothing less than the sensitive absorption of the hopelessness of an entire society that found itself unable to imagine a future. In other words, culture was observed to have had a 'patho-facilitating effect' on the suicidal behavior of novelists.

Cultural appropriations of voluntary death that applied to certain patterns and certain categories of people, however, arrived at an impasse with others. The proposition that suicide was an aesthetic expression of a civilization required a suspension of judgment for women's suicide and *tokkōtai* (Japanese pilots trained in World War II to make suicidal crash attacks). Both categories were excluded from the culturalizing discourse that sought to reestablish the legitimacy of prewar values and beliefs. No one overtly dared to rationalize wartime *kamikaze*, which was by this point recognized as a sacrifice or a coerced act of *harakiri*. In this regard, Yamashita Hajime opined that psychologically speaking, these young soldiers did not show strong willpower or internal motivations, and thus *tokkōtai* could not be considered suicide.[110] Yamashita refrained, though, from more clearly categorizing *tokkōtai* or elucidating for whom it had been committed. Saitō Shō advocated that although it was an old-fashioned Japanese attitude to take responsibility for others and society by committing suicide, in the case of *tokkōtai* the act could not be considered a free choice. He wrote, "Not only in recent times, suicides are committed in Japan because of the social pressure to make individuals take responsibility," adding that although "taking responsibilities is beautiful [*bifū*], killing oneself because of social pressure does not make suicide a deliberate act [as it is not internally motivated]."[111] Thus although suicide can be perceived as an honorable and valiant act, "this does not mean it is logical."[112] He further insisted that, for example, killing oneself for the Emperor or for the Nation "could be quite destructive rather than constructive."[113] Therefore, despite the fact that those young soldiers immolated themselves for the nation, this did not make their act more reasonable. Along similar lines, Hayashida Shigeo defined the people involved in *junshi*, *harakiri*, and wartime *tokkōtai* as victims of homicides, although he was never explicitly critical of the government. He wrote, "Suicide is all about the individual and about the society. [. . .] When suicide is an individual issue, it is a free act. When it is only about social rules, it is like a homicide." He further added, "[W]hen someone does not want to commit suicide but is forced to [then it is a homicide]."[114]

Interestingly, the popular discourse on suicide once again summoned biological norms to reject the idea that patterns of women's suicide demonstrated cultural traits unique to Japan. Newspaper reports on suicide cases became the locus in which a dichotomous representation of gender was reasserted through conventional paradigms. On the one hand, an extensive number of reports depicted female suicides as acts committed by psychologically fragile beings incapable of living or supporting a family, and motivated by trivial issues, mainly love relationships. On the other hand, male suicides were depicted as reflecting the socio-economic conditions of the country. This contrast is striking in reports such as "Betrayed by her Boyfriend, Young Woman Kills Herself" [115] and "Living Is Too Hard: Man Seriously Ill and Afflicted by Economic Problems Kills Himself."[116] The first article reported the shallowness of the protagonist, emphasizing the ridiculousness of her motivation in committing suicide; the second narrated the story of a stoic man, exhausted by fighting alone against poverty and illness, who decided to put a 'noble end' to his life. The portrait of the man in a hospital ward bed with his 8-year-old sitting by his side during the last days of his long and arduous battle against leukemia contrasts markedly with the editorial portrayal of a fancily dressed flibbertigibbet girl who could not tolerate being betrayed by her man. In opposition to the stereotyped image of psychologically weak women, newspapers painted a picture of men as stressed and hardworking. This portrayal emphasized the tough political and economic situation men faced, as well as the enormous sacrifices that working-class men had made to save the country from stagnation and economic depression. The most extreme portrayal of insanity in female suicide, in contrast, was epitomized by the suicides of mothers, especially those who made their children follow them into death. Several examples can be seen in newspaper accounts such as "Suffering from a Nervous Breakdown, a Mother Kills Herself," "A Crazy Mother Kills Herself and Her 3 Children," and "From Distress of Childbirth, Mother Kills Herself and Her 4 Children."[117] In the latter report, the woman is portrayed as a weak, disturbed individual who for an apparently derisory reason ("distress of childbirth," most likely a reference to postpartum depression) killed herself and four innocent creatures. Thus, the images presented of males reinforced the idea of men's social function, and gained widespread resonance in the popular press. On the other hand, the construction of the image of a 'fragile and pathetic' female reinforced the sense of stigma around their suicides and associated them with mental disease. This discourse reassessed mental disorders as 'real' illnesses but limited the illness to women.[118]

The cultural popular narrative firstly sought to restore the identity of the Japanese – which was assessed in terms of ethnicity, nationality, class, or gender – and consequently to bridge the past and the present. At the same time, this narrative excluded inconvenient suicide patterns or subjected them to reprehensible gender constructions, selectively using neurobiological explanations. In legitimizing 'traditional' suicide and in reproducing its language, the cultural discourse idealized and routinized certain patterns of conduct, rediscovering Japan's romantic historicity. We might raise the question, Why does the cultural narrative seek to use suicide as the lens through which it revitalizes historical continuity? The answer is: because suicide was a locus of threat that could be neutralized by 'fantasizing' the act as the repository of noble values and a timeless ethic unique to Japan. The nationalistic component and the determination to revive a sense of cultural pride served to provide a sense of specifically Japanese 'ownership' or 'entitlement' over the phenomenon of suicide. In other words, the cultural narrative on voluntary death homogenized the meaning of people's affliction and concealed the complexity and diversity of the suicidal by creating a romantic and ahistorical image of what it meant to be Japanese.

Even in the absence of a supportive Japanese nationalistic discourse and in the presence of international criticism that deterred Japan from reasserting its prewar values, patterns, and beliefs, the cultural narrative still managed to emerge from the ashes of the war. One condition that facilitated its quiet intention to come to the fore and reinvigorate Japanese cultural identity was the fragmented and confused medical discourse. As we have seen, the history of medicine in Japan between the end of World War II and 1960 was characterized by the rise and fall of widespread enthusiasm for psychoanalysis, along with the alternate dismantling and redeeming of the validity of biopsychiatry. Such swings back and forth between neurobiological and humanistic models opened up a space to contest the way in which suicide should be theorized. This dissonant cacophony of voices generated a conceptually fragmented debate on suicide and a theoretical vacuum, conditions that let the fervent cultural narrative resume.

In this moment of maximum turbulence in Japanese history, on the cusp of an epochal change, on the verge between the security of a fading past and the insecurity of the future, the cultural discourse emphasized continuities and attempted to establish a more cautious and modest cartography of the present. This cartography stabilized the past by recognizing it as timeless. Whereas on one hand the medical discourse relentlessly sought to differentiate the present from the prewar suicide phenomenon by freeing it of its political and romantic legacy, the cultural narrative sought to stitch up the present to include the prewar period. Whereas the medical discourse labeled contemporary suicide as 'anomic' as a way of distinguishing new historical conditions, the cultural narrative insisted on categorizing contemporary cases as 'altruistic,' just as had been used in traditional descriptions. These dichotomous approaches toward the conceptualization of suicide never resolved into a conversation; instead, each actor remained sheltered behind his position.

Therefore, in the 1950s, in response to the dilemma about whether suicide should be conceptualized as a political or an existential phenomenon, a particular or a universal act, the medical and the cultural narratives responded by each staking their own distant position. Psychiatrists came to reject the essentialization of national character and reiterated their position that suicide was a universal concept. They put much effort into investigating those suicides that occurred as a response to mental illness as well as into constructing a 'humanized' collectivity that should be scrutinized and regulated by medical experts. The cultural narrative, popularized by journalists and writers, instead sought to differentiate suicide patterns and actors, escaping the universal epistemic view of voluntary death and relegating it to a unique and authentic national condition. This rehabilitation of the suicide phenomenon in cultural terms was the springboard for the audacious narrative that would vigorously emerge in the following decades.

Notes

1 Akihito Suzuki and Christopher Aldous, *Reforming Public Health in Occupied Japan, 1945–52: Alien Prescriptions?* (London: Routledge Studies in the Modern History of Asia, 2011).
2 Okada Yasuo, *Nihon Seishinka Iryōshi* [History of Psychiatry in Japan] (Tokyo: Igaku Shoin, 2002), p. 201.
3 Okonogi Keigo, "Psychoanalysis in Japan," in Salman Akhtar (ed.), *Freud and the Far East: Psychoanalytic Perspectives on the People and Culture of China, Japan, and Korea* (Lanham, MD: Jason Aronson, 2009), pp. 9–26.
4 Kosawa's association was initially established in the late 1940s as a study group of professors of psychiatry from various Japanese universities, but slowly it became the primary arena for debates on the development of psychology and psychiatry in Japan.
5 Iwata Fumiaki, "The Dawning of Japanese Psychoanalysis," in Christopher Harding, Iwata Fumiaki, and Yoshinaga Shin'ichi (eds.), *Religion and Psychotherapy in Modern Japan* (New York: Routledge, 2015), pp. 131–132.
6 Katō Masaaki and Mori Saburō, "Kattō hannō to shite no jisatsu no kisei ni tsuite" [The Mechanism of Suicide as a Response to a Conflict], *Seishin Shinkeigaku Zasshi*, 55(4) 1953, p. 97.
7 Sonohara Tarō, *Jisatsu no Shinri* [Psychology of Suicide] (Tōkyō: Sōgeisha, 1952), p. 17.
8 Sonohara Tarō, "Seinen no Jisatsu" [Youth Suicide], *Shinrigaku Kōza*, 3, 19, 55, 1950, p. 249; Satō Yoshiharu, "Jisatsu no Ryokugaku" [Dynamics of Suicide], *Seinen Shinri*, 1950, p. 50; Segawa Yoshiro, "Jisatsu ni Tai Suru Seinen no Taido" [Youth Attitude toward Suicide], *Iwate Daigaku Gagugeigakubu Kenkyū Nenpō*, 1(15), 1959, pp. 239–251.
9 Sonohara Tarō graduated in psychology from Kyoto Imperial University in 1931. In 1938, he became assistant professor at Bukkyo University. Sonohara was a very productive pre- and postwar psychologist who investigated child education and behavioral psychology in great depth, and his research on suicide was a complementary study to his more extensive research on youth behavior.
10 Sonohara Tarō, *Jisatsu no Shinri*, pp. 1–2.
11 Ibid., p. 117 and p. 23.
12 Segawa Yoshiro, "Jisatsu ni Tai Suru Seinen No Taido," pp. 239–251.
13 Sonohara Tarō, *Jisatsu no shinri*, p. 17.
14 Minami Hiroshi, creator of the theory of desire based on physiological psychology and animal psychology, and unsurpassed contributor to the progress of mass communication and pop culture studies, wrote numerous books, including *Shakai shinrigaku* [Social Psychology, 1949], which has been used as a standard textbook on sociology and psychology at Japanese universities; *Nihonjin no Shinri* [Psychology of the Japanese, 1953]; and *Nihonjinron no Keifu* [The Genealogy of the Discourse on the Japanese Character, 1980].
15 Minami Hiroshi, *Ikiru Fuan no Bunseki* [Analysis of Anxiety of Living] (Tokyo: Kōbunsha, 1952), pp. 106–110.
16 Ibid., p. 18.
17 Ibid.
18 Regarding the *shinjū* pattern, for example, Minami debunked the myth of Japanese uniqueness, recalling several examples of double suicides in European history. He argued, "*shinjū* in the Tokugawa period should be interpreted as a form of resistance against the ethics of a traditional society [rather than a Japanese peculiarity]." Minami Hiroshi, *Ikiru Fuan no Bunseki*, p. 100.
19 Karl Binding, *Bindingu Keihōron* [Binding's Essay on Criminal Law], trans. Saitō Kinsaku (Tōkyō: Wasedadaigakuhōgakkai, 1936). See also Otani Izumi, "'Good Manner of Dying' as a Normative Concept: 'Autocide,' 'Granny Dumping' and

Discussions on Euthanasia/Death with Dignity in Japan," *International Journal of Japanese Sociology*, 19(1), November 2010, pp. 49–63.

20 Yamana Shōtarō, *Jisatsu ni Tsuite* [About Suicide] (Tokyo: Kyōya Shuppan, 1949), pp. 33–37. See also Yamana Shōtarō, *Anrakushi* [On Euthanasia] (Tokyo: Kōbundō, 1951), p. 24.

21 Togawa Yukio expressed his bold position in favor of voluntary death in an issue of the journal *Kaizō* entirely dedicated to the problems of the postwar period (suicide, crime, poverty, etc.). Togawa Yukio, "Jisatsukō Genkagu" [Contemporary Studies on Suicide], *Kaizō*, 31(3), May 1950, pp. 139–143.

22 Ibid., p. 143.

23 Ibid.

24 Saitō Shō, *Jisatsu Oyobi Satsujin no Tetsugaku* [The Philosophy of Suicide and Murder] (Tokyo: Yuzankaku, 1951), p. 3. In the 1947 Constitution, suicide itself is not considered a crime. In articles 202 and 203, it is stated that suicide and attempted suicide are not subject to criminal law [*shobatsu no taishō ni narimasen*], but suicide assistance [*jisatsu hōjo*] and suicide instigation [*jisatsu kyōsa*] are crimes.

25 Hayashida Shigeo, *Jisatsuron: Jisatsu wa Ningen no Saigo no Jiyū de Aru* [On Suicide: Suicide as the Last Freedom of Human Beings] (Tōkyō: San'ichi Shobō, 1957), p. 204 and p. 179.

26 Donald Keene, trans., *No Longer Human* [Ningen Shikkaku] by Dazai Osamu (New York: New Directions, 1973), p. 87.

27 Okada Yasuo, *Nihon Seishinka Iryōshi*, pp. 196–216.

28 The *ie* or household is the basic unit of the Japanese family system. Apart from being identified as the basis of solidarity, the *ie* also served as an economic foundation. Nakane Chie defined the *ie* as a corporate residential group, arguing that as an archetype it is replicated in all Japanese organizations. See Nakane Chie, *Kinship and Economic Organization in Rural Japan* (London: Athlone Press, 1967).

29 The number of psychiatric hospitals grew from 128 in 1947 to 506 in 1960. The number of beds dedicated to psychiatric patients also grew: in 1947 there were 17,196 beds and in 1960 there were 95,067. See Okada Yasuo, *Nihon Seishinka Iryōshi*, p. 198.

30 Ibid., pp. 212–213.

31 Japan's Ministry of Health, Labor and Welfare *Dai 5 Kai Jisatsu Shibō Tōkei: Jinkō Dōtai Tōkei Tokuchō Hōkoku* [5th Statistics Concerning Suicide Deaths: Special Report on Demographic Statistics] (2005), p. 44.

32 Korea National Statistics Office, www.nso.go.kr/eng2006/.

33 Along with these changes in suicide patterns, the ascending suicide curve observed from 1955 to 1958 was also characterized by rapid changes in suicide methods. Legal restraints were imposed after the war that forbade the private possession of military equipment such as Japanese swords and guns. Additionally, the first act of the Japanese Law of 1958 that formalized their prohibition fueled the increased use of other suicide tools and methods. Asphyxiation by hanging and the use of drugs, which by the late 50s were largely available in pharmacies, became the most popular methods of suicide. Only drowning continued to be used as a method of suicide at roughly the same levels as prior to the war, and represented throughout the twentieth century a popular method of suicide for women in their 60s. See more details about restraints on firearms and swords in the immediate postwar period in: Anonymous, "Prohibition of Military Activity in Japan and Disposition of the Japanese Military Equipment," *International Affairs*, 19(4), February 1948.

34 *Asahi Shinbun*, "Wakamono Jidai no Jisatsu no Tengoku" [The Suicide Paradise for the Young Generation], April 25, 1956; Yoshitomo Takahashi, *Gunpatsu Jisatsu* [Suicide Clusters] (Tokyo: Chūkō Shinsho, 1998), p. 26.

35 Japan's Ministry of Health, Labor and Welfare, *Dai 5 Kai Jisatsu Shibō Tōkei: Jinkō Dōtai Tōkei Tokuchō Hōkoku*, p. 47.

36 See Satō Yasuko, "Jisatsu no Tōkeiteki Kansatsu" [A Statistical Observation of Suicide], *Jinkō Mondai Kenkyūjo Nenpō* [Annual Reports of the Institute of Population Problems], 2, 1957, pp. 41–44.

37 This generation was also involved in another suicide peak in the late 1990s. This demographic cohort first suffered immensely during the postwar crisis, as could be observed by the increase in suicide during their 20s, then worked intensely through adulthood during the nation's reconstruction periods, a time when the suicide rate declined, and finally showed another peak in suicides after retirement during their early 60s. Beginning in 1998, the second statistical suicide wave of the postwar period occurred, peaking in 2003. As the upward trend was most pronounced among middle-aged and old men, it has been regarded by many historians and sociologists as a reflection of Japan's prolonged economic depression and increasing unemployment rate. Others (see Yoshimatsu Kazuya) suggested that the violent change brought about by the collapse of the Bubble Economy was worsened by the process of democratization that occurred within the family system throughout the 1990s: for example, in 1999, divorce hit a record high, epitomizing the loss of family stability. The group of men who were in the 20- to 24-year-old group in 1958 were also in the group of men who were in the 60- to 64-year-old group in 1998. See Shun'ichi Araki and Katsuyuki Murata, "Suicide in Japan: Socioeconomic Effects on Its Secular and Seasonal Trends," *Suicide and Life-Threatening Behavior*, Vol. 17 (Spring 1987), pp. 64–71; Kazuya Yoshimatsu, "Suicidal Behavior in Japan," in Kok Lee Peng and Wen-Shing Tseng (eds.), *Suicidal Behaviour in the Asia-Pacific Region* (Singapore: Singapore University Press, 1992), pp. 28, pp. 31–32; Toyomasa Fuse, *Suicide, Individual and Society* (Quebec: Canadian Scholars Press, 1997), pp. 102–104; Mark D. West, *Law in Everyday Japan: Sex, Sumo, Suicide, and Statutes* (Chicago and London: The University of Chicago Press, 2005), pp. 217–236.

38 Kaketa Katsumi and Katō Masaaki, *Shakai Seishin Igaku* [Social Psychiatry] (Tokyo: Igaku Shoin, 1970). Translation provided by Nakane Yoshibumi, *Progress in Social Psychiatry in Japan: An Approach to Psychiatric Epidemiology* (Tokyo and New York: Springer, 2012), p. 5.

39 Kobayashi Akio, "Jisatsusha no Seikaku" [Personality of Suicidal Victims], *Shinano Kyōiku*, April 1950, No. 760, pp. 41–44 and p. 43.

40 Ibid., p. 43.

41 Ibid., p. 44.

42 Katō Masaaki, Kosaka Hideyo, and Mori Saburō, "Chiiki Shakai ni Okeru Jisatsu no Seitaiteki Kenkyū" [Ecological Study of Suicide in Community], *Seishin Shinkeigaku Zasshi*, 57(5.6), 1955, pp. 49–50.

43 Katō Masaaki, "Shakai Fuan to Shinkeishō, Seishinbyō, Jisatsu" [Social Anxiety, Neurosis and Mental Illness], *Toshi Mondai*, 46(2), 1955, p. 78.

44 Katō also drew upon the monographs on suicide by Ruth Cavan (Chicago, 1926) and Calvin Schmidt (Seattle, 1928), which took as their foundation the established Durkheimian model for the sociological investigation of suicide. Similar to Cavan and Schmidt, Katō displayed the distribution of the victims on a map to show Japan's socially shady (and topographically shaded) areas, and their differential relationships to suicide rates. Katō Masaaki, Kosaka Hideyo, Mori Saburō, "Chiiki Shakai ni Okeru Jisatsu no Seitaiteki Kenkyū," p. 50.

45 Katō Masaaki, "Shakai Fuan to Shinkeishō, Seishinbyō, Jisatsu," pp. 77.

46 Ibid., p. 73 and p. 75.

47 Yōsei Sasaki, "Anomii no Shakaishi" [The History of an Anomic Society], *Shakaigaku Hyōron*, 55(4), No. 220, 2005, p. 480. Sasaki's article is a thorough analysis of the history of suicide in Japan between 1899 and 2002, but he particularly focuses on the 1950s, as he considers it a significant turning point.

48 Yoshimura Toshiko, "Nyuusu ni Deru Jisatsu – Asahi Shinbun (Tokyo) Shukusatsuban Yori" [Suicide in the News – From Reduced-size Issues of the Tokyo Edition of

Asahi Newspaper], in Tatai Kichinosuke and Katō Masaaki (eds.), *Nihon no Jisatsu wo Kangaeru* [Thinking of Suicide in Japan] (Tokyo: Igaku Shoin, 1974), pp. 62–70.

49 According to Yoshimura, only in the 1960s, when the economic situation stabilized and suicide cases decreased, did the editorial approach suddenly start linking voluntary death with isolation [*kudoku*] and neurosis. Yoshimura Toshiko, "Nyuusu ni Deru Jisatsu – Asahi Shinbun (Tokyo) Shukusatsuban Yori" p. 67.

50 Many studies had demonstrated how poverty undoubtedly represents a risk factor behind suicide cases. See Rob Poole, Robert Higgo, and Catherine A. Robinson, *Mental Health and Poverty* (Cambridge: Cambridge University Press, 2014).

51 Yamana Shōtarō, *Jisatsu ni Tsuite*.

52 Ibid., p. 227.

53 Ibid., p. 231.

54 Ibid., p. 185.

55 *Yomiuri Shinbun*, "Shitsugyōsha Hahaoya Jibun to 3nin Korosu" [Unemployed Mother Kills Herself and Her 3 Children], May 11, 1954.

56 *Yomiuri Shinbun*, "Shigoto Nashi de Oyako-Shinjū" [Jobless Mother Commits Mother-Child Suicide], September 15, 1955.

57 *Asahi Shinbun*, "Otōsan, Ningen Rashii Seikatsu wo" [Dad, Let Us Live a Human Life], April 20, 1956.

58 *Asahi Shinbun*, "Otōsan, Ningen Rashii Seikatsu wo."

59 Okazaki Ayanori, "Jisatstu to Tasatsu to no Kanrensei [Relationship between Suicide and Homicide], *Jinkō Mondai Kenkyūjo Nenpō* [Annual Reports of the Institute of Population Problems], No. 3, 1958, Tokyo: Institute of Population Problems, Ministry of Health and Welfare.

60 *Asahi Shinbun*, "Jisatsusha ha hi ni 57nin" [57 People Kill Themselves Every Day], December 29, 1953.

61 Mita Munesuke, *Gendai Nihon no Shinjō to Ronri* [Sentiment and Logic in Contemporary Japan] (Tokyo: Kōbundō, 1971); Mita Munesuke, *Shakagaku Nyūmon* [Introduction to Sociology] (Tokyo: Iwaba Shoten, 2006).

62 Mita Munesuke, Yamamoto Yasushi, and Sate Kenji (eds.), *Riidingusu Nihon no Shakaigaku 12 – Bunka to Shakai Ishiki* [Readings in Japanese Sociology: Culture and Social Consciousness] (Kyoto University Press, 1985).

63 Kōsaku Masaaki, Usui Jishō, *Nihonjin no Jisatsu* [Suicide of Japanese] (Tokyo: Sōbunsha, 1965), p. 443.

64 Kōsaku Masaaki was also a well-known philosopher. He, along with Kōyama Iwao, Suzuki Shigetaka, and Nishitani Keiji, were known as the Four Heavenly Kings of the Kyoto School.

65 Kōsaku Masaaki, Usui Jishō, *Nihonjin no Jisatsu*, p. 418.

66 "Kyōshi no Taibatsu Yasshisekini Yoru to Omowareru Jisatsu" [Suicides Assumedly Committed Because of Teachers' Punishments], last modified March 18, 2014, http://synodos.jp/wp/wp-content/uploads/2013/04/shidoshi-1.pdf.

67 Yoshimura Toshiko, "Nyuusu ni Deru Jisatsu – Asahi Shinbun (Tokyo) Shukusatsuban Yori" p. 65.

68 Hayashida Shigeo, *Jisatsuron: Jisatsu wa Ningen no Saigo no Jiyū de Aru*, p. 24.

69 Hayashida Shigeo further advocated that suicide is never an easy choice, writing, "Living is as difficult as committing suicide." Hayashida confessed that he had tried to kill himself three times, because the perception that the world had of him did not match his own, and at times that frustration exploded in suicide attempts. Hayashida Shigeo, *Jisatsuron: Jisatsu wa Ningen no Saigo no Jiyū de Aru*, p. 196 and p. 17.

70 Inaoka Junno, "Nihon ni Okenoru Shukyō to Jisatsu no Mondai" [Problems of Religion and Suicide in Japan], *Zengaku Kenkyū*, No. 49, February 1959; pp. 92–108, p. 98.

71 Ibid., p. 108.

72 Ibid., p. 103.

73 Ibid., pp. 102–103.
74 Isomura Eiichi, *Shinjūkō* [Thoughts on Double Suicide] (Tokyo: Kōdansha, 1959), p. 196.
75 Ibid., p. 213.
76 Okazaki Ayanori, *Jisatsu no kuni – Shakai Tōkeiteki Kenkyū* [Suicide Nation – a Socio-statistical Analysis] (Tokyo: Kokon Shoin, 1958), p. 199.
77 Ibid., p. 37.
78 Yamashita Hajime, "Seishun no Jisatsu ni Tsuite" [On Youth Suicide], *Fujin Kōron*, February 1958, pp. 142–146. This prolific output occurred immediately after Yamashita had carried out a seminar on Suicide and Philosophy at the Komaba campus of Tokyo University. Attendees repeatedly asked him to provide a straight opinion on youth suicide and on media interpretations, but unable to fulfill their greedy demand at the time, Yamashita audaciously expressed some of the key points later in *Fujin Kōron*.
79 Ibid., p. 143.
80 Ibid., p. 144.
81 *Asahi Shinbun*, "Shi wo Isogu Wakamonotachi" [Young People Looking Forward to Die], December 11, 1957.
82 Katō Hidetoshi, "From Things to Experiences: Changing Values in Contemporary Japan," in Ian Miles and John Irvine (eds.), *The Poverty of Progress: Changing Ways of Life in Industrial Societies* (Oxford: Pergamon Press, 1982), pp. 272–273.
83 Sasaki Kiichi, "Genbaku to Sakka no Jisatsu" [The Atomic Bomb and the Suicide of a Writer], *Ningen* (Kamakura Bunko), 6(5), 1951, pp. 102–107, pp. 106–107.
84 *Asahi Shinbun*, "Gakusei no Jisatsu ga Gekizō" [Students' Suicide Rate Increased Enormously], April 11, 1953.
85 Anonymous, "Shi wo Isogu Wakamono ga Oosugiru" [There Are Too Many Young People Rushing to Die], *Bungei Shunjū*, 36(2), 1958, pp. 74–83, p. 74.
86 Hayashida Shigeo, *Jisatsuron: Jisatsu wa Ningen no Saigo no Jiyū de Aru*, p. 14 and pp. 19–20.
87 Inaoka Junno, "Nihon ni Okenoru Shukyō to Jisatsu no Mondai," pp. 92–108, p. 100.
88 Yamana Shōtarō, *Jisatsu ni Tsuite*, p. 37.
89 Okazaki Ayanori, *Jisatsu no Kuni – Shakai Tōkeiteki Kenkyū*, pp. 31–32.
90 Isomura Eiichi, *Shinjūkō*, p. 119.
91 Maeda Shinjirō, *Hanzai no Toshika: Sono Hōsoku to Jittai* [Crime and Urbanization: Rules and Data] (Tōkyō: Yūhikaku, 1957), p. 217.
92 Although Japanese institutions never collected statistical data on *shinjū*, one third of the newspaper reports between 1946 and 1960 were constituted by accounts of *shinjū* cases. It is extremely problematic to assess whether a suicide committed by two or more people can be considered a *shinjū*, and it is perhaps for this reason that no official data on *shinjū* have ever been available. However, in non-fictional production, journalists tended to be rather determined to assess a fairly extensive number of suicide patterns as *shinjū*. Such obsessive attention to *shinjū* led to an editorial over-representation of it to the detriment of statistical 'realities,' presumably for the sake of reasserting romantic and old-fashioned patterns.
93 *Asahi Shinbun*, "Kekkon Dekinu to Shinjū" [We Kill Ourselves Together Because We Cannot Marry], July 16, 1952.
94 *Asahi Shinbun*, "Shiroi Yuki no Naka de no Shinjū" [*Shinjū* in the White Snow], February 11, 1951; *Yomiuri Shinbun*, "Masshirona yuki no naka de 2nin gakusei no shinjū" [*Shinjū* of 2 Students in the White Snow], December 11, 1952.
95 *Asahi Shinbun*, "Jaren no Seisan ni Shinjū" [Double Suicides – They Clear Off Their Irksome Relationship], February 6, 1950; *Asahi Shinbun*, "Hakone de 5nin shinjū. Jaren no Seisan, haha wa 3nin no Kodomo wo Tsureru" [*Shinjū* of 5 People in Hakone. Mother Brings Her 3 Children with Her in Order to Clean Off Her Extramarital Relationship], March 24, 1952.

96 *Asahi Shinbun*, "Hakone de 5nin shinjū. Jaren no Seisan, haha wa 3nin no Kodomo wo Tsureru."

97 In Japanese culture, the concept of *jaren* is best expressed by the axiom "when we die, we become *butsu*" [*Shinyaa, butsu da*]. To clarify, the axiom implies that in Japanese culture, the way we die may allow us to purify ourselves, purging our sins. Koshinaga Jūshirō, *Kansatsui no Jikenbo Kara* [From the List of Accidents of a Coroner] (Tokyo: Dokubai Shinbunsha, 1985), p. 124.

98 *Yomiuri Shinbun*, "Karōshi ka Jisatsu ka, 42 Sai no Dōrōsha no Shi" [Death of a 42 year old Worker: Suicide or *Karōshi*?], November 12, 1955; *Yomiuri Shinbun*, "Oyako ga Chichi to Otto No Tame ni Jiketsu" [Mother and Child Killed Themselves for Their Dad and Husband], July 1, 1954.

99 Matsumoto Seichō was a premier author of Japanese mystery and detective fiction. He was awarded the Akutagawa Prize in 1952 and the Mystery Writers of Japan Prize in 1957. Credited with popularizing the genre among readers in his country, Matsumoto was the nation's best-selling and highest earning author in the 1960s. *The Tower of the Waves* [*Nami no tō*] had immediate and ongoing impact on Japanese society. After its publication in 1957, it became a television drama with the same name, first in 1959, then again in 1961, 1964, 1970, 1973, 1983, 1991, and 2006. In the month following the publication of the novel, and again soon after the novel was turned into a TV drama, the number of suicides in Aokigahara forest increased. Several articles reported that an average of thirty suicide cases per year had been recorded since its publication; these articles attributed the phenomenon to Matsumoto's novel. See *Yomiuri Shinbun*, "Minijiten: Aokigahara Jukai" [Small Dictionary on Jukai in Aokigahara], October 1, 1992; *Yomiuri Shinbun*, "Jisatsuannaisho Shiji Shita 2kitai 'Hon Mite Kita'. Hitori Hogo" [Two People with a Guidebook Read the Instructions and Came to the Forest. One Is Safe], October 20, 1993; *Yomiuri Shinbun*, "Aokigahara Jukai – Fukai Mori ni Afureru Katsudōkan" [Great Activities in the Deep Forest of Jukai, in Aokigahara], November 16, 2003.

100 Matsumoto Seichō, *Nami no tō* [The Tower of the Waves] (Tokyo: Kōbunsha, 1957), p. 23.

101 Ibid., p. 111.

102 Togawa Yukio, *Ningen Nogi Maresuke* (Tokyo: Kōjinsha, 1988).

103 Togawa Yukio, "Jisatsukō Genkagu" [Contemporary Studies on Suicide], *Kaizō*, 31(3), May 1950, pp. 139–143, p. 141.

104 Umeda Haruo, "Jisatsuteki Sakuhin ni Tsuite" [On Suicidal Literary Works], *Bungaku Kaigi*, 6, December 1948, pp. 222–232, p. 223.

105 Haniya Yutaka, *Kyomu to Jisatsu* [Nihilism and Suicide] (Tokyo: Kakukawa Shoten, reprinted in 1979), p. 145.

106 Tanaka Hidemitsu (1913–1949), a novelist of the Buraiha genre during the Showa period, was greatly shocked by the suicide of his mentor Dazai Osamu. In his later years, he suffered from alcoholism, drug abuse, and mental instability. He committed suicide at the grave of Dazai Osamu in 1949.

107 Haniya Yutaka, *Kyomu to Jisatsu*, p. 142.

108 Shibukawa Gyō, "Kindai Shōsetsu to *Jisatsu*" [Contemporary Novels and Suicide], *Kokubungaku Kaishaku to Kanshō*, 13, October 1948, pp. 57–62, p. 62.

109 Ibid., p. 58.

110 Yamashita Hajime, "Seishun no Jisatsu ni Tsuite," p. 145.

111 Saitō Shō, *Jisatsu Oyobi Satsujin no Tetsugaku*, p. 11.

112 Ibid., pp. 21–22.

113 Ibid., p. 26.

114 Hayashida Shigeo, *Jisatsuron: Jisatsu wa Ningen no Saigo no Jiyū de Aru*, pp. 156, 165.

115 *Yomiuri Shinbun*, "Kareshi ni Uwaki Sare, Joshi ga Jisatsu" [Betrayed by Her Boyfriend, Young Woman Kills Herself], December 17, 1954.

116 *Asahi Shinbun*, "Ikite Ite Kurushii: Jūbyōki to Hin ni Semerare" [Living Is Too Hard: Man Seriously Ill and Afflicted by Economic Problems Kills Himself], August 8, 1956.

117 *Yomiuri Shinbun*, "Noirōze de Hahaoya ga Jisatsu" [Suffering from a Nervous Breakdown, a Mother Kills Herself], June 25, 1954; *Asahi Shinbun*, "Kurutta Hahaoya ha 3nin to no Shinjū" [A Crazy Mother Kills Herself and Her 3 Children], June 9, 1952; *Asahi Shinbun*, "Sango no ku ni, Oyako no 4nin ga Shinjū" [For the Distress of Childbirth, Mother Kills Herself and Her 4 Children], August 25, 1955.

118 Whereas the popular discourse on women's suicide reasserted conventional paradigms that saw mental illness as the core explanatory event, readopting biological terms rather than ecological ones, the sociologist Isomura Eichi advocated for a more uncontaminated social rationalization of women's voluntary death. Isomura explained, "For a long time, women lived in a family system that positioned them as men's slaves and therefore [killing oneself and one's child] was a sort of act of resistance." He further argued, "In the relationship with her husband, a woman is supposed to soothe him; with her child, she is supposed to calm him/her. However, very often she cannot fulfil her tasks. Middle aged Japanese women [. . .] are convinced that they should fulfil such a role [in society]." This meant that when they did not, they felt pressured to commit suicide. For Isomura, social stressors rather than neurological disorders were the unique conditions that explained women's suicide. Isomura Eiichi, *Shinjūkō*, p. 106.

Bibliography

Salman Akhtar (ed.), *Freud and the Far East: Psychoanalytic Perspectives on the People and Culture of China, Japan, and Korea* (Lanham, MD: Jason Aronson, 2009).

Kobayashi Akio, "Jisatsusha no Seikaku" [Personality of Suicidal Victims], *Shinano Kyōiku*, 760 (April 1950), pp. 41–44.

Anonymous, "Prohibition of Military Activity in Japan and Disposition of the Japanese Military Equipment," *International Affairs*, 19(4) (February 17, 1948).

Anonymous, "Shi wo Isogu Wakamono ga Oosugiru" [There Are Too Many Young People Rushing to Die], *Bungei Shunjū*, 36(2) (1958), pp. 74–83.

Shun'ichi Araki and Katsuyuki Murata, "Suicide in Japan: Socioeconomic Effects on Its Secular and Seasonal Trends," *Suicide and Life-Threatening Behavior*, 17 (Spring, 1987), pp. 64–71.

Okazaki Ayanori, "Jisatstu to Tasatsu to no Kanrensei [Relationship between Suicide and Homicide], *Jinkō Mondai Kenkyūjo Nenpō* [Annual Reports of the Institute of Population Problems], No. 3 (Tokyo: Institute of Population Problems, Ministry of Health and Welfare, 1958).

Okazaki Ayanori, *Jisatsu no Kuni – Shakai Tōkeiteki Kenkyū* [Suicide Nation – a Socio-statistical Analysis] (Tokyo: Kokon Shoin, 1958).

Karl Binding, *Bindingu keihōRon* [Binding's Essay on Criminal Law], trans. Saitō Kinsaku (Tōkyō: Wasedadaigakuhōgakkai, 1936).

Nakane Chie, *Kinship and Economic Organization in Rural Japan* (London: Athlone Press, 1967).

Isomura Eiichi, *Shinjūkō* [Thoughts on Double Suicide] (Tokyo: Kōdansha, 1959).

Iwata Fumiaki, "The Dawning of Japanese Psychoanalysis," in Christopher Harding, Iwata Fumiaki, and Yoshinaga Shin'ichi (eds.), *Religion and Psychotherapy in Modern Japan* (New York: Routledge, 2015), pp. 131–132.

Toyomasa Fuse, *Suicide, Individual and Society* (Quebec: Canadian Scholars Press, 1997).

Shibukawa Gyō, "Kindai Shōsetsu to Jisatsu" [Contemporary Novels and Suicide], *Kokubungaku Kaishaku to Kanshō*, 13 (October, 1948), pp. 57–62.

Yamashita Hajime, "Seishun no Jisatsu ni Tsuite" [On Youth Suicide], *Fujin Kōron*, 43(2) (February, 1958), pp. 142–146.

Umeda Haruo, "Jisatsuteki Sakuhin ni Tsuite" [On Suicidal Literary Works], *Bungaku Kaigi*, 6 (December, 1948), pp. 222–232.

Minami Hiroshi, *Ikiru Fuan no Bunseki* [Analysis of Anxiety of Living] (Tokyo: Kōbunsha, 1952).

Otani Izumi, " 'Good Manner of Dying' as a Normative Concept: 'Autocide,' 'Granny Dumping' and Discussions on Euthanasia/Death with Dignity in Japan," *International Journal of Japanese Sociology*, 19(1) (November, 2010), pp. 49–63.

Japan's Ministry of Health, Labor and Welfare, *Dai 5 Kai Jisatsu Shibō Tōkei: Jinkō Dōtai Tōkei Tokuchō Hōkoku* [5th Statistics Concerning Suicide Deaths: Special Report on Demographic Statistics] (Tokyo: Ministry of Health, Labor and Welfare, 2005).

Inaoka Junno, "Nihon ni Okenoru Shukyō to Jisatsu no Mondai" [Problems of Religion and Suicide in Japan], *Zengaku Kenkyū*, 49 (February, 1959), pp. 92–108.

Koshinaga Jūshirō, *Kansatsui no Jikenbo Kara* [From the List of Accidents of a Coroner] (Tokyo: Dokubai Shinbunsha, 1985).

Kaketa Katsumi and Katō Masaaki, *Shakai seishin igaku* [Social Psychiatry] (Tokyo: Igaku Shoin, 1970).

Donald Keene (trans.), *No Longer Human* [Ningen Shikkaku] by Dazai Osamu (New York: New Directions, 1973).

Tatai Kichinosuke and Katō Masaaki (eds.), *Nihon no Jisatsu wo Kangaeru* [Thinking of Suicide in Japan] (Tokyo: Igaku Shoin, 1974).

Sasaki Kiichi, "Genbaku to Sakka no Jisatsu" [The Atomic Bomb and the Suicide of a Writer], *Ningen* (Kamakura Bunko), 6(5) (1951), pp. 102–107.

Korea National Statistics Office, "Shuyōkoku Jisatsuritsu Chōki Idō (1901–2005)" [Long term Trends of the Suicide Rate in Industrialized Countries (1901–2005)], last accessed November 2015. www.nso.go.kr/eng2006/.

"Kyōshi no Taibatsu Yasshisekini Yoru to Omowareru Jisatsu" [Suicides Assumedly Committed Because of Teachers' Punishments], last modified March 18, 2014, http://synodos.jp/wp/wp-content/uploads/2013/04/shidoshi-1.pdf

Katō Masaaki, "Shakai Fuan to Shinkeishō, Seishinbyō, Jisatsu" [Social Anxiety, Neurosis and Mental Illness], *Toshi Mondai*, 46(2) (1955), pp. 255–260.

Katō Masaaki and Mori Saburō, "Kattō Hannō to Shite no Jisatsu no Kisei ni Tsuite" [The Mechanism of Suicide as a Response to a Conflict], *Seishin Shinkeigaku Zasshi*, 55(4) (1953).

Katō Masaaki, Kosaka Hideyo, and Mori Saburō, "Chiiki Shakai ni Okeru Jisatsu no Seitaiteki Kenkyū" [Ecological Study of Suicide in Community], *Seishin Shinkeigaku Zasshi*, 57(5.6) (1955), pp. 49–50.

Kōsaku Masaaki and Usui Jishō, *Nihonjin no Jisatsu* [Suicide of Japanese] (Tokyo: Sōbunsha, 1965).

Ian Miles and John Irvine (eds.), *The Poverty of Progress: Changing Ways of Life in Industrial Societies* (Oxford: Pergamon Press, 1982).

Mita Munesuke, *Gendai Nihon no Shinjō to Ronri* [Sentiment and Logic in Contemporary Japan] (Tokyo: Kōbundō, 1971).

Mita Munesuke, Yamamoto Yasushi, and Sate Kenji (eds.), *Riidingusu Nihon no Shakaigaku 12 – Bunka to Shakai Ishiki* [Readings in Japanese Sociology: Culture and Social Consciousness] (Kyoto University Press, 1985).

Mita Munesuke, *Shakagaku Nyūmon* [Introduction to Sociology] (Tokyo: Iwaba Shoten, 2006).
Kok Lee Peng and Wen-Shing Tseng (eds.), *Suicidal Behaviour in the Asia-Pacific Region* (Singapore: Singapore University Press, 1992).
Rob Poole, Robert Higgo, and Catherine A. Robinson, *Mental Health and Poverty* (Cambridge: Cambridge University Press, 2014).
Yōsei Sasaki, "Anomii no Shakaishi" [The History of an Anomic Society], *Shakaigaku Hyōron*, 55(4) (2005), p. 220.
Matsumoto Seichō, *Nami no tō* [The Tower of Waves] (Tokyo: Kōbunsha, 1957).
Hayashida Shigeo, *Jisatsuron: Jisatsu wa Ningen no Saigo no Jiyū de Aru* [On Suicide: Suicide as the Last Freedom of Human Beings] (Tōkyō: San'ichi Shobō, 1957).
Maeda Shinjirō, *Hanzai no Toshika: Sono Hōsoku to Jittai* [Crime and Urbanization: Rules and Data] (Tōkyō: Yūhikaku, 1957).
Saitō Shō, *Jisatsu Oyobi Satsujin no Tetsugaku* [The Philosophy of Suicide and Murder] (Tokyo: Yuzankaku, 1951).
Yamana Shōtarō, *Jisatsu ni Tsuite* [About Suicide] (Tokyo: Kyōya Shuppan, 1949).
Yamana Shōtarō, *Anrakushi* [On Euthanasia] (Tokyo: Kōbundō, 1951).
Akihito Suzuki and Christopher Aldous, *Reforming Public Health in Occupied Japan, 1945–52: Alien Prescriptions?* (London: Routledge Studies in the Modern History of Asia, 2011).
Yoshitomo Takahashi, *Gunpatsu Jisatsu* [Suicide Clusters] (Tokyo: Chūkō Shinsho, 1998).
Sonohara Tarō, "Seinen no Jisatsu" [Youth Suicide], *Shinrigaku Kōza*, 3, 19, 55, 1950.
Sonohara Tarō, *Jisatsu no Shinri* [Psychology of Suicide] (Tōkyō: Sōgeisha, 1952).
Marc D. West, *Law in Everyday Japan: Sex, Sumo, and Suicide* (Chicago and London: The University of Chicago Press, 2005).
Satō Yasuko, "Jisatsu no Tōkeiteki Kansatsu" [A Statistical Observation of Suicide], *Jinkō Mondai Kenkyūjo Nenpō* [Annual Reports of the Institute of Population Problems], 2 (1957), pp. 41–44.
Okada Yasuo, *Nihon Seishinka Iryōshi* [History of Psychiatry in Japan] (Tokyo: Igaku Shoin, 2002).
Satō Yoshiharu, "Jisatsu no Ryokugaku" [Dynamics of Suicide], *Seinen Shinri*, 1950.
Segawa Yoshiro, "Jisatsu ni tai Suru Seinen no Taido" [Youth Attitude toward Suicide], *Iwate Daigaku Gagugeigakubu Kenkyū Nenpō*, 15(1) (1959), pp. 239–251.
Togawa Yukio, "Jisatsukō Genkagu" [Contemporary Studies on Suicide], *Kaizō*, 31(3) (May, 1950), pp. 139–143.
Togawa Yukio, *Ningen Nogi Maresuke* (Tokyo: Kōjinsha, 1988).
Haniya Yutaka, *Kyomu to Jisatsu* [Nihilism and Suicide] (Tokyo: Kakukawa Shoten, reprinted in 1979).

4 The triumph of the 'Suicide Nation' (1960–1985)

The sunrise and sunset of psychiatrists' authority (1960–1969)

The 1960s brought a resurgence of emphasis in Japanese psychiatry on biological causes and treatments, and, as a result, the decline of psychotherapy and the first attempt at broad psychiatric medicalization. Advances in the neurosciences and psychopharmacology along with the rise of marketplace competition brought the debate about the etiology and pathogenesis of psychiatric disorders – the dichotomy between psychogenic and biological approaches – to an end for the time being. The biological approach had been proven to have effective tools to prevent and treat mental illnesses, and consequently psychiatric institutions expanded; psychotherapy, on the other hand, lost its preeminence and was virtually abandoned by many academic centers and psychiatric training programs.

The vigorous return of Japanese psychiatry and the popularization of treatments for psychosis that were offered by the growing pharmaceutical industry only partly explain the concomitant weakening authority of psychology and psychoanalysis. The decline of psychoanalysis following its extraordinary expansion in the 1950s continued until the mid-1980s, and was essentially characterized by a lack of élan both in clinical research and in proactive interdisciplinary collaboration.[1] When Agari Ichirō, professor in clinical psychology and a specialist in psychology of personality at the Department of Human Health Sciences at Waseda University, gathered and analyzed the proceedings of the symposia hosted in Japan between 1965 and 1979 that focused on the psychological aspects of suicide, he concluded that no satisfactory methodological study had been carried out by Japanese clinical psychologists.[2] Comparing Japanese psychoanalytical scholarship to suicidologists' works in Europe or in the United States, Agari mourned the weak status of Japanese psychology. The shortage of relevant works in the field, crucially, left no obstacles to the rejuvenated enthusiasm for the discipline of neurobiological and pharmacological psychiatry.

The convergence of several other factors guaranteed the reestablishment of psychiatry as the premier authority. Firstly, the introduction of universal health coverage in 1961, which allowed virtually the entire population access to preventive, curative, and rehabilitative services at an affordable cost, guaranteed increased demand and led the pharmaceutical industry to become one of the most profitable and fast-growing industries in Japan. Furthermore, increased public expenditures supported the creation of small hospital facilities to accommodate long-term patients in particular. The number of hospital beds dedicated to psychiatric patients increased from 106,265 in 1961 to 247,265 in 1970.[3] Rather than reading these data as a sign of the growing number of mentally ill in the country, we should see it – as suggested by Okada Yasuo – as an increase in the number of patients who were considered 'eligible' to be hospitalized and treated for psychiatric disorders.

One event in particular promoted broader authority and accountability for psychiatrists and led to increased surveillance over mentally ill patients by medical professionals. This was known as the Reischauer incident. In March 1964, a Japanese man attempted to assassinate Edwin O. Reischauer, the US Ambassador to Japan, by stabbing him in the thigh. Reischauer received a blood transfusion, which infected him with hepatitis. He never fully recovered. The attacker, apparently not affiliated with any group or cause, was captured; authorities deemed him mentally disturbed. Following the incident, Japan's Minister of Public Safety was compelled to resign. According to several commentators, the incident revealed the lack of a proper system for managing outpatients and reinforced the importance of protecting all of society from the mentally ill. The public uproar over the incident not only led to the assigning of greater responsibility to the police for registering the names of mentally disturbed citizens as well as arresting and hospitalizing them, but also clarified the obligations of medical professionals.[4] The incident, in Okada Yasuo's words, was "the beginning of sweeping changes" in the development of psychiatry and in the establishment of mental health laws in the years to follow, and "gave visibility to movements and to multiple voices who had remained in the background."[5] In fact, following the Reischauer incident, laws were enacted to give more authority to local governments to require the institutionalization of people with mental illness, to oblige mandatory reporting of their hospitalization, and to guarantee that they received health care benefits provided by the government. Additionally, following the Reischauer incident, the Mental Hygiene Law [*Seishin Hokenhō*] was revised in 1965. It now included long-awaited amendments regarding the laws regulating insurance and guaranteeing the extension of mothers' benefits to their children [*Boshi Hokenhō*, or Maternal and Child Health Law]. The 1965 Mental Hygiene Law thus established a policy basis for community care and expanded the pool of potential patients covered by national insurance, conditions that were broadly welcomed by the medical community.

During the 1960s and early 1970s, the so-called third generation of Japanese psychiatrists – doctors who had returned from clinical training abroad – dedicated a large number of studies to proving the legitimacy of patient institutionalization and the validity of antipsychotic medications to prevent and treat suicide. Their efforts were primarily focused on justifying the growth of private and public hospitals and defending their profit-based structure.[6] They were also determined to move toward the 'internationalization' of psychiatry under the aegis of the Japan Psychoanalytic Society and the leadership of Okonogi Keigo, a psychoanalyst and professor at Keio University and Tokyo International University who had been a disciple of Kosawa Heisaku. Japanese psychiatrists translated various medical works into Japanese and introduced to their peers those schools of thought they had studied overseas. However, their efforts to overcome the national borders of psychiatric knowledge were overshadowed by their long-standing loyalty to a Kraepelinian orientation: they continued to assume that suicide was a pathological process internal to the individual, one that required expert diagnosis and management. Japanese psychiatrists were motivated to demonstrate the effectiveness of drugs (such as chlorpromazine and phenothiazine) that had been newly introduced and aggressively marketed by pharmaceutical companies. Their dynamic approach sought to validate the necessity of gathering data from both outpatients and inpatients treated for psychiatric issues.[7] As a matter of fact, despite recognizing the relevance and significance of a socio-statistical analysis on the suicide phenomenon, they criticized sociologists for having carried out surveys focused solely on assessing the suicide risk for the general population. It was more vital, they now believed, to assess how well psychiatric hospitals' treatment of inpatients was safeguarding people from the risk of suicide.

Nishiyama Akira, psychiatrist at the Bokutō Hospital in Tokyo, recounted the case of one woman who had lost her father very early in life and was raised by a mother who suffered from psychosis. This woman married, gave birth, had an outburst of depression, and became suicidal.[8] As a result, she was treated with antipsychotics as an outpatient following the protocol of contemporary medical guidelines; in spite of receiving treatment for two weeks, she killed herself. In response to the question 'Could such suicides be prevented by institutionalizing patients?' Nishiyama argued that controlling patients by institutionalizing them was the only effective way to prevent suicide. According to a sample of 4,561 psychiatric patients aged 15 and older gathered between November 1968 and December 1974 by Nishiyama, 0.48 percent of mentally ill outpatients and 0.17 percent of inpatients committed suicide. In general terms, such data indicated that the rate of suicide by psychiatric patients was ten times higher than the rate for the general population and specifically that there was a higher risk of suicide for outpatients than for inpatients. Who was responsible for those outpatient deaths? Paternalistically, Nishiyama insisted that psychiatrists should patrol hospital wards and proposed that the health system be expanded to include other private institutions able to accommodate a larger number of inpatients. The psychiatrist Hirayama Masami too was convinced that the institutionalization of patients was the only means of limiting the suicide phenomenon, observing: "I noticed that patients want to become healthy, have a successful life and be treated." In order to preserve their self-respect and hope for the future, patients should be followed closely and treated with "multiple antipsychotics" if necessary: this was the only way to prevent suicide.[9] Hirayama had examined a sample of 56 suicides committed by schizophrenic patients, searching for patterns by scrutinizing the patients' clinical histories, their professions, and the time and date at which their suicides occurred, finally concluding that the only commonality was mental illness. Mental illness was reckoned to be the unique triggering condition behind suicide, and this, he argued, was why the pathology should be treated by medical professionals. Clinical psychiatrists at the Matsuzawa Hospital too looked at a sample of 52 psychiatric patients who had committed suicide, analyzing their medical records, suicide notes, suicide methods, and treatment over a period that covered 30 years. It emerged that the suicide rate among patients had more than doubled over time, and therefore to prevent suicide it was strongly recommended that effective treatment be administered under the gaze of medical professionals.[10] Kitamura Akihide, professor of adolescent psychiatry at Nara University, collected data about 100 young Japanese aged 8 to 18 and used it as part of a comparative analysis with data gathered by Friedrich Specht, psychiatrist and professor at Göttingen University in Germany. Kitamura not only highlighted the great difference in motives behind the suicides of German and Japanese youth (drugs and family disruption were the main causes for Germans, school and the phenomenon of so-called examination hell [*shiken jigoku*] for the Japanese), but also was adamant that the neurotic nature of Japanese youth had to be controlled and treated within hospital wards.[11]

All this simultaneous research, carried out independently but tending to strictly follow the Kraepelinian tradition, reasserted the belief that suicides were 'avoidable tragedies.' While psychiatry was experiencing a new renaissance in terms of authority and prestige, the discipline remained anchored to the old biological precepts. Accordingly, the medical professional was once again perceived as someone who possessed the power to cure mental illness, and the patient was once again conceptualized as a passive victim of illness and a recipient of medical intervention. By asserting the medical nature of suicide, psychiatry further strengthened the reemerging view of its own power to treat the phenomenon.

However, during the late 1960s, psychiatry began to face failure. Throughout this time, the insistence on individual pathology left psychiatrists with a limited set of tools, which were unable to decipher other elements that may have had a bearing on the victim's actions, such as those cultural and historical forces that acted to constitute suicide and the suicidal subject. Furthermore, in the late 1960s psychiatrists began to be criticized for profiting from the institutionalization of the mentally ill – by accepting regular payments from the national health insurance system, for example. On July 13, 1963, a journalist for *Fujin Minshu Shinbun* reported on the harsh critiques made by the president of the Japanese Medical Association, Takemi Tarō, against psychiatrists. Takemi called psychiatrists "stockbreeders" [*seishin byōin ha bokuchikugyōsha*], implying that they treated patients the same way a farmer greedy for profit might treat his stock animals.[12] In 1965, the Tokyo Report [*Tōkyō Senden*] denounced unethical psychiatric practices and the frenzy to treat patients, demanding that medical professionals respect patient rights.[13] Such severe remarks remained isolated, though, until 1968, when international criticism of Japanese psychiatry was openly articulated in the World Health Organization's Clark Report. The British psychiatrist David Clark was commissioned by the WHO to conduct research on mental health care facilities in Japan. Clark concluded that, as was true in the US and the UK, Japanese psychiatrists were following the path of profit-oriented management, prioritizing lucrative inpatient treatments over outpatient treatments. Clark also pointed out that the number of private hospitals outweighed the number of public ones and questioned whether the mass-scale confinements considered patients' human rights. Despite Clark's unforgiving admonition, the profit-based structure of Japanese private hospitals proved resistant to change. Neither was any national movement organized to deinstitutionalize psychiatric patients and place them in community-based programs. In 1970 more than 76,000 patients were treated through the system of involuntary institutionalization, committed to private or public hospitals at public expense. The time was ripe to embrace the sunset of biological reductionism.

The accumulating evidence of medical malpractice helped to set in motion the anti-psychiatry movement in Japan. The movement had begun at an international level in the early 1960s, intensified in the late 1960s (as seen in the 1968 revolts), and extended until the beginning of the 1980s. It significantly heated up in Japan in 1969 at the Kanazawa Conference of the Society of Psychiatry and Neurology in the middle of a dispute over schizophrenia. While conservative psychiatrists believed that the cause of schizophrenia was a physical condition in the individual body, the psychiatrists who supported anti-psychiatry located the cause in social systems.[14] The leaders of the anti-psychiatry movement present at the conference, such as Moriyama Kimio, leveled harsh criticism against conservative psychiatrists, whom they accused of maintaining a paternalistic approach toward patients in order to guarantee the dominance of a system of certified physicians and of establishing a mechanism of control for the sake of their own self-protection at patient expense.[15] Moriyama deprecated conventional norms and practices that he saw as a sort of brainwashing technique, aimed at homogenizing society through 'proper' behavior. In this way, he believed, psychiatrists were inhibiting the true self of the individual and creating a distorted and schizophrenic self.[16] The anti-psychiatry movement promptly spread to psychiatric associations and to Japanese academia. In some cases, institutions found that they could no longer stand by their original institutional mission and consequently chose to disband. Japanese universities saw an impact, and several departments of psychiatry disintegrated. Popular media as well extensively reported the unprofessional conduct of psychiatric institutions and advocated respect of patient privacy and human rights [*jinken to shijisei*].

The anti-psychiatry movement, inspired by those who, even without a medical background, asked unconventional questions and assumed a critical stance on psychiatry, triggered a broad interest in the humanities and in the social sciences. The influential *The Myth of Mental Illness* by Thomas Szasz, which offered a genuine philosophical foundation for the anti-psychiatry movement, was translated into Japanese in the early 1970s. Translations were made as well of other works by the movement's activists – such as Ronald David Laing (whose ideas had great impact on the movement in Japan), Maxwell Jones, Robert Coles, Aaron Esterson, and David Clark – all of them denouncing unethical practices and attacking the legitimacy of medicine's authority to coercively limit individual choice. The anti-psychiatry movement significantly, if temporarily, constricted the dominance of neuropsychiatry. In fact, from the late 1960s onward, psychiatrists refrained from promoting broader medicalization of the mentally ill and gradually reverted to what I call a 'bio-sociocultural' model. Psychiatrists once again began to examine the etiology, epidemiology, and manifestation of mental disorders in general and suicide in particular through the lens of social, economic, and political conditions (such as prolonged poverty, economic instability, social changes, and maladjustment following the end of World War II). Once again mental health was reckoned as being impacted by these conditions in addition to genetics.

From the biosocial to the bio-sociocultural conceptualization of suicide (1969–1985)

As one of the outcomes of the anti-psychiatry movement, culture was increasingly perceived as a decisive element that interacted with biological, environmental, and psychological variables to affect mental health. Comparative analyses of different cultures had demonstrated that sociocultural variables were linked to all aspects of normal and abnormal behavior. While these analyses showed meaningful geographical distributions of behavior, including suicide rates, interestingly these distributions were unrelated to character stereotypes based on nation. The most influential research that reinvigorated the debate on the significance of sociocultural factors was a study carried out by the World Health Organization that examined the cultural variations of mental diseases. In 1968, in the wake of a number of critiques enumerated by the anti-psychiatry movement, the WHO published the eighth revision of the *International Statistical Classification of Diseases and Related Health Problems* (ICD), which aimed to improve uniformity of psychiatric diagnosis. The WHO recognized the necessity of identifying universal patterns of distress and standardizing diagnostic practices across Europe, the US, and Japan. In so doing, though, the WHO also uncovered cultural variations in terms of diagnosis and treatments of psychiatric disorders and emotional distress that were emerging in different countries. The WHO noted significant geographical variations in the prevalence, symptomatology, course, and outcome of psychiatric illness.

Thus, paradoxically, just as the international community was gearing up to create a universal diagnostic manual with consistent nomenclature, open debates made it starkly apparent that mental illness had features that manifested uniquely depending on geographical location and sociocultural context. While some psychiatrists remained loyal to neuro-chemical paradigms, others with a more clinical orientation began to portray mental illness in general and suicide in particular by evoking culturally resonant idioms and metaphors. In so doing, they naturalized suicide, describing it as a 'national' phenomenon, and eventually de-stigmatized mental illness. For some psychiatrists it was clear that the discipline could no longer commit itself to a conception of mental disorders as biologically caused diseases, with an etiology and manifestation that could be captured in universal representation. It was evident that mental illness existed, but the simple universalization of the biological predisposition could not adequately explain the illness and was insufficient to justify the therapeutic frenzy that dictated how patients were treated. These psychiatrists thus gradually acknowledged susceptibility to mental illness as a national feature – that is, a collective feature impacted by both relational (for example, social and environmental) and historical conditions.

The advent of the anti-psychiatry movement and the international consensus on the relevance of culture in the conceptualization of mental illnesses helped shape the 'new bent' taken by both psychiatry and sociology. During this dynamic moment, the conceptualization of suicide was enriched by clinical advances and by the incorporation of multidisciplinary data. In the 1950s, both the biological and social narratives on suicide had led the medical community to conceptualize voluntary death as a biosocial disease – that is, what was supposed to be uniquely an individual biological defect began to be seen as a feature of the collective. But by the late 1960s, a further shift occurred, one that reincorporated the cultural approach: suicide was seen as being situated at the core of the Japanese self, of its values and beliefs.

The drastic reversal of direction undertaken by psychiatrists occurred at the crossroads where the anti-psychiatry movement converged with two other significant events: first, the economic miracle and the cultural nationalism that it triggered (as will be explored in the following section); and second, the recognition of American and European suicidology and its promising theoretical outcomes. I argue that the circularity among these three discourses was responsible for limiting clinicians' tendencies to regard mental illness as a totally independent, timeless, culture-free process when they treated suicidal patients. The changing awareness of voluntary death as a cultural artifact boosted an unprecedented interest that gradually led to a multidisciplinary approach to the phenomenon.

In the wake of the anti-psychiatry movement, a renewed faith in the sociological model emerged, and a generation of new sociologists, who continued to be fascinated by Durkheimian theories on suicide, called for a more meaningful and systematic organization of statistical data to inform psychiatric and psychological theories. Sociological views were essentially concerned with the increase of the suicide rate in modern industrialized societies in general, and Japan in particular. In seeking to comprehend and prevent suicide, sociologists gradually became critical of their own discipline, reckoning that the sociological method alone was insufficient to explain the complex phenomenon. Despite the fact that Durkheim's theory had been enormously pervasive among Japanese sociologists, its applications did not prove sufficient to a full understanding of the suicide phenomenon. In the early 1960s, sociologists Kōsaku Masaaki and Usui Jishō began to suspect that an amalgam of modern anomie and indigenous culture was responsible for the increasing rate of suicide that their country was facing. They thus inferred that a thorough examination of Japanese 'culture' was fundamental to understanding the suicide phenomenon and that the sociological approach alone was insufficient to explain the reasons behind statistical suicide peaks. In trying to understand how well Durkheimian empirical and theoretical assumptions might have forecast the Japanese suicide rates in the 1950s and the 1960s, Kōsaku and Usui became increasingly critical of the predictive power of Durkheim's theory; they also were highly critical of its applicability to non-European countries. Could the Durkheimian paradigms explain the suicide wave in postwar Japan?[17] Could the Durkheimian categories capture the unusual array of Japanese suicide patterns? Could the meaning of these patterns be understood without inquiring into Japan's historical and cultural past?[18] Consequently, could the Durkheimian theory alone explain the suicide phenomenon in Japan? It was clear to the new generation of sociologists that the answer to all these questions was no, or not completely. The complexity of the phenomenon had to be investigated by examining the cultural features [*shiso*] of the Japanese: that is, suicide had to be explored using both sociological and cultural lenses together. In the mid-1960s, Naka Hisao, a professor emeritus in sociology who specialized in Durkheim studies, insisted that cultural conditions were essential to measuring, treating, and preventing suicide. Naka claimed that suicide could be seen as a sociological phenomenon through two unique measurements: first, through the absolute suicide rate of a country and its trends; second, through the relative suicide rate and trends of a country when compared with others. In relating the two datasets, Naka revealed how the absolute rate varied marginally over time, whereas the relative rate fluctuated enormously. This indicated to him that culture had a stronger impact on the suicide phenomenon than did contingent environmental conditions.[19]

The critical gaze that Japanese sociologists addressed toward their own discipline, which devalued the monolithic sociological approach and emphasized the need for a more overarching approach, created fertile ground in which the new field of study named 'suicidology' could flourish. In 1968, the American suicidologist and thanatologist Edwin S. Shneidman founded the American Association of Suicidology with the conviction that suicide is a 'cry for help' [translated into Japanese as *tasukaritai*] and the idea that understanding individual patterns of reaction to socially defined situations was fundamental to understanding the causes of suicide.[20] Suicidology contributed to suicide studies through the hybridization of psychological, psychiatric, and sociological theoretical approaches, focusing on suicidal attitudes and behaviors transmitted through social and family-based learning experiences.[21] Shneidman and suicidology promptly became well known in Japan; a generation of Japanese sociologists fascinated by the new American-born discipline sought to overcome the rift between social and psychological analyses of suicide by including 'culture' in their investigations. They believed that – borrowing the words of cultural anthropologist and suicide expert Maurice Pinguet – "[i]t is no use accusing psychopathology and sociology of being partial and reductive, and sending them off into separate corners: better to contemplate their uneasy alliance and ponder the chances of striking truths from their discords."[22] Not only did Japanese sociologists, reinvigorated by Shneidman's conceptualization of suicide as a 'cry for help,' understand the validity of a comprehensive approach to suicide that would include a cultural vision, but, unexpectedly, the National Police Agency had also called for an all-inclusive exploration of the suicide phenomenon in 1967. The National Police Agency had been in charge of collecting detailed suicide statistics and evaluating suicide notes since the beginning of the twentieth century. Inspector Inamura Yoshimasa encouraged Japanese academics and clinicians to carry out a quantitative and qualitative study of suicide notes. Japanese sociologists who, like Shneidman, were seeking to comprehend the suicide phenomenon – so Inamura stated – should put more effort into exploring the cultural complexity surrounding the act of suicide.[23]

In 1972, the popular case of Kōda Risa became an emblem of the renewed and more comprehensive approach to the suicide phenomenon taken by sociologists and psychiatrists who found the orthodox Durkheimian approach untenable. On September 25, 1972, Kōda Risa committed suicide at the age of 17. The last words she screamed before putting an end to her life were, "I do not know why I am living. I cannot believe anyone. Love is vain. I do not know why I want to die, but I don't want to give way to the suffering. I would like to live as a strong person. Mom! Mom!" Risa was in her third year at a public high school and was among the five best students in the school. She was good-looking, she came from a wealthy and well-educated family, and her parents hoped to see their daughter admitted to the prestigious Tokyo University one day. For this reason, every afternoon, Risa attended private school [*juku*] and constantly studied long hours. In her spare time, Risa was accustomed to reading Japanese novels and composing poetry. Her poetic genius can be observed in her diary, which was published posthumously. Newspaper commentators called it "Risa's suicide note," but she referred to it as "the album of my heart and of my spring days" and "the footprint of my time." Why would such an innocent and talented soul kill herself?

To fulfill her parents' dream and be admitted to the most prestigious university in Japan, Risa studied so hard that she slept an average of only four hours per night. During lunch break at school, however, she typically read comics, played chess with her classmates, and chatted. She gave the appearance of being a cheerful and outgoing classmate to disguise her unbearable exhaustion. She was a competitive girl who once wrote in her diary that if she had failed an exam, her shame would have made it impossible for her to leave her house.[24] Two weeks before her suicide, her mother was hospitalized for cholecystitis, which threw Risa into a dark depression. The lack of sleep and the concern for her mother hit her hard.

The Asahi Newspaper maintained that Risa was suffering from a severe neurosis caused by mental and physical fatigue, which cost her her life. The philosopher Katō Shigeru, who drew heavily on Stuart Picken's philosophical work comparing suicide in Japan to suicide in Western countries, dared to claim that Risa's mother and her ambitious dreams of success for her daughter had led to Risa's suicide.[25] Risa was thus a victim of social stress. On the other hand, while she seemed sociable and likable, inwardly she was competitive and aggressive, which made her not merely a victim. For Katō, Risa's suicide, judging from her own words, was the result of pressures she felt both publicly and privately. Thus, beyond the social pressure coming from a distorted educational system, the introverted nature of a teenager swinging back and forth between the need to be socially accepted among her peers and the ambition to stand out had also made her commit such an act. The case was analyzed closely throughout the years, especially after Risa's diary, *The Suicide Notes of a Seventeen-Year-Old* [*17sai no kisho*], was published in 1973 by Sanryo Bunkō. Durkheimian theories were publicly rejected as inappropriate to this case: Risa seemed to be well integrated in her community, and her act was neither altruistic, nor individualistic, nor fatalistic. The sociologist Kurihara Akira ruled out any possibility that Risa belonged within the Durkheimian category of 'anomic suicide' and stubbornly insisted that her death was a "multilayered social sign."[26] Risa's emotional state and voluntary death could be understood as the result of both social pressure and personal psychological imbalance.

So what factors were now seen as relevant in comprehending Risa's act? The psychological side was surely crucial, as suggested by Katō: "In order to understand the meaning of voluntary death and why people ultimately decide to commit suicide, it is absolutely necessary to decipher the feelings and will of the individual. An objective analysis cannot emerge from the darkness of the human soul."[27] Sociologically speaking, Risa lived in the so-called *musanshugi* era, in which youth were assumed to have no interests, no passions, and no responsibilities [*mukanshin mukandō musekinin*] but were made to endure extreme pressure at school and the well-known examination hell.[28] In cultural terms, the aestheticization of death and the inclination to suicide of the Japanese could help explain the act. Finally, according to the approach of suicidology, Risa's suicide could be labeled as a 'cry for help'; according to Katō, such suicidal individuals should be kept under the rigid control of medical professionals, because "the temptation to commit suicide is a dangerous freedom."[29] Behind her act, sociologists and psychiatrists thus recognized the existence of multiple dimensions: individual and social, existential, emotional, and physical. Durkheim's categorization was far too narrow to contain all of these dimensions. In the wake of the emergence of suicidology, the anti-psychiatry movement, and the culturalization of medicine, suicide was finally reckoned as a complex act that could only be interpreted using a combined set of tools. It is within this framework that the bio-sociocultural turn undertaken by psychiatrists should be understood.

By the early 1960s, as a natural progression of medical professionals' concern over the 1958 boom in suicides, a few psychiatrists had begun to explore whether there might be something about the Japanese psyche or society that was problematic, even pathogenic. While some explored the role that social forces such as one's age, employment, or marital status had on individual biology, and consequently on the suicide phenomenon, others investigated the impact that cultural forces, such as shared knowledge, customs, habits, beliefs, and values, had on the Japanese, emphasizing the crucial differences between Japanese culture and the cultures of other nations. Ōhara Kenshirō, Katō Masaaki, and Tatai Kichinosuke were the main representatives of a pioneering group of psychiatrists who, in the wake of American suicidology, sought to demonstrate how suicide was shaped by forces of culture and society. Their bio-sociocultural hypotheses were elaborated in disaccord with the 1968 WHO study that claimed that environment was a more significant factor than culture in psychiatric illness.[30] From this beginning, strengthened by scientific corroboration, the shaky bio-sociocultural psychiatric model gradually solidified and promptly incorporated culture as *the* condition triggering the suicide phenomenon in Japan; suicide was envisioned as an endogenous and viscerally rooted tendency of the Japanese. The genesis and manifestations of psychiatric disorders were to be understood as features of the 'race' rather than the individual. In other words, bio-sociocultural psychiatry conceptualized suicide as a pattern shared by a group of people, unique and different from patterns seen in other groups. A few years after the works of these three psychiatrists were published in 1974, Inamura Hiroshi pushed the conceptualization of suicide even further. He asserted that the phenomenon was exclusively the outcome of cultural variations, and therefore was treatable at the individual level but untreatable at a deeper level, the cultural one. The multi-disciplinary approach taken by these psychiatrists explained the proclaimed, but not actual, high suicide rate among the Japanese as the result of cultural factors unique to the nation (suicide patterns and motivations, for example).

The allegedly high suicide rate was rationalized by invoking the cultural proclivity and sensitivity of the Japanese to aesthetically beautiful voluntary deaths. Professor of psychiatry at Hamamatsu University School of Medicine and senior psychiatrist Ōhara Kenshirō wrote, "The aesthetics based on the very values of Japanese people are clearly embedded in their religious and cultural history. The purity of *shintō* lies in the beauty of simplicity [. . .] and this is also where the sense of aesthetics of the *bushi* lies. [. . .] At many levels, Japanese culture is embedded in this aesthetic. It was under these conditions that Chikamatsu's *shinjū* were created; they externalized that beauty and were capable of cleansing any sin."[31] In other words, for Ōhara, death was a purifying act that justified the high rate of suicide. Ōhara further explained that the prewar and wartime nationalistic discourse enabled a certain devotion toward noble and beautiful deaths: "If a warrior was not willing to die, how could he have fought? The highest sacrifice of one citizen was to reject his own life for the sake of the nation, and the ultimate expression of such extreme sentiment was represented by the *tokkōtai*."[32] By evoking the principles of *bushidō*, Ōhara's historical rationalization called for understanding with regard to those cultural beliefs that fostered wartime suicides, and at the same time it nostalgically glorified the timeless purity of voluntary death in Japan. Suicide patterns and motivations were assumed to epitomize the bulwark of Japanese cultural uniqueness. Ōhara sustained, "Suicide has several faces. It is different according to the historical period and the population [*minzoku*]. [. . .] Therefore, we should remember that there are some peculiar aspects related exclusively to the Japanese." Hinging crucially on Durkheim's categorization, Ōhara advocated that the motives behind the Japanese act of suicide were peculiar and culturally determined. He defended the nobility of prewar altruistic motivations for suicide – loyalty, sense of responsibility, and sacrifice – and predicted a consistent occurrence of suicide cases motivated by such values in the postwar era too, noticing a persistent Japanese passion for suicide literature and a continued appreciation for altruistic acts.[33]

Another thinker greatly inclined to reexamine the suicide phenomenon according to its cultural facets was Inamura Hiroshi, suicide expert and social psychiatrist at Tsukuba University, and one of the most active promoters of suicide prevention in Japan; he claimed, "The time has finally come for the numerous cultural differences that have an impact on suicide [to be noticed]. For instance, suicide patterns might all seem the same, but there is actually a big difference among societies." After Nogi's *seppuku*, Inamura claimed, psychiatrists had insisted on identifying suicide with mental illness. He noted, however, that cultural variations and individual personalities had a great impact on the phenomenon.[34] Japanese suicide patterns and motivations, Inamura insisted, had been shown to be very 'colorful' [*tasai*] and 'abundant' [*hōfu*] throughout history compared with the rest of the world.[35] For professors of psychiatry Katō Masaaki and Tatai Kichinosuke as well, the Japanese suicide phenomenon presented peculiar patterns. However, contrary to Ōhara's claims, they argued that motives differed according to the time period. Whereas in the prewar period "it was common to kill oneself for traditional values such as the family, the society and the nation," such suicides, they asserted, occurred very rarely in postwar society.[36] In Durkheimian terms, Katō and Tatai were claiming that altruistic suicides had decreased and anomic suicides had increased in the postwar period.[37] The cause of the increase was adduced to the absence of an all-embracing nation [*kyōdōtai*] – like the prewar Showa nation – that could manage to alleviate an individual's sense of loneliness and construct a solid logic of community.

Despite their apparent differences, the works of these various bio-sociocultural psychiatrists unmistakably showed a common approach, framed within the cultural and social realms. In this light, Tatai advocated, "It is evident that the suicide phenomenon [. . .] is greatly influenced by the cultural traits of the Japanese [*bunkateki minzokusei*]."[38] Inamura explained further that suicide is a universal phenomenon, but at the same time it reflects the deeply peculiar aspects of a society.[39] He rejected Sigmund Freud's claim that "all young people show a similar attitude to suicide" by affirming, "[I]t is now natural to think that people are subject to historical and cultural variations."[40] The bio-sociocultural approach precluded the idea of suicide as a tragedy caused primarily by pathological processes internal to the individual, and assumed that the phenomenon was a cultural product generated by forces situated outside of the individual. Culture was thus reckoned to be the wellspring of all actions, and suicide was the outcome of that unique culture. Japanese psychiatrists increasingly began to recognize the creative power of language, and became fascinated by the role that cultural forces played in shaping illness and deviant behaviors, as well as the role of cultural knowledge in the conceptual organization of illnesses and symptoms – that is, the ways clinicians made sense of their data. They fundamentally agreed that culture provided – borrowing Geoffrey M. White and Anthony J. Marsell's words – "structures of relevance" that determined what kinds of events and information were *salient*.[41] However, in evoking cultural features, they extended the realm of potential patients to the entire nation, calling for psychiatric treatment to prevent the suicide phenomenon. I would argue that psychiatrists' methodological tools had adapted to the trends and scientific discoveries of the time, but their final intent remained constant: to increase the pool of potential patients and to protect their prestigious position within the medical community.

An additional common denominator noticeable in bio-sociocultural studies was a sloppy theoretical approach. Inamura's research, for instance, was uniquely based on fictional materials instead of statistical data. Because he lacked discriminating theoretical frameworks and systematic methods, it is reasonable to be skeptical about how his limited dataset led him to produce a wide-sweeping attack on the biomedical model of mental illness. Katō and Tatai's work – a fairly comprehensive portrait of the suicide phenomenon in twentieth-century Japan – haphazardly pulled together surveys on happiness, economic and political investigations, and suicide statistics. This portrait often provided a confusing and incorrect picture, and factual and interpretive errors abounded. Worse was the soft-headed nostalgia both academics imposed on hard data and the mode of 'explaining Japan' they consistently slipped into, a sure formula for misrepresenting suicide in Japan as a 'Japanese' rather than human behavior. Tatai and Katō wrote extensively on suicide in both Japanese and English for an international audience (Tatai frequently participated in overseas symposia), and I would speculate that their cultural bent and their reframing of the Japanese phenomenon as 'peculiar' served to compensate for their limitations in their comparative approach to suicide. It is very likely as well that they were both influenced by the cultural discourse that was gradually overrunning every professional field. It is true, nevertheless, that Tatai's, Katō's, and Inamura's ideas were populist and very much the outcome of the counterculture of the late 1960s and the 1970s. Yet their quest for national authenticity translated into a very ambiguous theoretical language and revealed their incapacity to carry through on their ideas scientifically. I would argue that the bio-sociocultural approach to suicide in Japan was dictated mainly by a superficial fascination with suicidology, by the limits imposed by the anti-psychiatry movement, and by the overlapping cultural nationalist discourse, rather than by a mature theoretical apparatus aimed at demonstrating the multitude of facets impacting suicide.

The assumption that the universal biological indicators of suicidal patients were largely embedded in other factors, such as cultural assumptions, social reality, and concept of identity, meant that suicide was to a certain extent ethnocentric. But if suicide was caused by cultural processes that led to recognizable symptoms regardless of universal rules, were all Japanese then suicidal? And were all affected by mental illness, and thus treatable according to psychiatrists? The dangerous assumption that medical professionals had to keep at bay was the association between nation and madness [*kokka to kyōki*].[42] Ōhara Kenshirō addressed this thorny issue by resorting to the same rationalization that had been offered by prewar psychiatrists: particular suicides could be considered cultural artifacts – that is, the product of social and historical forces situated outside the mental state of isolated individuals – whereas others were medically treatable because their origins were pathological. This incoherent yet resolute approach was further explained by Ōhara at the 1980 symposium on suicide hosted by his faculty at Hamamatsu University. Psychiatrists, sociologists, and psychologists from all over the country joined the event to discuss the most contemporary issues on voluntary suicide. When at the final session an attendee asked Ōhara how he conceptualized suicide, the psychiatrist responded that cultural, sociological, and psychological variations all have an impact on the biological predisposition of the individual who commits suicide. It was still legitimate to label suicidal patients with the term "*seishin shōgaisha*" [mentally challenged/disabled], but only when referring to "modern suicides." Prewar suicides – for example, Nogi's act of *seppuku* – were a different kind of suicide.[43] On one hand, Ōhara's position coherently claimed that the reality of mental illness implied physical pathology; but at the same time he recognized sociocultural peculiarities that were exempted from medicalization. That is, Nogi's suicide, as well as all those suicides committed for valuable and noble reasons, could be exonerated from being treated with anti-psychotics because they were not committed out of a physical pathology, but instead represented the blaze of glory the Japanese had experienced during the Meiji and Taisho period. Those suicide patterns therefore should be preserved. Whereas a decade earlier Ōhara had located an obstacle to psychiatrists' prevention plans in the romanticization, aestheticization, and rationalization of suicide – as a beautiful act that was linked to traditional values and beliefs, such as loyalty and obligation – in the wake of the economic boom and newly rampant cultural nationalism he came to believe that the romanticization of suicide could quietly coexist alongside its pathologization.[44] In this movement toward the postwar normalization of Japanese culture, psychiatrists' role was to condone cultural uniqueness through the enshrining of old-fashioned altruistic motivations for suicide; it served to rehabilitate the Japanese sense of historical continuity and to rebuild the fragile national ego while still setting aside a category of non-altruistic suicides that deserved a closer medical gaze.

The question that arises is then the following: Why were psychiatrists in the 1970s once again eager to reject biological reductionism in order to reformulate their discipline according to a scientifically false discourse on the 'Suicide Nation'? The rising nationalistic discourse, whether directly or indirectly, encouraged them to do so, and in return this discourse revealed itself as extremely beneficial to the psychiatric one: it helped psychiatrists make suicide normal and familiar. The contemporary sociologist Serizawa Kazuya, professor at Tokyo University, has claimed that this conjunction between nationalistic and medical discourses worked to enable the "normalization" of the psychiatric system and of the perception of the mentally ill that followed the anti-psychiatry movement.[45] People could recognize themselves in the 'traditional' jargon. Culture and ethnocentrism filled the void left by the neurobiological model by creating an emotional attachment to cultural 'features' of the Japanese – that is, by simplifying the discourse on mental health, by aestheticizing Japaneseness, and by creating a homogenized society. In fact, since the end of World War II the international community had demonized many of the cultural features of the Japanese, and a cultural approach to mental illness could never truly find fertile ground. However, when Japan entered a phase of high economic growth, the shattered image of the nation was reassembled and internationally rehabilitated through the evidence of technological progress and an ever-rising GNP. In this positive economic climate, a mass reexamination of history, nationalism, and society occurred, rehabilitating the 'prewar system of values.'[46] Suicide epitomized one of the prewar features. The ingrained ethnocentrism that then dominated the medical and psychiatric professions challenged the paradigms of biomedical science, rejecting biological reductionism and emphasizing a combination of biological, social, and cultural variables that were compatible with the movement to glorify the national character. These bio-sociocultural researches represented a line of symbolic studies in which medicine was the subject matter, though rarely the principle source of interest. Nonetheless, they helped establish the concept of medicine as a cultural system.

The *nihonjinron* debate and cultural nationalism: mythologizing the 'Suicide Nation'

The early 1970s witnessed a dramatic recovery from poverty and gross economic inequality, as well as the beginning of the celebration of a fanatical devotion to work and the triumph of capitalism. When the euphoria surrounding economic success kicked in, one primary theme of public discourse was the fervent fascination with national character. The "Who are we Japanese?" boom spawned a vast literature on the assumed uniqueness of all aspects of Japan, and a new discursive formation of the nation appeared under the name of *nihonjinron*. The *nihonjinron* debate acquired the shape of a dichotomy between the supporters of continuity versus the supporters of modernity; of tradition versus modernization; of Japan's uniqueness versus its ordinariness. The result was that a large proportion of Japanese academic work was jeopardized by its positioning in the debate and, under the aegis of the myth of Japan's exceptionalism, persisted in holding the view that absolutely atypical aspects of Japanese culture existed. According to the cultural anthropologist Aoki Tamotsu, in the late 1960s and 1970s Japan began to recognize the importance of historical relativity and to locate certain defects in Western industrial society and certain merits in Japanese traditions, as re-invented in Japanese modernization. Then in the late 1970s and the 1980s – in the jubilation that followed the economic 'miracle' – Japan recognized its uniqueness as a positive model for a distinctively Japanese road toward modernity and its potential global reach.[47] The social psychologist Minami Hiroshi, one of the foremost scholars of the genre, added that it was in fact in the late 1970s and the 1980s that a nationwide cultural mobilization became evident – what Minami called a precondition of the *nihonjinron* debate.[48] It is within this theoretical framework that the tendency to culturalize the concept of suicide took on strength.

Primary and secondary sources published up through the early 1980s, whether they described prewar (Meiji, Taisho, and prewar Shōwa) or postwar suicide, shared the same viewpoint: voluntary death was described as an 'exceptionally traditional act' and as characteristically Japanese. While the prewar period was narrated as the origin of such a tradition, the postwar period was conceptualized as the moment in which the charm of tradition was rediscovered. Lingering traces of cultural exceptionalism were evident in all fields of study. The historical novelist and aspiring historian Yagiri Tomeo revisited the history of Japan and in particular the native Japanese people over a long timeframe, concluding that the nation's sense of chivalry was represented by *harakiri*, a timeless national value and a mysterious feature of the Japanese comparable to the Egyptian pyramids.[49] Despite the fact that his work was brusquely discredited in academic circles, his essays and collections of notes were well known in 1970s Japan, as were his strong assertions that suicide is not an expression of illness and *harakiri* is not a pattern of suicide but a statement of virtue.[50] Yagiri fervently supported the idea of the nobility of self-destruction as a demonstration of a coherent and noble Japanese past.[51] Although Ōhara, Katō, Tatai, and Inamura never overtly referred to the *nihonjinron* debate or to cultural nationalism, it is evident – judging from the ethnocentric bent they took – that they were not immune to it. They exalted and condoned those suicides committed for altruistic reasons and exonerated the victims from clinical intervention in the name of culture. Other medical professionals who specialized in the study of suicide explicitly positioned themselves within the debate, rejecting the biological universality of the phenomenon and insisting on its cultural singularity. Agari Ichirō, who was a great admirer of Karl Menninger and Émile Durkheim and heavily drew upon the suicidologists Al Alvarez, Edwin S. Shneidman, and Norman Farberow, claimed that Japanese culture had never acted as a deterrent to suicide. On the contrary, it instilled in the Japanese the idea that "you can be in the mood for dying," "if you want to die, you can do it," "if you can't do something, you can always die," and finally, "you can delete your misdeeds by dying."[52] In the wake of the *nihonjinron* debate, the peculiar propensity of the Japanese to commit suicide was thus explained by Agari culturally rather than biologically: "a society that prioritizes productivity is far from being a society that grows individuals who respect their personality. [. . . S]uicide is thus the multifaceted portrayal of such culture."[53] In other words, Agari was claiming that the system of values and beliefs that molds an individual was more meaningful than his/her neurobiological predisposition. The jump from 'suicide as a cultural feature of the Japanese' to 'Japan as Suicide Nation' was short.

The myth of a long-standing history of altruistic suicide

Imagining a long and common history was a must for a nation that desired to be proud of itself again. To bridge past and present, a massive production of historical works on suicide came to the fore that connected the deaths of Chikamatsu's famous lovers to contemporary suicides, by way of wartime *tokkōtai*. The widespread interest in retracing the evolution of voluntary death aimed at rediscovering its uninterrupted past and at strengthening its legitimacy by unveiling its roots and origins. The core of these studies was thus located in those suicide patterns presumed to be 'traditional' and committed for altruistic reasons, such as *seppuku*, *jōshi*, and *oyako-shinjū*, which had survived throughout the decades, through modernization and the war.

The underlying assumption of many of these historical works was that the Japanese practice was sufficiently peculiar that it would be impossible for a non-Japanese to decipher it. The suicides committed by many Japanese throughout the decades could only be sympathized with by those who shared the same values. Bessho Naoki, poet, critic, and essayist, claimed, "Westerners who research suicide in Japan cannot explain in a simple manner three patterns: *shinjū*, *harakiri*, *junshi*."[54] Suicide was seen as a cultural artifact and only the Japanese were presumed to be capable of understanding their own culture. Ōhara Kenshirō integrated psychological findings with sociological theories and historical evidence to create a proudly melancholic portrait of Japanese lovers' suicides. Methodologically, the study was based on a superficial overview of several stories of double suicides from the Meiji period to the immediate postwar, categorized according to Durkheim's paradigm. However, from a cultural perspective, it was an incredibly captivating story about the uniqueness of the Japanese and their impenetrability to outsiders.[55] Susumu Iizuka rediscovered the peculiar charm of the *oyako-shinjū* by narrating the historical evolution of the most theatrical act to emerge since the end of the nineteenth century.[56] Yamana Shōtarō glorified the suicides committed by virile men, imbued with a sense of altruism and responsibility that, according to the essayist, could also be recognized in "those acts barely narrated by history books" – probably a hinting reference to *tokkōtai*.[57] Evidently, a vivid feature of these historical works was the intention to restore a view of self-effacing suicide as an ethical act, a way of reestablishing a sense of virtue and morality in a nation whose culture had been demonized since its defeat in 1945.[58] In this regard, the sociologist Fuse Toyomasa, who specialized in comparative suicidology, listed 20 cases of suicide dating from 1954 to 1980 and allegedly committed following political scandals.[59] Fuse not only praised the sense of responsibility toward the community demonstrated by these men, but also drew a connection between their suicides and *tokkōtai*, who in his eyes demonstrated a much greater devotion to the nation than any other soldiers in the world: "In the prewar period, Japanese were required to demonstrate loyalty toward the nation; in the postwar period the nation expects such loyalty toward the policies of high-speed economic growth."[60] In idealizing contemporary suicides by legitimizing *tokkōtai*, Fuse redeemed the wartime atrocities by exalting their noble motivations. In addition, by connecting the past to the present, he reimagined a monolithic history of altruistic suicide. Fuse clarified that Westerners reckon that *harakiri* is a cruel and gruesome practice, but for the Japanese, *harakiri* is erotic: "It is a long-standing ritual; when the Japanese want to free their soul, they cut their bellies."[61] Fuse elevated Japanese suicides and *harakiri* to the sphere of altruism and additionally singled them out as being so peculiar that their true meaning could only be understood by the Japanese. The same argument was pushed even further by the sociologist Iga Mamoru, who carried out one of the most comprehensive historical accounts of Japanese suicide in the postwar period, by applying Durkheim's categorization of motivations.[62] He overestimated the tendency of Japanese to commit suicide for their society (altruistic and fatalistic suicides), and thus underestimated the rates of egoistic and anomic suicide. In other words, Iga claimed that suicide in Japan was motivated by the traditional tendency to die for the honor of the community, in the same way that samurai sacrificed their lives for their master. For the sociologist Nakahara Hiromichi, the long-standing concept of *seppuku* as a legitimate act of problem-solving, a demonstration of loyalty, and a condoned form of behavior encouraged a certain propensity of the Japanese to suicide. Nakahara not only justified but indeed glorified all those honorable deaths committed during the war for the sake of the nation: "The alacrity and the bravery embodied by a *bushi* became a self-destructive energy and was manifested through the most painful pattern of suicide: *harakiri*, an act that I would define as heroic [. . .]. However, the true nature [of the *bushi*], which is his drive to commit the most painful of suicides, was most probably animated by the exaggerated excitement he experienced in wartime."[63] In so arguing, Nakahara legitimated the very same pattern that was demonized by the international community, and rediscovered the honorable historicity of the nation. By assuming that there was a substantial continuity between prewar and postwar suicide patterns, by repeating and re-emulating the traditional, a story without rifts and fractures was rebuilt, in which the nation's days of yore could be recalled. More importantly, these historical works on voluntary death in Japan all shared the tendency to not distinguish between sacrifice and suicide. Were all the suicides that constituted the history of altruistic suicide in Japan committed out of free will, or under coercion? I would argue that, ironically, when the individual's will is portrayed as matching the society's will, here you have the identikit of the perfect citizen, one willing to fall into the shadows and selflessly commit suicide for the sake of the community.

Interestingly enough, the exaltation of the long-standing history of Japanese altruistic suicide was traceable not only in the literature produced within Japan, but in the international academic arena as well. The impact of the *nihonjinron* debate and of Japanese economic prosperity was centrifugal; it did not spare any field of study in or outside of the country. Abroad, Japanese suicide was synthesized as the reflection of the culture's attitudes – attitudes toward life and death, duty and honor, pain and pleasure. Maurice Pinguet, for instance, portrayed the evolution of upper-class suicide (focusing on the warrior class and writers) from the Kamakura period through Mishima Yukio's *harakiri* in 1970.[64] His historical investigation romanticized the ethics, faithfulness, and integrity expressed in the act of self-sacrifice by the Japanese, indomitably crossing the centuries. In his historical overview, Stuart D. B. Picken, cleric and professor of philosophy at International Christian University in Tokyo, praised the uniqueness of Japanese suicides, writing, "Compared to any other country, Japan has the most sophisticated patterns."[65] Picken too portrayed Japanese suicide as unique: a performance, an act of courage, a romantic statement infused with the highest self-sacrificing values and inspired by the noblest of virtues. For both Japanese and Westerners, rebuilding the respectability of Japanese culture clearly entailed the rehabilitation of the demonized wartime suicide patterns and the removal of the war as an imaginary watershed between a despicable past and contemporary success. Altruism, as the motive standing behind voluntary death, personified that respectability.

In the wake of the dominant *nihonjinron* debate, a sense of Japanese national identity was reinforced by rediscovering the history of 'Japanese suicide patterns and motivations' and subsuming it within old paradigms. Instead of a biological universality, the *nihonjinron* debate insisted on forging suicide as a Japanese peculiarity. Whereas biology considered every society to exhibit an equal risk of suicide among its members, the cultural exceptionalism of the 1970s and 1980s depicted the Japanese as more inclined to voluntary death and to unique suicide patterns. Reframing it within a bigger picture, this could be conceived of as one of the failures or limits of biological internationalism in the age of nationalism.

Death imagery became part of a process of rebirth, helping Japan to reassert cultural patterns and values that contributed to its reintegration into the international arena. Suicide provoked by decorous motivations was obsessively narrated as one of the historical and philosophical continuities traceable in the story of the nation. Such discourse shed light not on the self-sacrificing nature of the Japanese, but rather on the criteria of selectivity according to which writers picked allegedly altruistic suicides to rebuild the nation's integrity. The nostalgic projection of a return to the prewar ethos reasserted a synthesis in which the prewar and the postwar could cohere and in which the dishonorable past could be forgotten. Those who committed suicide became the sites for that historical reconstruction and national rehabilitation.

The myth of the propensity to suicide of Japanese writers

Japan is famous for writers' suicides, argued psychiatrist Ōhara Kenshirō: "Japan has the highest suicide rate for novelists in the world," added Yamana Shōtarō. Hasegawa Izumi, professor of contemporary Japanese literature, quantified the number of Japanese novelists' suicides at "more than 300."[66] The arbitrariness of such claims – not supported by legitimate statistical data or reference – should have undermined their significance. What is relevant here, however, is that they hint at the sharp perception among intellectuals that suicide – a feature of the Japanese – largely came from, or was 'represented,' in the demographic group consisting of artists. This perception was strengthened in the wake of the *nihonjinron* debate.

How were Japanese novelists' suicides represented, and why were they 'selected' to epitomize the Japanese propensity toward voluntary death? Novelists and poets were conceived of as 'gifted and sick': they were moody, depressed, prone to introspection, and inclined to melancholy because of the excess of their dark psyche. The combination of the spark of divine poetic inspiration with the physiological basis of neurosis produced the image of a figure who was both manically productive and yet inclined to suicide and depression. The celebration of such creative genius was blended with a lament for heavy suffering. Several intellectuals and medical professionals interpreted novelists' acts as a "barometer of social anxiety"[67] that was generated by modernization [*kindaika*] and the encounter with the unknown.[68] The suicide of the novelist Tanaka Hidemitsu in 1949 in front of Dazai Osamu's tomb, of the novelist Katō Hideo in 1953, of the novelist Kubo Sakae in 1958, and of Hino Ashihei in 1960 were all motivated by – according to Ōhara Kenshirō – their "lack of integration," borrowing from a Durkheimian category.[69] Yamana Shōtarō explained even further the concept of the lack of social integration of novelists, whom he called "dissenters" [*bunrishugisha*], by claiming that they endured the struggles of a turbulent era.[70] Komatsu Shinroku, professor of German literature at Rikkyō University, labeled the Meiji, Taisho, and Showa novelists who committed suicide as "souls living in an unlucky moment" and "a lost generation" [*ushinawareta sedai*].[71] By analyzing the works of Japanese and German novelists and intellectuals, Komatsu noticed that despite the fact that every individual showed a unique story and individual motives, Japanese novelists shared a strong self-awareness of the environmental contingencies and the historical moment in which they lived. Komatsu critiqued the National Police Agency statistical data for negligently attributing the suicides of most novelists to mental illness. Their act, he said, was nothing but the expression of environmental and historical stress. Kataguchi Yasufumi, professor of clinical psychology at Chukyo University, generated an identikit for suicidal Japanese novelists by applying the Rorschach test to investigate the authors' personalities.[72] He examined 21 Japanese authors, consisting of 18 men and 3 women, among them Edogawa Ranpo, Mishima Yukio, and Funabashi Seiichi, and concluded that they all showed a sharp sensitivity to revolutionary ideas and sweeping changes coming from abroad [*gaikoku kara no shigeki*]: "[I]n an epoch of enormous transformations, the personality of a genius [*tensai*] changes accordingly." Japanese novelists were presumed to be exceptionally prone to adjusting their views and ideas according to contemporary trends and to advocating for new movements – for euthanasia, for instance.[73] They showed all the disadvantages of being sensitive geniuses: lack of self-esteem [*jiga ga yowai*], and neurotic or anxious personality.[74] It was thus the relationship between a turbulent historical period and a sensitive disposition that triggered so many deaths among novelists. In this regard, the philosopher Karaki Junzō raised the question "Are we Japanese peculiar?" and suggested that the reader, before seeking an answer, should reconsider the question by remembering that at the time of Fujiwara no Michizane's death, suicide was strictly "beautiful and pure" [*kiirei seijō*].[75] Karaki explained that contemporary novelists were torn by "the dialectic between reason and instinct [*risei to honnō*], will and sentiment [*ishi to kanjō*], rationality and tradition [*gōri to dentō*], which had remained socially unresolved."[76] Their deaths could thus be explained as the outcome of an unsettled tension between tradition and modernity. For Bessho Naoki the key motive was instead "solitude" [*kudoku*]: "Japan is internationally isolated," and this greatly affected novelists.[77] The supposition here was that novelists were not common people; they were "precursors" of the times, as argued by Shibusawa Tatsuhiko, a novelist, art critic, and translator of French literature. Shibusawa heavily drew upon the 1972 book *The Savage God: A Study on Suicide* by the English poet and critic Al Alvarez, which, through a historical exploration of novelists' suicides around the world, unveiled the intimate link between novelists and poets and voluntary death. Novelists' suicide, Shibusawa reiterated in his own words, is an allegory for the high philosophical level reached by Japanese society. Japanese have to commit suicide, he wrote, because "[they] have the task of performing that desire to die." In other words, it mirrors what it means to be quintessentially Japanese.[78]

Other intellectuals explained suicides by Japanese novelists as nihilistic acts: writers were "people who disinherited life," who consciously and voluntarily renounced life in favor of death.[79] The difficulties of the era they were living in and the complexity of their lives as 'artists,' so exposed to the sense of annihilation and disappearance, but also to an extreme egotism and narcissism, might have pushed them to resolve such ideological displacement through death. "[S]uicide is one way to overcome nihilism and nothingness," commented the novelist Shiina

Ronzō, better known by his pen name Ōtsubo Noboru.[80] Essayist on Japanese literature Hirano Ken, following his analysis of suicides by popular Japanese novelists, hypothesized a variety of motives ranging from depression to irrationality, finally concluding that Japanese writers commit suicide for "nihilistic motives"; it is these motives that make these acts mysterious and fascinating at the same time.[81] Their novels are like massive suicide notes or, as defined by Karaki Junzō, a "literature of anxiety" [*fuan no bungaku*].[82] One such novelist was Akutagawa Ryōnosuke. His writings demonstrated a subdued anxiety that could not be overtly verbalized because of a mobilized nation glorifying a positive approach toward modernization but that was indirectly conveyed through his voluntary death. In other words, intellectuals perceived that Japanese novelists were not experiencing a universal condition, but a contingent sense of annihilation ultimately expressed through suicide. In short, the suicide of novelists had come to function as a 'collective representation' not only of a troubled society, but also of beliefs and ideas that were threatening to vanish, be it because of war mobilization, modernization, or the American occupiers. Their suicide was not merely emblematic of the sense of rootlessness experienced by sensitive individuals; it was also the solution to those very problems.

Although the suicide of novelists was not an altruistic act, and although it was somehow evident that most writers embraced death following a moment of brief irrationality, intellectuals and commentators glorified their personalities and aestheticized and culturalized their act as one unique to the Japanese.[83] Bessho Naoki defined Dazai's death as "cool" [*kakkō ii*] because – in the words of the essayist and scholar on British literature Nakano Yoshie – it was the ultimate romanticization of a glorious life.[84] Other intellectuals commented that novelists were narcissistic and self-centered, esthetes and bohemians[85]; they were all for lyricism, idealism, magnificence, and passion.[86] They very likely suffered from neurasthenia [*shinkei suijaku*] and psychological problems, as well as unresolved issues with their families, friends, or the nation itself, and they probably suffered from sleep disturbances and were addicted to medications. This might be why they all committed suicide in their homes or villas: to feel at ease and to transform their homes into a sacred location.[87] However, what commentators highlighted was also that these very schizophrenic and hopeless romantics belonged to a culture that profoundly appreciated their suicide as a resolute act capable of ending the pain sparked by infertile creative moments. Yasumoto Biten, psychologist and passionate researcher of ancient history of Japan, claimed that suicides by Japanese novelists could be explained using the following formula: biological weakness (decreased vital energy) + narcissistic personality (which makes them self-centered, self-involved, anxious) = suicide. That is, the combination of both neurological and psychological factors slowly but increasingly tended to drain novelists' energies and eventually pushed them to kill themselves.[88] But why then were Japanese writers exonerated from being medically 'treated'? Because the sources of these traits in writers were ultimately not located in their bodies or their minds, but in their culture. Moreover, these character traits played an important role in the culture: healing the troubled personalities of writers would have meant a decrease in the quality and extent of their artistic production. Writers' creative élan meant that those suicides were accomplished for the sake of a better or higher purpose, whether it be the nation or a particular value. Suicides by novelists epitomized a tormented emotional life, but at the same time evoked a reassuring sense of nostalgia that the past had not disappeared. The exaltation of their voluntary death triggered a process that allowed the identification of the 'ordinary Japanese' with a sensitive artist who quivers with the waves of the time because his culture has made him so perceptive. And of course, Japanese suicides, enshrouded in such a romantic cultural aura, could only be comprehended in all their sophisticated intricacies by one who shared the same values and beliefs and vaunted the same sensibility: a Japanese.

The media and the myth of the high rate of 'traditional' suicides

Despite the steady decline in the suicide rate that followed the peak of 1958, the representation of suicide did not diminish; on the contrary, asynchronies between statistical data and media coverage were evident. Commentators continued to reflect the ongoing preoccupation with the phenomenon and regularly described Japan as the 'Suicide Nation.'

Official sources provide evidence that apart from a slight increase in 1973 and 1974, Japan experienced a period of decreased suicide rates between 1960 and 1985, quite rapidly reaching the low levels seen in the late 1940s.[89] From the beginning of the 1960s onward, the total suicide rate declined steadily for both sexes, in particular among those groups responsible for the peak of 1958: young people and females. The wave of lower suicide rates coincided with the era of the radical youth movement of the late 1960s, with Japan's reintroduction to the international scene, and with the nation's economic 'miracle.' In 1973, the suicide rate for Japanese males ranked ninth among the twelve most industrialized countries, and the male-female ratio was lower in Japan than in the other eleven countries.[90] The suicide rate maintained a steady plateau until 1986, when an unexpectedly high rate was recorded. Demographers and statisticians typically do not identify the 1986 occurrence as a statistical "wave" of suicide, as it took place over only one year and only among minors; it is generally assumed that this isolated spike was the result of a suicide epidemic triggered by the voluntary deaths of pop star Okada Yukiko and of a junior high school student – cases which newspapers reported on extensively.

Despite the reassuring statistical data, the fascination with suicide as part of the national character exploded in the midst of the *nihonjinron* debate and the revival of cultural nationalism. Prewar patterns of suicide were brought under the spotlight of the public discourse and captured enormous attention that was directed toward the uniqueness of the Japanese and their predisposition to voluntary death. The media discourse represented suicide for the most part through a conventional vocabulary of altruism and sacrifice and praised its sophisticated and traditional patterns (the acme of this glorification came in 1970 in response to the public suicide of Mishima Yukio). Throughout the 1970s and the 1980s, a distinct fascination with the locations and modalities of suicides emerged, along with a continuing attempt to establish a sense of Japanese exceptionalism by elaborating a discourse that sought to make voluntary death 'autochthonous.'[91]

The media gave substantial coverage to suicide as an exceptionally traditional phenomenon, and thus showed an apparent increase in conventional patterns and motivations. Cases of *shinjū*, the repository par excellence of conventional aesthetics, were reported extensively in newspapers throughout the 1970s and the 1980s. Reporters tended to catalogue *shinjū* according to the following three motivations: a pursuit of purity, by cleansing shameful situations with death; an escape from a rigid society; and the sympathetic union with another person in death. In the first two categories, journalists' attempts to echo conventional aesthetics through the obstinate use of archaic terminology tended to affirm the cultural roots of the *shinjū* pattern and to produce stereotyped gender representations. On the other hand, *shinjū* cases belonging to the third type appeared in newspapers very rarely up to the mid-1970s but climbed steadily thereon, generating a number of neologisms related to the practice and an unconventional representation of the phenomenon.[92] The exploration of purity and love, along with sympathetic explanations of the motivations behind lovers' suicides, emphasized the vigorous nature of the relationships in question as well as the weight of the constrictions that society exercised on its victims. One example of *shinjū* passionately narrated by the press was the suicide committed by a teacher and his under-age student in a school classroom, which was later discovered by the girl's classmates. An article appearing in *Yomiuri Shinbun* briefly mentioned the illegality of the act, but then it repeatedly justified the courageous and noble suicide that had put an end to the inappropriate relationship.[93] A significant number of reported lovers' suicide cases were committed in public places, and most of them occurred during the winter season, in the middle of snowfields, or in bucolic *ryōkan* (traditional Japanese inns). Stock sentences related to the season were often used in the titles of articles as a cliché for winter *shinjū*. Titles like "Not Being Able to Wait for the Spring . . ." and "Double Suicide in a Cold Snowfield" are two examples that clearly expressed the melancholic seasonal connotation of the act.[94] In the latter article, the reporter wrote, "In a snowfield, a young girl and a young man had just swallowed some poison when a too-precocious death took them."[95] The narrative and aesthetic formulas used in these reports conveyed a nostalgic disenchantment with a coercive society that did not give true love a chance, and a nostalgic zeal for the 'beauty of death' when accomplished for dignified purposes. Apart from being extremely observant of the seasonal aspect of the suicide, the titles and contents of *jōshi* articles relayed the nomadic customs of lovers who traveled around the country looking for a romantic and melancholic place to commit suicide. "A Student Couple Commits Double Suicide on Hakone Mountain" and "Double Suicide in Snow-Covered Kanazawa" unambiguously suggested the outmoded nature of these young wandering souls who, through the staging of their deaths in a dreamy location, reasserted the image of suicide as an act of extreme nobility.[96] In this vein, in an interview in 1983, the novelist Yoshida Chiko declared, "If we classify humans' deaths according to their theatricality, we would have *shinjū* in first place, followed by suicide, then death caused by an accident, and eventually death caused by illness. There are different types of *shinjū* [. . .], but they all idealistically represent three sides of the human being: youth, beauty, love."[97] In 1976, a column on the sociology of suicide defined Japan as a *shinjū* society: "Even if people have become accustomed to the high-speed industrialization process and even if they are aware of the fact that time has passed, the Japanese are still extremely attracted to death. [. . .] It seems that on the basis of this 'dark period' in which no exit exists from the terrible economic crisis, there is Japan, a '*shinjū* society.'"[98] Even during the prosperous period of industrialization in which the difficulties of the immediate postwar period had been overcome, the high rate of *shinjū* suicide that still prevailed led to explanations based on the nature of Japanese society, a society fascinated by voluntary death. Thus in the popular discourse on suicide imbued with cultural exceptionalism, *shinjū* cases were representative both of the unbearable suffering of the Japanese, who were prone to feeling emotions in an amplified way, and of an unquestionable proclivity among reporters to rediscover and re-present the ahistorical nature of lovers' motivations.

Suicide reports were gradually reframed to emphasize spectacle and theater. Locations where these allegedly traditional suicides occurred were increasingly portrayed as public architectural settings, where an ostentatious act of suicide challenged the silence and loneliness of the citizens' anonymity, interrupting tedious routines, exploding in an egocentric performance and seeking the attention of an audience. A rising number of reports began with the phrase "He/she commits suicide in front of . . .," meticulously reporting the relationship between the audience and the victim. Articles reported cases such as *shinjū* committed by a mother and her children in front of the father or in front of their children's school, suicides committed in a supermarket or performed in the nude in the middle of a crowd of shoppers, and a student burning himself while facing a crowd in front of the Imperial Palace.[99] An explicit example is the case of three female schoolmates who decided to spend the night before their death planning their suicide in a hotel. Once everything was set, they phoned a classmate and told him, "Prepare some flowers for tomorrow."[100] The next day, the three girls went to the train station closest to their school and jumped in front of a train, holding hands, in front of the classmates who had previously been warned about their imminent suicides. The alert given to friends amplified the resonance of the event because the performance was a scheduled one: when the show opened, a curious audience crowded the space. Thus the suicides most eagerly narrated by the press were those that could be depicted as a performance exposed to the general eye for approval or disapproval. The act was portrayed as more symbolic than referential or representational; suicide was pictured as shocking a public audience and interrupting everyday routines.

Much news coverage focused on suicides completed in beautiful, scenic, or notable locations, such as Tokyo Tower, Sumo Lake, Ueno Park, Nikkō, Hakone, the Kanawaza Mountains, Shirahama, Sumida River, and Takahara, as well as Miharayama (the so-called Japanese Mecca of *shinjū*), Sakadayama, Takao Mountain (in which a series of suicides took place in August 1975), Kogon Falls, and the evocative cliffs on the Japan Sea coast, and Takashimadaira.[101] All offered sensational sites for lovers' suicides and were described as historical locations for suicide.[102] Among the most reported 'modern' public locations for suicide were railway stations, especially on the Seibu line in Tokyo, and department stores.[103] Newspapers emphasized the attraction of two particular department stores in Tokyo, Shinseikai and Seibu. Suicides in those two locations were often associated with the word *konran* [confusion], as victims interrupted the routine of a shopping afternoon, leaping into the carefree crowd that was walking down the street.[104] They were also portrayed as challenging the perfect functionality of urban conglomerations, with the location triggering a desire to *perform* – rather than commit – suicide. I would argue that the insistent portrayal of spectacle and theater reinforced the image of dignity and nobility associated with conventional patterns of motivation, and that this created a symbolic reality and generated a separation between routinized and exceptional activities. Suicide narrated as a performance thus involved a specific relationship between performer and audience in which a liminal space was opened up. The performer-audience interaction in fact often occurred in a significant location, a place that was already self-reflexively important to society, such as famous suicide locales or those 'modern' settings in which productive activities took place (train stations, department stores). In this kind of liminal space, performances such as public suicides desacralized social values and beliefs and enabled the society to look at itself through a historical lens.[105]

By bringing together past, present, and future through preindustrial symbols and by acknowledging the individual as the repository of that historicity, intellectuals and newspapers in the wake of the *nihonjinron* debate symbolically portrayed suicide as an instrument of personal and national regeneration. The obstinate attachment to the traditional suicide terminology legitimized the purity of immemorial traditions and allowed a smooth process of 'suicide naturalization,' keeping at bay any attempt at audacious conceptualization. How could the suicide phenomenon be naturalized? Simply by portraying it as familiar and culturally recognizable, and casting off the biological features. Suicide was thus associated with a genuine past, and with nationalism as an immutable force. 'Traditional patterns' of suicide were treated as national symbols. What kind of symbols were they? Symbols of altruism – in Durkheimian terms – and of respectability, thus aimed at preserving coherence. Traditional suicide patterns reaffirmed and strengthened the alliance between nationalism and respectability. These fearless acts of courage and nobility were narrated as expressions of human dignity and righteousness. Suicide thus became the epitome of historical coherence, of transwar continuity, of the rationalization of wartime sacrifices – with the *tokkōtai* belonging to the category of altruism.

The mythologization of suicide in fictional and non-fictional production reinforced the idea of Japanese cultural exceptionalism and projected the idea of Japan as a 'Suicide Nation.' The association between writers and suicide, the reaffirmation of the code of lovers, the recollection of historical continuity, and the reiteration of cultural uniqueness through the exaltation of old-fashioned altruistic suicide motivations insinuated the putative propensity of the entire nation to commit suicide as an act of decency. Suicide victims were not conceived of as individuals but as components of a collective experience. Nevertheless, the laudability of motives behind the traditional patterns was not granted equally to all. Commentators and the press tended to grant altruistic motivations to men alone. Noble suicides were males' ultimate act of self-denial and self-justification, and this arbitrary association that heightened the glory and the exaltation of manhood served to obliterate the horrors of the wartime deaths. Noble motives standing behind suicide were an invitation to manliness, which made the myth of Japaneseness even more attractive. Women and youth had no place in this pantheon.

Outcasts from the 'Suicide Nation' – women and youth

While medical professionals, intellectuals, and the media were fervently insisting that suicide be viewed as a sign of the peculiar values and beliefs of Japanese culture, medical and cultural discourses at the same time excluded two specific demographic categories from their categorization of the 'Suicide Nation': weak-minded women and irrational young people.

Throughout the 1970s and the 1980s, the discourse that glorified suicide explicitly excluded women's voluntary death. Women's suicide – in sharp opposition to the dignity of white-collar male workers – was perceived as the outcome of neurological weakness or of a personal fragility that rendered women unable to deal with the times and with economic challenges; as such, suicides by women were intentionally omitted from the class of acts that portrayed the nation in a favorable light.[106] Whereas the booming economy exposed both men and women to an exaggerated workload, men were portrayed as virtuous in their selfless workaholism, while women were portrayed as unable to embrace the increased work demands. Their sensitivity and weak neurological system did not allow them to keep pace with the times, thus diminishing the value of their deaths and intrinsically affirming the distinctive value of male suicide. Interestingly, Japanese novelists too – all males, by the way – were portrayed as neurologically weak, but their act was aestheticized and rationalized as 'philosophical' or 'creative.' Why did women's suicide continue to be de-culturalized? Why was their act not considered adequate to represent being 'Japanese'?

Medical professionals explored women's suicide mainly by drawing upon statistical data collected by the National Police Agency or cases narrated in the national newspapers. Iino Shirō, for instance, professor of medicine at Showa University, compared male and female suicide cases gathered by the National Police Agency and enumerated the reasons behind their acts. Iino constructed a stereotyped gender portrayal: women mainly kill themselves for reasons related to love (romantic delusions, unwanted marriages, etc.); men because of economic hardship, or a sense of guilt or responsibility.[107] The methodological fallacy of his research can be seen in his data interpretation and categorization: because he drew upon existing sources, Iino was unable to create a portrayal of women that differed at all from the one that already existed. Limiting his analysis to secondary sources inhibited Iino from asking unorthodox questions about women's suicides and motives. Sociologists Koshinaga Jushirō and Takahashi Shigehiro analyzed a sample of 535 *shinjū* and 638 *jōshi* cases that had been reported by newspapers over 27 years following the war and across Tokyo's 23 wards. They concluded, "Culturally, women who are mothers have identities that are not fully formed [*kakuritsu sezu*], and an extremely pathological way to affirm their own identity is to kill themselves with their children." In this painful process of "identification" [*aidentifikeshon*], women perceive children as a sort of "appendix" [*fuzokumono*] to their own identity.[108] Interestingly, although the two sociologists were analyzing 'traditional suicide patterns' – that is, the ones extensively glorified and supposedly representative of the respectability of the nation – they did not include women in the legitimation process, but rather demonized them. It was as if they were implying that the pattern itself was 'traditional,' but women's motives for suicide were contaminating its purity. A lousy methodological approach resulted in a poor perception of women's capacities, which ultimately led to women's suicides being denigrated as not being motivated by the same noble values that infused men's suicides.

According to newspaper commentaries, many women involved in *boshi-shinjū* were divorced, separated, widowed, or unmarried mothers living with their children, experiencing extreme economic hardship. However, in a pattern familiar from earlier decades, the media tended to focus on their unstable mental and physical conditions rather than on their economic troubles. They were very often labeled as *byōjaku no onna* [weak women] or *noirōze no onna* [women suffering from a nervous breakdown]. The article titled "My Son Has Eye Problems – Mother-Child Suicide," for example, underscored that the woman was mentally unstable and obsessed by her son's sight problems to the point that she considered *boshi-shinjū* to be the only option left to her.[109] In another article, the reporter suggested that a mother, who had probably been driven "crazy by the summer heat," killed her children and then herself because she was incapable of controlling her rage.[110] "Mother Starves Her Baby and Then Attempts to Join Him in a Double Suicide" was the title of the story of a mother who was unable to kill her baby, and so instead let him slowly die of hunger; she subsequently tried to follow him in death but was ultimately incapable of committing suicide. Paradoxically, the stigma of mental illness that she faced afterward was worse than the stigma surrounding the homicide of her baby.[111] Two significant points emerge here. The first is that reporters chose to focus on only certain aspects of the story, the more sensationalistic ones, bypassing a deeper analysis of context and motivations standing behind the act. This led to a biased gendered representation of the phenomenon. The second is that language was crucial to connecting women to the stigma of mental illness. The simple use of epithets such as "woman suffering from a nervous breakdown" or "a weak woman" invoked deeper gender narratives.[112] Furthermore, the genderization of suicide, which directly ascribed female suicide to 'madness,' had a much more crucial role: it implicitly reinforced the concept of males' altruistic suicide as a supreme act of responsibility that reincarnated the ethos of the samurai. Media categorization of the worthless deaths committed by women, meanwhile, was set in contrast to the categorization of Japanese middle-age workers' suicides as courageous acts animated by nobility of purpose. The stereotyped phrase "Hard worker suffering a nervous breakdown," which recalls the aforementioned women's epithet, was used in reports to instead express the deep attachment and commitment of Japanese men toward the company, a devotion that sent them to their deaths.[113] The genderization of males' altruistic suicides and of women's weak neurological systems is a clear example of the manipulation of suicide symbolism by the media. The media dealt with suicides by creating stereotyped images of them that reinforced connections to cultural values, which often came charged with long-standing patriarchal assumptions.

Youth suicide too was excluded from representing the 'Japaneseness' of the nation: Japanese youth were the target of unprecedented demonization. This was largely promoted by the utilitarian approach of psychologists and anthropologists who showed disdain for the apathy they perceived amongst youths, comparing it unfavorably to the resilient workaholism of their fathers. Okonogi Keigo, for instance, who wrote extensively on Japanese youth, reprimanded the young generation for their playfulness and childishness, features that could not be framed within traditional social values. Okonogi called youth who persisted in play and refused to belong to a controlled society "moratorium people," taking the phrase from American developmental psychologist and psychoanalyst Erik Erikson.[114] In Okonogi's words, Japanese youth consisted of a generation of narcissists, with a weak sense of reality and an exaggerated ideal ego.[115] The death they sought was thus a controlled and aesthetically beautiful but empty act.[116] Other scholars were convinced that the thorny problem of suicide among students and teenagers originated in the 'negative' features of Japanese youth, such as irresoluteness and vacillation. These features were attributed to the unique relationship Japanese children had with their mothers, which the psychiatrist Doi Takeo theorized as *amae* [dependence] in his work *Amae no kōzō* [The Anatomy of Dependence].[117] According to Doi, while it is well known that the growth and development of a teenager implies an initial psychological loss after which a further maturation and enrichment occurs, the new generation in Japan perpetuated an extended dependence on adults, became alienated from life, and gradually familiarized themselves with death. Doi's theory vividly reinforced the idea of an unenthusiastic, unengaged youth totally removed from the social context, and promoted a centripetal view of youth suicide. In other words, the discourse on youth suicide hinted at the idea that the phenomenon was the result of social decadence residing 'within' the young generation. Women were thus the repositories of physical and mental weakness; men, of valuable principles; and youth, of social decadence.

Despite the fact that the youth suicide rate remained at a fairly low level, the medical community constructed biased hypotheses and speculated on a neurotic young generation eager to end its life far too early. A survey carried out on a sample of 75 suicidal teenage patients who were being followed by clinical psychiatrists at the department of medicine of Osaka University, for instance, showed that only 11 of these young people actually ended up committing suicide. The authors hypothesized, using the resulting ratio of 11:75, that given that 784 actual youth suicides had been recorded throughout the nation in 1977, then approximately 4,000 suicides were likely to have been attempted during the same period.[118] Research like this deviated from the actual picture of Japanese youth suicide and painted the picture of an enormous phenomenon, an amplified 'cry for help' triggered by allegedly irrational youth behavior. Medical research also explored the incidence and the nature of youth motives for suicide by applying ethical judgments rather than using a scientific lens, concluding that such acts did not belong in the category of 'altruism' and thus should not be considered representative of the nation. Suicide in the 15–19 age group was attributed by Iino Shirō to problems with love, school-related anxiety, and irrational behaviors. Japanese youth was composed, insisted Iino, of people who were "already mentally and physically semi-adults."[119] In utilitarian terms, this meant that young people should accept their responsibilities and 'return' to society what they had been given. For Ōhara Kenshirō, contemporary youth suicide was motiveless [*gen'in no nai jisatsu; mumokuteki tekina jisatsu*], or at least it was so in the eyes of adults. This is why Ōhara strongly suggested that youth who were feeling suicidal should be followed by therapists. Despite the great effort he made to avoid generalization or a simplistic approach to youth suicide, when one reads between the lines it is evident that Ōhara did not approve of the new generation: "The high suicide rate [in Japan] is composed of those young people who are disappointed because their parents have not bought them toys or have asked them to get a haircut."[120] Inamura Hiroshi and Shimoyama Tokujicho examined the differences in motivation between youth suicides that occurred in the late 1940s and 1950s and those that occurred in the 1970s and 1980s, emphasizing the horrifying moral laxity into which the young generation had recently fallen.[121] While victims in the earlier period were described as incapable of overcoming problems arising from circumstances beyond their control, such as hunger and poverty, Japanese youth in the 1970s showed a moderate decrease in the suicide rate, but frightening motivations. Contemporary suicides were committed, according to Inamura and Shimoyama, by victims of trends and mass media beliefs: "Having lost their ethics and moral values, Japanese people have turned out to be animals living in a materialistic 'concrete jungle' who, much more attracted by death than their predecessors, pray to God that they might go to paradise in order to be able to meet pop stars and famous actors."[122] Along the same lines, media specialist Yoshimura Toshiko also attributed Japanese youth suicide to teenage irrationality and susceptibility to glamorized images in the news. For Yoshimura, Mishima Yukio's *harakiri* had a tremendous impact on foolish youth, and might have unintentionally encouraged teenagers to commit suicide.[123] Such a decadent generation was thus pictured as being particularly fascinated by voluntary death but lacking in appropriate motivations. Between July 1965 and December 1979, a group of clinical psychiatrists carried out a survey on 22 males and 48 females who had attempted suicide at ages that ranged from 12 to 19 in order to explore the motives behind their 'cry for help.' The team concluded that the pressures of going to school accounted for four times as many suicide attempts as all other motives and that it could be considered a peculiarity of Japanese society. However, despite not being supported by any scientific data or statistics, the researchers arbitrarily concluded that at the origin of their act there must ultimately lie immaturity and an incapacity to face the challenges of life.[124] In de-culturalizing and devaluing youth suicide, the scientific discourse also tended to incorporate social understandings of time within their interpretation of youth suicide cases. Temporality, exhibited in the definition of different phases of a person's lifetime, is an essential ingredient of identity and social organization. Understanding at which moment in their social lives suicides decided to kill themselves could provide researchers with vital information about their lives, the difficulties they were encountering, their values, and their beliefs. Medical professionals extensively commented that teenage suicides had committed the act 'too early' and with no reason. In other words, the idea that the agency of anticipating one's death could occur 'before' an appropriate time suggests that this was very much an economic and political judgment. Evidently, work life filled the gap before the critical time of life when death might be appropriate. Age was therefore perceived as an indicator of one's economic and political value to others, and without this investment of time in society, suicide drifted into social and economic irrelevance. It attracted stigma, even antipathy, for the victims, those young people who had been educated by society but had not yet paid it back by being productive.

Reporters too remained perplexed when facing the question, Why are these young people looking forward to dying? Titles like "Suicide of Minor: Motive Unknown" were endlessly repeated, showing an evident tendency to impute a lack of motivation to youth suicide.[125] Most suicide notes by teenagers reported their indifference and lack of engagement toward life. In a few of them, there emerged a sense of dissatisfaction with and antagonism toward the educational system and its challenging policy of examination. However, in these articles too, reporters perceived a lack of a reason triggering the suicide.[126] A psychologist interviewed by an Asahi Newspaper reporter affirmed, "Apparently, they don't have any reason to live, but they have some reasons to die." The journalist then commented: "Our new generation is embracing what one might call suicide-for-no-reason [*dōki naki jisatsu*]," which would become the metaphor for the predisposition to death among the young generation in Japan and the label for apparently incomprehensible suicide acts.[127] Takeda Makoto – psychiatrist, psychoanalyst, and president of the Takeda hospital, who along with Furusawa Heisaku, Doi Takeo, Masahisa Nishizono, and Maeda Shigeharu founded the Japan Psychoanalysis Society [*Seishin Bunseki Gakkai*] – deciphered the inexplicable phenomenon of youth suicide by claiming that the moment young people refuse social responsibility, voluntary death is doomed to become a "sweet temptation" [*kanbina yūwaku*].[128]

There was an evident tendency to characterize student suicides with the adjective "weak," and with phrases such as "suffering a nervous breakdown," thus enhancing an image of the innate psychological fragility of Japanese students. However, by the mid-1970s, media preoccupation with suicide among teenagers and students included explanations that ranged from individual incapacity to suicide as an indication of wider educational and social dysfunction. Suicides attributed to entrance exams, the changing of schools, and bullying made the headlines of the Asahi Newspaper and Yomiuri Newspaper between 1970 and 1985 on an almost daily basis. The discourse on students gradually became a more differentiated phenomenon, swinging back and forth between interpreting suicide as an indicator of the aesthetic attraction to death among Japanese youth and pointing out the weakness of students who could not stand the stress caused by exams. Newspaper coverage gradually interpreted youth suicide as a symptom of a more serious sociological problem and began to shift some of the responsibility to society. Reporters emphasized that college entrance examinations put students through a grueling trial of anxiety and fatigue, blaming them as one of a number of contemporary social ills. Poor parental guidance, distant teaching staff, and the education system itself were acrimoniously faulted for failing to impart proper education to the young.[129] Other reports highlighted that examination hell was just one part of a much wider vicious circle, including parents' expectations and children's desires to meet those expectations. Such a worrisome picture became further aggravated by two other articles: "After a Discussion over Admission Exams, Father Commits Suicide," which reported the anxiety of parents about their children's results at school,[130] and "I Have Lost Faith in the Examination System," in which a high school teacher harshly criticized the Japanese school system.[131] In the discourse on suicide and education, the student and his development became the site of an intensified nexus of social anxiety. *Ijime* [bullying], *kodomo ga hen* [children are turning strange], *gakkyū hōkai* [collapse of classrooms] were terms and phrases that formed part of a larger discourse of social crisis and collapse that took students as its focus.[132] The student, and youth in general, thus constituted the locus where anxieties about the national future gathered. On commenting about a series of suicides that occurred in 1978 among young Japanese, the essayist Kondō Nobuyuki claimed, "[Y]outh is a mirror for the environment that has lost its humanity. Apart from examination hell, young Japanese have a weak personality. They feel lonely and every day they fight to find a way to survive. We could define youth suicide as the epitome of contemporary Japan."[133] In describing the decadence that Japanese society had fallen into, Kondō highlighted how youth suicide had become the nest of all those conditions that had gone wrong in the postwar period, from material culture to family disruption, from the inhumane educational system to the sense of the meaninglessness of life. The tremendous gap between what society reckoned to be desirable for students and what students reckoned to be desirable for themselves became the raw material for extensive commentary on youth suicide and self-harm. The link between youth suicides and the discourse on the disintegration of the home and of the educational system embodied the truly frightening awareness that the anachronistic remnants of the national imaginary and collectivism were disappearing. But how can the inconsistent approach to youth suicide be explained? How was it possible to reconcile the idea of a de-culturalized youth suicide committed by weak and irrational teenagers and the idea of youth who were victimized by a widespread social unhappiness?

Saitō Shō, professor emeritus in philosophy at Tōyō University and Meiji University, distinguished between two categories of suicide: literary and philosophical [*bungakuteki* and *tetsugakuteki*]. With literary suicide, Saitō referred to writers' and artists' suicides that showed the innate instinct toward death of the Japanese race; under the category of philosophical suicide, Saitō included irrational and sensationalist suicides like Fujimura Misao's act. The distinction here is a telling one – on one side you have suicides that are culturally explained and that aim at homogenizing the masses; on the other, you have youthful senselessness that stands out and merely creates "noise."[134] The philosopher Takeuchi Yoshitomo resolved this fracture by reasoning that society had changed, whereas culture had not. In other words, the new generation that represented contemporary society no longer reflected Japanese culture.[135] Only some demographic categories such as writers, artists, and indefatigable male workers were reckoned to be suitable to translate Japanese values and beliefs into suicide.

The end of romantic and the beginning of political suicide?

In 1962, in narrating the story of a woman who tried to poison herself with sleeping pills eight times within a year, Nakamura Kazuo, rehabilitation consultant at the Brain Research Institute of Tokyo University and advocate for suicide prevention, listed various personality problems as well as neurological and genetic conditions that the patient suffered from. However, he concluded that there was a more significant condition that acted as a trigger for her suicide: the cultural one. The woman felt a strong sense of guilt for having low energy and for not decorously fulfilling her marital responsibilities. One night, though, her husband showed up at home with a prostitute, thus allowing his wife to feel free to file for divorce; surprisingly, it was at this point that the woman's sense of guilt as well as her suicidal desire faded away. Nakamura advocated that understanding how marital relationships are managed in Japan and what kind of values and beliefs are embedded in such relationships was pivotal; pushing the idea further, Nakamura was convinced that one must understand Japanese culture to prevent the high suicide rate in the country, and that only Japanese could succeed in such a task. Nakamura and many other medical professionals asserted, in fact, that a high suicide rate like Japan's indicates a superior culture, as it demonstrates a complex re-elaboration of social stress. However, in 1969 the WHO published the World Health Annual Statistics of 40 industrialized countries and their suicide rates, and reported that Japan was number 12.[136] Being number 12 among industrialized nations did not indicate an extraordinarily high suicide rate in Japan, and did not make Japan a 'superior' country. What, then, did make Japan become a 'Suicide Nation' and an internationally renowned cultural nest for voluntary death?

I argue that the overarching bio-sociocultural approach to suicide merged with the enthusiastic discourses on cultural nationalism and a romanticized Japanese exceptionalism within the context of a vacuum left by the neurobiological and psychological approaches. The synergy between the medical and the cultural discourses generated a scientifically built and rhetorically attractive conversation that was able to promote the popular acceptance of suicide through traditional language. The conceptualization of suicide as a national feature not only guaranteed medical professionals a larger pool of potential patients, but also let the nationalistic discourse gradually recover and rediscover Japanese historicity, homogenizing and overdetermining the meaning of its citizens' condition. This process concealed the complexity and diversity of the suicidal by creating a static, ahistorical, standardized image of the Japanese. Pushing it a bit further, the medical and the popular discourses on suicide were thus mechanisms of homogenization and standardization that incorporated victims into social subsets by writing their national history, a history imagined in the context of a 'peculiar and unique' national identity. Japanese suicide was thus explained culturally rather than biologically. As during the 1930s, the monological private character of death was cast aside in favor of its dialogical public function, in the service of a sense of social continuity. The individual's quest for a personal death was overshadowed by the society's efforts to socialize that death. The individual committing suicide was equated with creative artists and loyal samurai, reinforcing Japanese conformity to shared values and beliefs. The notions of 'suicide' and 'tradition' were thus vandalized by their subjection to the utilitarian requirements of rebuilding the national image.

The mid-1980s marked the beginning of a new phase in the history of the conceptualization of suicide. The tiny space left for individual agency in the immediate postwar period had shrunk even further in the 1960s and the 1970s. However, by the mid-1980s, with the economic recession and the concomitant sunset of the optimistic cultural discourse on the nation, the conceptualization of suicide became more involved in supporting individual free will and the choice of death with dignity. When the dying process shifted from being relatively simple to being very complex due to advanced medical treatments, the movements in favor of euthanasia and liberal bioethics strengthened, raising their voices on several ethical, psychological, and sociological issues. Suicide as well promptly became the object of analysis of a kaleidoscopic number of theoretical approaches. The 'right to die' movements and the political and philosophical debates on the relevance of death and on the meanings of suicide opened the possibility of alternative narrations. The existential writings of Hume, Kierkegaard, Nietzsche, Heidegger, Sartre, and Camus, for instance, came back into vogue in the contemporary discussion related to rational suicide. Greater agency was granted to the individual by a number of events and new guidelines in the mid-1980s that aimed at protecting individual rights. When in 1984 a number of inpatients died after being abused by nursing staff in the so-called Utsunomiya Hospital Scandal, for example, the Japanese medical community was severely criticized on several fronts. The issue of human rights violations in Japanese mental hospitals was raised at the International Commission of Jurists in Geneva and at the United Nations International League of Human Rights. Members of the International Commission of Jurists visited Japan to survey the state of affairs at mental hospitals and urged the Japanese government to undertake a drastic revision of the Mental Hygiene Law. The new law had to protect the human rights of mental hospital inpatients and had to require that designated physicians report regularly on the conditions of involuntarily committed inpatients. The new Mental Health Law [*Seishin Hokenhō*] in 1987, its further revision in 1993, and the Mental Health and Welfare Law [*Seishin Hoken Fukushihō*] of 1995 promoted the deinstitutionalization of the mentally ill and their normalization and rehabilitation.[137] These laws aimed to contain the paternalistic attitudes of Japanese medical professionals and to advocate for patient rights to effective treatment and a return to their original place in society. Because of the aforementioned events and interventions, the mid-1980s represent a watershed in the history of psychiatry in Japan. They demarcate the shift from mass institutionalization to independent living, from Japanese psychiatrists' conventional nosology of suicide to a more accommodating one, and from a dichotomous 'social versus biological' conceptualization of suicide to a more holistic one. This change was partly driven by the international pressure to revise the Japanese Mental Health Law and partly driven by the development of second-generation antipsychotics that allowed severely mentally ill people to live outside hospital wards. More importantly, the culturally evocative discourse on suicide of the 1970s, which managed to naturalize, normalize, and popularize suicide against a narrow biological standardization, was a crucial part of the genealogy of a more complex conceptualization of voluntary death. In the face of the 'Suicide Nation' mythology that had been empowered by an enthusiastic sense of cultural nationalism, medical disciplines were forced to soften their scientific apparatus. This may have biased their approach with the need to accommodate a romanticized sense of 'Japaneseness,' but it also amplified their capacity to speak to each other's findings and gradually added multiple layers to their conceptualization of suicide.

Notes

1 Throughout the 1970s, psychology was primarily led by returnees from the United States and Europe, such as the Jungian analyst Kawai Hayao, who had studied in Switzerland. Once he returned to Kyoto University, he presided over the growing number of clinical psychologists in Japan. A fourth generation of clinical psychologists returned to Japan in the early 1980s, after studying psychoanalytic psychotherapy and dynamic psychiatry in Britain and the United States. For further information on Kawai Hayao's formation and education, see Tarutani Shigehiro, "Kawai Hayao's Transnational Identity and Japanese Spirit," in Christopher Harding, Iwata Fumiaki, and Yoshinaga Shin'ichi (eds.), *Religion and Psychotherapy in Modern Japan* (New York: Routledge, 2015), pp. 181–203. The clinical psychologist Minagawa Kuninao received training on psychotherapy of children and adolescents in Michigan, Kano Rikihachirō in Kansas, and Kitayama Osamu in London. Simultaneously, Japanese translations of the most essential works of Kleinian theory started to appear and a growing number of psychoanalysts from overseas, especially from the United States, began to visit Japan. Starting in 1983, simultaneous interpretation was introduced at the annual congress of psychoanalysis. A full-scale international exchange in the psychological field was about to begin, but it would take until the following decade to bear fruit. While psychotherapy managed to survive through the 1980s in the United States and Europe thanks to efforts to integrate its material with the work of other disciplines, in Japan the rift between psychiatric, sociological, and psychological approaches persisted and continued to grow.

2 Agari Ichirō, *Jisatsu Kōdō no Shinri to Shidō* [Psychology and Guidance of Suicidal Tendencies] (Kyōto: Nakanishiya Shuppan, 1980), pp. 7–11.
3 Okada Yasuo, *Nihon Seishinka Iryōshi* [History of Psychiatry in Japan] (Tokyo: Igaku Shoin, 2002), p. 198.
4 For further details on how the National Police Agency was assigned responsibility for regulations about and surveillance of the mentally ill, see Nakazawa Masao, "Seishin Iryō no Ayumi" [History of Psychiatric Care], in Nakazawa Masao and Utsuno Yuki (eds.), *Seishin Eisei to Hoken Katsudō* [Mental Hygiene and Social Work] (Tokyo: Igaku Shoin, 1985), p. 8.
5 Okada Yasuo, *Nihon Seishinka Iryōshi*, p. 217, p. 229.
6 Okonogi Keigo, "Psychoanalysis in Japan," in Salman Akhtar (ed.), *Freud and the Far East: Psychoanalytic Perspectives on the People and Culture of China, Japan, and Korea* (Lanham, MD: Jason Aronson, 2009), pp. 9–26.
7 Kikawa Takehiko and Yano Toru, "Seishin Byōsha no Jisatsu He no Ryokudōteki Sesshin" [A Dynamic Approach to Suicide Patients], *Seishin Igaku*, 10(11), November 1968, pp. 876–882; Kamijima Kunitoshi et al., "Seishin Bunretsu Byōsha no Jisatsu ni Tsuite – Gaisui 96 Rei no Bunreki Kara" [A Study of 96 Successful Suicides in Schizophrenic Patients], *Seishin Igaku*, 23(9), September 1981, pp. 893–902.
8 Nishiyama Akira, "Jisatsu to Seishinka Gairai" [Suicide and Psychiatric Outpatients], *Seishin Shinkeigaku Zasshi*, 81(5), May 1979, pp. 311–341.
9 Hirayama Masami, "Bunretsubyō to Jisatsu" [Schizophrenia and Suicide], *Seishin Shinkeigaku Zasshi*, 82(12) December 1980, pp. 769–786, pp. 783–784.
10 H. Fujimori, M. Sakaguchi, T. Wakejima, M. Shintani, and M. Kamei, "Matsuzawa Byoin ni Okeru Kako 30nenkan (1951–1980) no Seishinbunretsubyōsha no Jisatsu Gaisuirei" [Thirty Years of Analysis (1951–1980) of Suicide Committed by Psychiatric Patients at Matsuzawa Hospital], *Seishin Shinkeigaku Zasshi*, 84, July 1982, pp. 483–502.
11 Kitamura Akihide, "Seishōnen Jisatsu Kito no Nichidoku Hikō Kenkyū" [A Comparative Analysis of German and Japanese Youth Suicides], *Seishin Shinkeigaku Zasshi*, 85, January 1983, pp. 54–68.
12 Akimoto Haruo, *Seishin'igaku to Hantai Seishin'igaku* [Psychiatry and Anti-psychiatry] (Tokyo: Kongo Shuppan, 1976), p. 193.
13 Akimoto Haruo, *Seishin'igaku to Hantai Seishin'igaku*, pp. 294–295.
14 Abe Akane, "70 Nendai Nihon ni Okeru Seishin Iryō Kaikaku Undō to Hanseishin' igaku" [The Japanese Reform Movement of Psychiatric Medicine and Anti-psychiatry Thought in the 1970s], *Core Ethics*, 6 (2010), pp. 1–11.
15 Ibid., pp. 1–2.
16 Moriyama Kimio, *Gendai Seishin Igaku Kaitai No Ronri* [The Theory of Dismantling Modern Psychiatry] (Tokyo: Iwazaki Gakushutsu Shuppansha, 1975), p. 243 and pp. 245–247.
17 Sociologists rationalized that the anomie generated by the unstable economic conditions of postwar Japan and the individualism entrenched in the process of modernization were particularly detrimental to countries like Japan, which was a well-integrated, if not conformist, society. Kōsaku and Usui explained the significance that the Japanese assigned to the institution of the family, citing numerous examples of women who committed suicide when they experienced marital problems, as well as the critical significance that Japanese youth gave to the group, citing examples of children who killed themselves because they thought that "they [did] not fit." Kōsaku Masaaki and Usui Jishō, *Nihonjin no Jisatsu* [Suicide of Japanese] (Tokyo: Sōbunsha, 1965), pp. 182, 185.
18 Despite the fact that Japanese and Western scholars insisted that some suicide patterns unique to Japan occurred in great numbers, Kōsaku and Usui debunked this myth, showing that the statistical data of these patterns were very limited. However, they claimed that the array of suicide patterns in Japan offered more unique types than

found elsewhere in the world. Kōsaku Masaaki and Usui Jishō, *Nihonjin no Jisatsu*, p. 199 and pp. 203–204.

19 Naka Hisao, "Shakaigaku ni Okeru Jisatsu no Riron" [Sociological Theories on Suicide], *Ōtani Gakuhō*, 40, March 1961, pp. 11–23. See also Naka Hisao, "Shakaigaku ni Okeru Jisatsu Riron no Kentō" [Considerations on the Sociological Theories on Suicide], *Shakaigaku Hyōron*, 60(15), April 1965, pp. 30–48.

20 Thomas Szasz clarified that the term 'suicidology' was coined in Germany in 1929, but became popular only later on with Shneidman. See Edwin S. Shneidman, *Suicidology: Contemporary Developments* (New York: Grune & Stratton, 1976), p. 12.

21 Behaviors like suicide, suicidologists believed, were more open to cultural influences, including, for example, the modeling of suicide via the mass media and the inhibition of suicide via religious influences. Edwin S. Shneidman, *Definition of Suicide* (Northvale, NJ: Aronson, 1994), pp. 63–69. Following the tenets of suicidology, in the mid-1970s relevant works on media and the cultural contagion of suicidal behaviors were carried out by David P. Phillips and Steven Stack. See David P. Phillips, "The Influence of Suggestion on Suicide: Substantive and Theoretical Implications of the Werther Effect," *American Sociological Review*, 39, 1974, pp. 340–354; Steven Stack, "Media Impact on Suicide," in David Lester (ed.), *Current Concepts of Suicide* (Philadelphia: The Charles Press Publishers, 1990); Steven Stack, "Suicide: A Comparative Analysis," *Social Forces*, Special Issue, 57(2) (1978), pp. 644–653.

22 Maurice Pinguet, *Voluntary Death in Japan* (London: Polity Press, 1993), p. 26.

23 Inamura Yoshimasa, "Jisatsu to Kisho" [Suicide and Suicide Notes], *Gengo Seikatsu*, 190, 1897, July 1967, pp. 50–56.

24 Katō Shigeru, *Jisatsu no Genshōgaku: Sei no Kiretsu* [The Phenomenology of Suicide – a Crack in One's Life] (Tokyo: Kōbundō Shuppansha, 1980), p. 67.

25 Ibid., p. 65. See also section pp. 63–70.

26 Kurihara Akira questioned the devout conformity of Japanese sociologists toward Durkheim's theory. Kurihara was particularly interested in understanding how Durkheim's category of 'anomic suicide' was acknowledged in his era. In this attempt, he first explained the Marxist ideological basis of Durkheim's work and then stated the lack of criticism put forth against Durkheim's *Suicide*. Kurihara found it disappointing that none of the numerous scholars who reinterpreted suicide cases like that of Risa questioned the very biased concept of 'anomic suicide.' He argued that 'anomic suicide' was a category based on the Marxist assumption that a society is a balance of powers, and that suicide threatens that equilibrium. Therefore a Durkheimian approach suggested that a need existed to rediscover the equilibrium that governed the anomie and to reconvert it into a productive source. Kurihara Akira, *Seiji no Shigaku – Me no Shuhō* [Poetics of History – Technique of Eyes] (Tokyo: Shinyōsha, 1983), p. 89.

27 Katō Shigeru, *Jisatsu no Genshōgaku: Sei no Kiretsu*, p. 147.

28 Ibid., pp. 88–95.

29 Ibid., p. 32.

30 See Ōhara Kenshirō's presentation of the new discipline in: Ōhara Kenshirō, "Jisatsu Bōshi Katsudō no Genjō" [The Contemporary Status of Suicide Prevention], *Seishin Igaku*, 11(2), February 1969, pp. 143–144.

31 Ōhara Kenshirō, *Jisatsugaku – Jisatsu to Bunka* [Suicidology: Suicide and Culture] (Tokyo: Shibundō, 1974–1975), pp. 176–177.

32 Ibid., p. 138 and pp. 140–141.

33 Ōhara overtly contested the argument formulated by the American anthropologist Ruth Benedict in *The Chrysanthemum and the Sword: Patterns of Japanese Culture* (1946), in which the author asserted a clear distinction between the motives behind prewar/wartime suicides and the motives behind postwar suicides (altruistic in the first case and individualistic in the latter). See Ōhara Kenshirō, *Jisatsu wo Kangaeru* (Tokyo: Keizai Ōraisha, 1971); Ōhara Kenshirō, *Ikiru Koto to Shinu Koto – Hito Ha*

Naze Jisatsu Suru no ka [To Live and to Die – Why People Kill Themselves] (Tokyo: Asahi Shinbunsha, 1996).

34 Inamura Hiroshi, "Burando Hakushi no Kōen wo Kiite" [Listening to Brandt's Speech], *Seishin Igaku*, 17(8), August 1975, pp. 871–874.

35 Inamura Hiroshi, *Jisatsu no Genten: Hikaku Bunkateki Kōsatsu* [The Origin of Suicide – Comparative Cultural Analysis] (Tokyo: Shinyōsha, 1979), p. 1.

36 A typical example of prewar suicide was the case of a couple who first set their child on fire and then killed themselves. A month before the suicide, they had sold their house hoping to settle a debt they had with the husband's family. However, the money they made on the sale was insufficient and they "couldn't stop apologizing to the family of the husband for the trouble." For Katō and Tatai, this was clearly an altruistic suicide. However, the source was a newspaper article and the psychiatrists' interpretation seems inappropriate if not arbitrary. A typical example of postwar anomic suicide was, according to Katō and Tatai, the case of an 18-year-old boy who poisoned himself. His father had died when he was 11, his mother was experiencing harsh economic constraints, and he kept receiving bad marks at school. He frequently borrowed money from his mother but never returned it. When one day he disappeared, no one worried because everybody was convinced that he would return home as soon as he ran out of money. However, the boy killed himself in the woods. The source of this case too was newspaper coverage whose narration was carefully tailored to sensationalize the events. Nonetheless, Katō and Tatai interpreted the case as a lack of prewar romanticism and noble values. Tatai Kichinosuke and Katō Masaaki (eds.), *Nihon no Jisatsu wo Kangaeru* [Thinking of Suicide in Japan] (Tokyo: Igaku Shoin, 1974), pp. 100–101.

37 In particular, Katō Masaaki and Tatai Kichinosuke argued that anomic suicides were caused by a so-called status conflict among the youth and a "cultural conflict" among the older generation. Tatai Kichinosuke and Katō Masaaki (eds.), *Nihon no Jisatsu wo Kangaeru* [Thinking of Suicide in Japan] (Tokyo: Igaku Shoin, 1974), pp. 103, 106.

38 Ibid., pp. 103 and 1.

39 Inamura Hiroshi, *Jisatsu no Genten: Hikaku Bunkateki Kōsatsu*, p. 322.

40 Inamura Hiroshi, "Seinenki to Jisatsu" [Youth and Suicide], *Seishin Igaku*, 19(12), December 1977, pp. 1323–1333, 1323.

41 See Geoffrey M. White and Anthony J. Marsella (eds.), *Cultural Conceptions of Mental Health and Illness* (Holland: Reidel Publishing Company, 1982), p. 8.

42 Akimoto Haruo, *Seishin'igaku to Hantai Seishin'igaku*, pp. 197–224.

43 Ōhara Kenshirō, "Tōron" [Discussion], *Seishin Shinkeigaku Zasshi*, 82(12), December 1980 pp. 802–819, pp. 809–810.

44 Ōhara Kenshirō, *Jisatsu wo Kangaeru* (Tokyo: Keizai Ōraisha, 1971), pp. 2–3.

45 Serizawa Kazuya, *Jidai ga Tsukuru 'Kyōki': Seishin Iryō to Shakai* [The Era that Produces 'Fool People:' Psychiatric Treatment and Society] (Tokyo: Asahi Shinbunsha, 2007), p. 206.

46 Kosaku Yoshino, *Cultural Nationalism in Contemporary Japan* (London: Routledge, 1992); Brian McVeigh, *Nationalisms of Japan, Managing and Mystifying Identity* (Lanham, MD: Rowman & Littlefield, 2004); Harumi Befu, "Nationalism and Nihonjinron" in Harumi Befu (ed.), *Cultural Nationalism in East Asia: Representation and Identity* (Los Angeles: University of California Press, 1967); Peter Dale, *The Myth of Japanese Uniqueness* (London: Routledge, 1986).

47 Aoki Tamotsu, *'Nihonbunkaron' no Hen'yō* [Phases of Theories of Japanese Culture in Transition] (Tokyo: Chūō Kōron Shinsha, 1990), p. 29.

48 Minami Hiroshi, *Nihonjinron no Keifu* [The Genealogy of the *Nihonjinron*] (Tokyo: Kōdansha, 1980), p. 3.

49 Yagiri Tomeo, *Seppuku Ronkō* [Debates on Seppuku] (Tokyo: Chūō Kōron, 1970), pp. 16, 18.

50 Ibid., pp. 24–25.

51 Ibid., p. 17.
52 Agari Ichirō, *Jisatsu Kōdō no Shinri to Shidō*, p. 87 and p. 85.
53 Agari Ichirō, *Seishōnen no Jisatsu* [Teenagers' Suicide] (Kyōto: Dōhōsha, 1988), p. iii.
54 Bessho Naoki, *Jisatsu no Bigaku* (Tokyo: Nichigei Shuppan, 1972), p. 69.
55 Kenshirō Ōhara, *Shinjūkō – ai to Shi no Byōri* [On *Shinjū* – the Pathology of Love and Death] (Tōkyō: Taiyō Shuppan, 1973).
56 Susumu Iizuka, "Michizure Jisatsu, Konjaku" [The Double Suicide, Past and Present], *Bulletin of Momoyama Gakuin University* 15(2) (1982), pp. 207–208.
57 Yamana Shōtarō, *Seikai Jisatsukō* [Considerations on Suicide around the World] (Tokyo: Sekkasha, 1970), pp. 101–102.
58 Fuse Toyomasa, *Suicide, Individual and Society* (Quebec: Canadian Scholars Press, 1997); Fuse Toyomasa, *Jisatsugaku Nyūmon* [Introduction to Suicidology] (Tokyo: Chūkō Shinsho, 1990).
59 Fuse Toyomasa, *Jisatsu to Bunka* [Suicide and Culture] (Tokyo: Shinchōsha: 1985), pp. 208–209.
60 Ibid., p. 210.
61 Ibid., p. 188, p. 196 and p. 196.
62 Tatai Kichinosuke and Iga Mamoru, "Characteristics of Suicides and Attitudes toward Suicide in Japan," in Norman Farberow (ed.), *Suicide in Different Cultures* (Baltimore: University Park Press, 1965); Iga Mamoru, Joe Yamamoto, Thomas Noguchi, and Koshinaga Jushiro, "Suicide in Japan," *Social Science and Medicine*, 11, 12(6a) (1978), pp. 507–516; Iga Mamoru, "Suicide and Japanese Youth," *Suicide and Life-Threatening Behavior*, 11(1), Spring 1981, pp. 17–30; Iga Mamoru, *The Thorn in the Chrysanthemum: Suicide and Economic Success in Modern Japan* (Los Angeles: University of California Press, 1986).
63 Nakahara Hiromichi, *Seppuku* [Suicide by Disembowelment] (Tokyo: Kubo Shoten, 1971), pp. 224–232.
64 Maurice Pinguet, *Voluntary Death in Japan* (Cambridge: Polity Press 1993).
65 Stuart D. B. Picken, Taoko Hori, *Nihonjin no Jisatsu: Seio to no Hikaku* [Japanese Suicide: A Comparison with the West] (Tokyo: Saimaru Shuppankai, 1979), p. 145.
66 Ōhara Kenshirō, *Nihon no Jisatsu* (Tokyo: Seishin Shobō, 1965), p. 13; Yamana Shōtarō, *Seikai jisatsukō*, p. 193; Hasegawa Izumi, "Sakka no Jisatsu – Kawabata Yasunari no Baai" [Suicide of a Writer – the Case of Kawabata Yasunari], in Tatai Kichinosuke and Katō Masaaki (eds.), *Nihon no Jisatsu wo Kangaeru*, pp. 15–28, p. 15.
67 Yamana Shōtarō, *Seikai Jisatsukō*, p. 193.
68 Kōsaku Masaaki, Usui Jishō, *Nihonjin no Jisatsu*, pp. 358–359.
69 Ōhara Kenshirō, *Nihon no Jisatsu*, pp. 16–17.
70 Yamana Shōtarō, *Seikai Jisatsu*, p. 361.
71 Komatsu Shinroku, *Bi wo Mishi Hito wa: Jisatsu Sakka no Keifu* [Connoisseurs of Beauty: The Genealogy of Novelists' Suicide] (Tōkyō: Kōdansha, 1981), p. 18, pp. 7–8.
72 The Rorschach test is a diagnostic psychological test in which subjects' perceptions of inkblots are recorded and then analyzed using psychological interpretation, complex algorithms, or both. Some psychologists use this test to examine a person's personality characteristics and emotional functioning. It has been employed to detect underlying thought disorders. Despite the fact that in the late 1950s some skeptics considered the Rorschach inkblot test to be pseudoscience, in the 1960s the Rorschach was the most widely used projective test and the Japanese Rorschach Society was by far the largest in the world. A moratorium on its use was called for in 1999.
73 The dying process had shifted from being relatively simple to being very complex, and a number of ethical, psychological, and sociological studies emerged, with the aim of supporting the desire to achieve death with dignity. In 1967, works by the

German jurist Karl Binding and the psychiatrist Alfred Hoche supporting euthanasia were introduced in Japan. Their writings were mainly translated and commented on by Kinsaku Saitō, an expert in German criminal law. See Karl Binding and Kinsaku Saitō, *Bindingu Keihōron* [Binding's Essay on Criminal Law] (Tōkyō: Waseda Daigaku Hōgakkai, 1936). Binding and Hoche's works were already well known by Japanese criminal lawyers, but many politicians, physicians, and intellectuals were able to become familiar with the texts when Japanese translations were issued. See Miyano Akira, *Anrakushi – Ningen ni Shinu Kenri ha Aru ka* [Euthanasia – Do People Have the Right to Die?] (Tokyo: Nikkei Shinsho, 1976), pp. 54–55; Ōtani Izumi, *Sonkeishi Gensetsu no Tanjō* [The Genealogy of the Term 'Death with Dignity'] (Tokyo: Ritsumeikan Daigaku Daigakuin Sentan Sōgōgakujuku Kenkyū Hakuronbun, 2006), p. 41. Intellectuals who heavily drew upon Binding and Hoche's works were convinced that suicide is the way to end one's own life with honor; euthanasia and a dignified death were thus desirable. Intellectuals inherently advocated that suicide had to be conceived of as voluntary and therefore as a free choice in political terms – that is, as a form of resistance, refutation, or protest. See also Iino Shirō, *Nihonjin no Shinikata* [How Do Japanese Die] (Tokyo: Kanki Book, 1973), pp. 222–224.

74 Kataguchi Yasufumi, *Sakka no shindan: Rōrushahha Tesuto Kara Sōsaku Shinri no Himitsu wo Saguru* [Analysis of Novelists: Searching the Secrets of Literary Creativity through the Rorschach Test] (Tokyo: Shibundō, 1971), pp. 240–243.

75 Karaki Junzō, *Jisatsu ni Tsuite* [On Suicide] (Tokyo: Kakukawa Shoten, reprinted in 1979), p. 90. Karaki's book is a collection of thoughts and considerations on Japanese novelists and their suicides collected over two decades, between 1951 and 1979.

76 Ibid., p. 8.

77 Bessho Naoki, *Jisatsu no Bigaku*, p. 33.

78 Shibusawa Tatsuhiko, "Gyakusetsutekina 'Jisatsu no Susume'" [Paradoxical Advice on Suicide], *Chūō Kōron*, 1046, May 1974, pp. 196–197, p. 196.

79 Komatsu Shinroku, *Bi wo Mishi Hito wa: Jisatsu Sakka no Keifu*, p. 18.

80 Shiina Rinzō, *Sei to Shi to ni Tsuite* [On Life and Death] (Tokyo: Kakukawa Shoten, reprinted in 1979), p. 239.

81 Hirano Ken, "Sakka no Jisatsu" [Novelists' Suicide], *Shincho*, 69(7), June 1972, pp. 167–171, p. 171.

82 Karaki Junzō, *Jisatsu ni Tsuite*, p. 85.

83 Bessho Naoki, *Jisatsu no Bigaku*, p. 27; Isoda Kōichi, "Mokokusekisha no Shiten" [Viewpoints of a Stateless Person], *Bungakkai*, May 1967, pp. 19–89.

84 Bessho Naoki, *Jisatsu no Bigaku*, p. 179; Nakano Yoshie, *Ningen no Shinikata* [Human Ways of Dying] (Tokyo: Shinchō Sensho, 1969).

85 Komatsu Shinroku, *Bi wo Mishi Hito wa: Jisatsu Sakka no Keifu*, p. 18 and pp. 7–8; Hasegawa Izumi, "Sakka no Jisatsu – Kawabata Yasunari no Baai" [Suicide of a Writer – the Case of Kawabata Yasunari], in Tatai Kichinosuke and Katō Masaaki (eds.), *Nihon no Jisatsu wo Kangaeru* [Thinking of Suicide in Japan] (Tokyo: Igaku Shoin, 1974), pp. 15–28.

86 Yasumoto Biten, *Sōsaku no Himitsu: Sakka no Seikaku to Shinri* [The Secret of Creativity: Authors' Personality and Psychology] (Tokyo: Seishin Shobō, 1963), p. 250.

87 Hasegawa Izumi, "Sakka no Jisatsu – Kawabata Yasunari no Baai" [Suicide of a Writer – the Case of Kawabata Yasunari], in Tatai Kichinosuke and Katō Masaaki (eds.), *Nihon no Jisatsu wo Kangaeru* [Thinking of Suicide in Japan] (Tokyo: Igaku Shoin, 1974), pp. 15–28, p. 15, p. 27; Yasumoto Biten, *Sōsaku no Himitsu: Sakka no Seikaku to Shinri*, p. 243 and pp. 185–186.

88 Yasumoto Biten extensively analyzed the psychological, artistic, historical, and autobiographical aspects of the suicides of Akutagawa Ryōnosuke, Kawakami Bizan, Arishima Takeo, Kitamura Tōkoku, Makino Shin'ichi, and Tanaka Hidemitsu. Yasumoto Biten, *Sōsaku no Himitsu: Sakka no Seikaku to Shinri*, p. 252.

89 The economic recession that followed the 1973 oil crisis exposed the working class, mainly composed of men, to unemployment, causing an inexorable increase in the suicide rate of middle-aged males. After 1974, the suicide rate decreased again and maintained a steady plateau until the sudden spike of 1986, when a total of 21.2 suicides per 100,000 inhabitants was recorded, consisting of 27.8 for males and 14.9 for females.

90 Araki Shun'ichi and Murata Katsuyuki, "Suicide in Japan: Socioeconomic Effects on its Secular and Seasonal Trends," *Suicide and Life-Threatening Behavior*, 17, Spring 1987, pp. 64–71; Taisaku Honbu, *Seishōnen no Jisatsu ni Kansuru Kenkyū Chōsa* [Survey on Suicide in Children and Teens] (Tokyo: Sōrifu Seishōnen Taisaku Honbu, 1979), pp. 4–5.

91 For example, unofficial sources underlined that this period witnessed an increase of suicides committed in 'famous' locations, such as Takashimadaira, and an increase in *oyako-shinjū*, which from the late 1950s until the present steadily maintained a higher rate than the *jōshi* patterns. From 1958, *oyako-shinjū*, or mother-child suicides, represented approximately 0.29 cases per 100,000 inhabitants, an average of 1.6 percent. Takahashi Yoshitomo, *Gunpatsu Jisatsu* [Suicide Clusters] (Tokyo: Chūkō Shinsho, 1998), pp. 118–120.

92 From the late 1970s on, terms for new *shinjū* categories were coined by the Japanese media, such as *dōjō-shinjū* and *yukizuri-shinjū*. These two neologisms designated suicides committed by two or more people triggered by an unconventional motive [*dōjō*, sympathy, instead of love or altruistic motivations] and/or by an unconventional type of relationship (that is, the absence of kinship or hierarchical or love relationship between the victims). In the same period, the neologism *fukyō shinjū* [*shinjū* for poor economic conditions] appeared in Japanese newspapers. It designated the suicide of working couples, families who lived in poor economic conditions, or colleagues suffering from similar work anxieties. In 1983, the neologism *shinjū-doraibu* [*shinjū*-drive] replaced the conventional metaphor *shi no tabi he* [trip toward death] that had been used to designate the nomadic journey of mothers and children toward a specific location at which to commit a mother-child suicide. Furthermore, in the early 1980s, another neologism for *shinjū* committed in a car appeared in Japanese newspapers: *gekitotsu shinjū* [*shinjū* by car crash] labeled those *shinjū* cases accomplished by two or more people in a car crash. *Shinjū* was thus simultaneously used both as antonomy and hyponomy: antonomy in the sense that it excluded all suicides committed by a single individual; hyponomy in the sense that all newly coined *shinjū* neologisms were included under the general label of *shinjū*. In other words, neologisms related to *shinjū* defined different 'members' belonging to the 'class' of *shinjū*. Therefore, in this explicit editorial effort to generate new terms, there was an implicit tendency to create an appearance of complexity. (Can we assess that a certain case was a *gekitotsu shinjū* or a *shinjū-doraibu*? A *dōjō-shinjū* or a *yukizuri-shinjū*?). But this apparent complexity was also simplified by the linguistic organization of neologisms into hyponomy.

93 *Yomiuri Shinbun*, "Oshiego no Onna seito to Shinjū, Tsuma Aru Kōkōkyōshi" [Married High School Teacher Kills Himself with His Student], January 11, 1981.

94 *Yomiuri Shinbun*, "Haru wo Matazu ni . . . " [Not Being Able to Wait for the Spring . . .], February 19, 1972; *Asahi Shinbun*, "Tsumetai Yuki no Naka de no Shinjū" [Double Suicides in a Cold Snowfield], February 26, 1961.

95 *Asahi Shinbun*, "Tsumetai Yuki no Naka de no Shinjū" [Double Suicides in a Cold Snowfield], February 26, 1961.

96 *Asahi Shinbun*, "Kōkōsei Danjo ga Hakone Yama de Shinjū" [A Student Couple Commits Double Suicide on the Hakone Mountain], August 27, 1970; *Asahi Shinbun*, "Yuki no Kanazawa de Shinjū" [Double Suicide in Snow-covered Kanazawa], February 26, 1961.

97 Satō Kiyohiko, *Nippon Shinjūkō* [Thoughts on *Shinjū* in Japan] (Tokyo: Bunshū Bunkō, 2001), pp. 36–37.

98 From 1975 on, an enormous number of sociological reports on youth suicide as an expression of the anomic Japanese society were published in the Asahi Newspaper, and beginning in 1976, a specific column dedicated to youth suicide, called "Sociology of Suicide" [*Jisatsu no Shakaigaku*], was published on a monthly basis. Articles were generally written by private reporters and followed a sociological perspective. Usually the column began with a reflection on a specific youth suicide case and followed with a wide-ranging analysis of the educational system and value system, to conclude with some interviews with famous TV stars, novelists, and movie directors. *Asahi Shinbun*, "Yarikirenai 'Shinjū Shakai'" [A *Shinjū* Society that Never Stops], January 27, 1976.

99 *Yomiuri Shinbun*, "Otōsan no Mae de Boshishinjū" [Shinjū of Mother and Children in Front of the Father], January 12, 1982; *Asahi Shinbun*, "Musuko no Gakkō no Mae de Okaasan no Jisatsu" [Mother Commits Suicide in Front of Her Child's School], May 5, 1982; *Asahi Shinbun*, "Supaa de no Jisatsu" [Suicide at the Supermarket], July 17, 1982; *Yomiuri Shinbun*, "Hadaka de Depaato no Tsūrō de Jisatsu" [He Commits Suicide Naked in the Corridor of the Department Store], September 3, 1982; *Yomiuri Shinbun,* "Kōkousei Kōkyō no Mae de Yakimi" [High School Student Burns Himself in Front of the Imperial Palace], November 4, 1979.

100 *Yomiuri Shinbun*, "Nakayoshi Shingaku no Nayami, Chū 3 Shōjō ga Shinjū" [*Shinjū* of 3 Girl Classmates from a Lower Secondary School Who Shared Similar Problems], September 9, 1981.

101 Already in 1973, journalists had reported two suicide cases in Takashimadaira. In 1975, 1976, and 1977, a few more cases were recorded, but the designation as a 'famous place' came in 1978 with an explosion of suicide cases. From 1979 on, every report about people killing themselves in Takashimadaira began with a title noting the increasing total number of victims. The magic power of Takashimadaira not only derived from its emblematic image of an urban jungle of cement buildings, but also epitomized the alienation of people living in anonymous high-rise buildings. From the top floor of Takashimadaira, victims could thus defy, in a broad sense, their fear of vertigo.

102 Shirō Kunimitsu, *Jōshi no rekishi* [The History of Lovers' Suicide] (Tokyo: Gonzai Eibunshō, 1995), p. 29.

103 When suicides were committed by leaping under a train or performed inside a station, titles almost always reported how many people it inconvenienced or delayed in commuting to their workplaces. For example, "60,000 People in Chaos during the Morning Commute. Suicide on the Chūo Line" was a sensational headline that emphasized the problematic consequences that a single suicide represented for an entire society. *Asahi Shinbun*, "60.000nin no Asa no Tsūkin no Konran. Chūosen no Jisatsu," December 12, 1975.

104 *Asahi Shinbun*, "Mata Tobiori Jisatsu – Seibu Depaato no Yane Kara" [One More Leaping Suicide – From the Roof of the Seibu Department Store], April 12, 1963.

105 Nicholas Abercrombie and Brian Longhurst, *Audiences* (London: Sage Publications, 2003), pp. 46–47.

106 Media specialist Yoshimura Toshiko examined suicide articles collected from the Tokyo edition of *Asahi Shinbun* between 1940 and 1973, concluding that a clear pattern emerged in their attitude toward women's suicide: women were depicted as unable to keep pace with the times and with their work. Yoshimura Toshiko, "Nyuusu ni Deru Jisatsu – Asahi Shinbun (Tokyo) Shukusatsuban Yori" [Suicide in the News – From Reduced-size Issues of the Tokyo Edition of Asahi Shinbun], in Tatai Kichinosuke and Katō Masaaki (eds.), *Nihon no Jisatsu wo Kangaeru*, pp. 62–70.

107 Iino Shirō, *Nihonjin no Shinikata*, pp. 46–66.

108 Koshinaga Jushirō, Takahashi Shigehiro, "Jōshi to Oyaku Shinjū" [Lovers Suicide and Parent-Child Suicide], in Tatai Kichinosuke and Katō Masaaki (eds.), *Nihon no jisatsu wo kangaeru*, pp. 29–61, p. 60.
109 *Asahi Shinbun*, "Kodomo no me ga Okashii – Boshi-Shinjū" [My Son Has Eye Problems – Mother-Child Suicide], November 11, 1976.
110 *Asahi Shinbun*, "Atsusa ni Kurutte, Boshi-Shinjū" [Becomes Crazy from the Heat and Kills Her Son], August 14, 1963.
111 *Asahi Shinbun*, "Mahiji wo Gashi Sasu – Hahaoya 'Shinjū no Tabi' No Tōchū" [Mother Starves Her Baby to Death and Then Attempts to Join Him in a Double Suicide], September 14, 1971.
112 *Yomiuri Shinbun*, "Hahaoya ga Byōjaku de Jisatsu" [Weak and Ill Mother's Suicide], March 23, 1969; *Yomiuri Shinbun*, "Noirōze de Hahaoya to Kodomo Futari no Shinjū" [Suffering from a Nervous Breakdown, Mother Kills Herself and Her Two Children], May 18, 1967.
113 *Yomiuri Shinbun*, "Shigoto Shisugi de 43sai no Otoko no Jisatsu" [Suicide of a 43 Years Old Man after Too Much Work], November 23, 1971.
114 The concept, invented in 1978, actually originated in the context of the student movement at the end of the 1960s as a way to portray students' social rebellion, disaffection, and childishness. The concept became widespread and influential with Okonogi Keigo beginning in 1978. See also Takeda Makoto, *Hito ha Naze Jisatsu Suru no Ka* [Why do People Kill Themselves?] (Tokyo: Genshū Shuppansha, 2005), p. 88.
115 Even when it came to narcissism, Okonogi highlighted the difference between the love for oneself that Japanese demonstrate by holding their society in high regard, and Westerners' narcissism, which was characterized by a lack of altruism and respect for the community. Okonogi Keigo, *Jikoai Ningen: Gendai Narushishizumu Ron* [Human Self-Love – Modern Theory of Narcissism] (Tokyo: Kōdansha, 1984), pp. 228–229.
116 Ibid., p. 123.
117 Doi Takeo, *Amae no Kōzō* [The Anatomy of Dependence] (Tokyo: Kodansha, 1971). Okonogi Keigo proclaimed Doi's work to be the most original research in Japanese psychoanalysis of all time. Okonogi Keigo, "Psychoanalysis in Japan," in Salman Akhtar (ed.), *Freud and the Far East: Psychoanalytic Perspectives on the People and Culture of China, Japan, and Korea*, pp. 9–26, p. 13.
118 A. Kitamura, M. Shimizu, K. Wada, E. Kitamura, Y. Inoue, and A. Yamamoto, "Seinenki Jisatsu no Misuirei to Gaisuirei to no Hikō" [A Comparison between Committed and Attempted Suicide among Teenagers], *Seishin Shinkeigaku Zasshi*, 82(2), February 1980, pp. 121–129.
119 Iino Shirō, *Nihonjin no Shinikata*, p. 191.
120 Ōhara Kenshirō, "Aoi Jisatsu yo Hashiru Nakare" [Stop Youth Suicide], *Ushio*, 227, April 1978, pp. 174–183, p. 176–177.
121 Inamura Hiroshi, Shimoyama Tokuji, "Seishōnen no Jisatsuron" [An Essay on Suicide Among Teens], *Chishiki*, n. 56, August 1986.
122 Inamura Hiroshi and Shimoyama Tokuji, "Seishōnen no Jisatsuron" [An Essay on Suicide Among Teens], *Chishiki*, n. 56, August 1986.
123 Yoshimura Toshiko, "Nyuusu ni Deru Jisatsu – Asahi Shinbun (Tokyo) Shukusatsuban Yori" [Suicide in the News – From Reduced-size Issues of the Tokyo Edition of Asahi Shinbun], in Tatai Kichinosuke and Katō Masaaki (eds.), *Nihon no Jisatsu wo Kangaeru*, pp. 62–70, p. 69.
124 A. Kitamura, M. Shimizu, K. Wada, E. Kitamura, Y. Inoue, and A. Yamamoto, "Seinenki Jisatsu Kito no Jūdanteki Kenkyū" [A Longitudinal Research on Youth Suicide], *Seishin Shinkeigaku Zasshi*, 83(6), June 1981, pp. 372–384.
125 *Asahi Shinbun*, "Miseinen Jisatsu: Gen'in ha Wakaranu" [Minor Suicide: Motive Unknown], January 14, 1973.
126 *Yomiuri Shinbun*, "Shiken ga Dame Datta to Danshikōsei no Jisatsu" ['The Exam Didn't Go Well' – Suicide of a High School Student], May 11, 1972.

127 *Asahi Shinbun*, "Naze Shi wo Isogu no Ka, Kimitachi Wa" [Why Are You Looking Forward to Dying?], February 9, 1972.
128 Takeda Makoto, *Hito ha Naze Jisatsu Suru no Ka*, p. 35.
129 Suicide notes like "I hate studying," "I can't go on studying," "I can't live with these marks," or "I hate the school, I hate the sports club" prove the impact of academic pressure on psychological and physical well-being, along with the anxiety of facing such important performances. Some desperate students sent letters to the Minister of Education threatening to commit suicide because of the difficulty of the exams they were required to pass. Some elementary and high school students killed themselves at the entrance of the Ministry of Health, Labour and Welfare because of the unbearable stress suffered at school. *Asahi Shinbun*, "Benkyō ga Iya" [I Hate Studying], January 11, 1964; *Asahi Shinbun*, "Benkyō ga Susumanu" [I Can't Go On Studying], January 29, 1966; *Asahi Shinbun*, "Kono Seiseki Ja . . ." [I Can't Live with These Marks], March 13, 1973; *Yomiuri Shinbun*, "Gakkō Iya, Kurabu Iya" [I Hate the School and I Hate the Sports Club], February 11, 1979; *Asahi Shinbun*, "Monbushō no Mae de Jisatsu" [Suicide in Front of the Ministry of Education], February 12, 1980.
130 *Yomiuri Shinbun*, "Juken de Kuron, Chichioya ga Jisatsu" [After a Discussion over the Admission Exams, Father Commits Suicide], November 22, 1978.
131 *Asahi Shinbun*, "Juken Kyōiku ni Jishin wo Ushinau" [I Have Lost the Faith in the Examination System], April 22, 1966.
132 In the late 1970s, modest coverage was dedicated to adolescent suicides related to *ijime* [bullying]. The label of bully-related suicide appeared for the first time in 1979 in *Asahi Shinbun* and was destined to increase extensively in the following decade. The problem of *ijime* was very often related to the cases of young students being bullied by classmates when they changed schools, as this seemed to be the moment during which the difficulties of teenage social adjustment and adaptation brutally emerged, triggering desires to kill and to die.
133 Kondō Nobuyuki, "Shōnen no Jisatsu" [Youth Suicide], *Bungei Shunju*, March 1979, 57(3), pp. 126–149, p. 144.
134 Saitō Shō, *Jisatsu Oyobi Satsujin no Tetsugaku* [The Philosophy of Suicide and Murder] (Tokyo: Yuzankaku, 1951), p. 62.
135 Takeuchi Yoshitomo, "Kodomo no Jisatsu" [Kids' Suicide], *Sekai*, No. 402, May 1979, pp. 18–26.
136 In terms of suicide by women, Japan was number 6. Sociologist Ueda Fuse explained that the relatively high rate of women's suicide was an evident sign of the "superior" degree of gender equality achieved in Japan – a very debatable position indeed. See Ueda Fuse, "Nihonjin no Jisatsu, Sono Kōshō" [Japanese Suicide – Some Reflections], in Tatai Kichinosuke and Katō Masaaki (eds.), *Nihon no Jisatsu wo Kangaeru*, pp. 71–97, p. 71 and p. 77; Nakamura Kazuo, "Tōdai 'Jisatsu Sōdanjo' Hanjōki" [Substantial Records of the Consultations at Tokyo University], *Fujin Kōron*, 8, August 1962, pp. 141–146.
137 Serizawa Kazuya, *Jidai ga Tsukuru 'Kyōki': Seishin Iryō to Shakai*, pp. 207–208.

Bibliography

Nicholas Abercrombie and Brian Longhurst, *Audiences* (London: Sage Publications, 2003).
Abe Akane, "70 Nendai Nihon ni Okeru Seishin Iryō Kaikaku Undō to Hanseishin'igaku" [The Japanese Reform Movement of Psychiatric Medicine and Anti-psychiatry Thought in the 1970s], *Core Ethics*, 6 (2010), pp. 1–11.
Salman Akhtar (ed.), *Freud and the Far East: Psychoanalytic Perspectives on the People and Culture of China, Japan, and Korea* (Lanham, MD: Jason Aronson, 2009).

Kitamura Akihide, "Seishōnen Jisatsu Kito no Nichidoku Hikō Kenkyū" [A Comparative Analysis of German and Japanese Youth Suicides], *Seishin Shinkeigaku Zasshi*, 85 (January, 1983), pp. 54–68.
Miyano Akira, *Anrakushi – Ningen ni Shinu Kenri ha aru ka* [Euthanasia – Do People Have the Right to Die?] (Tokyo: Nikkei Shinsho, 1976).
Nishiyama Akira, "Jisatsu to Seishinka Gairai" [Suicide and Psychiatric Outpatients], *Seishin Shinkeigaku Zasshi*, 81(5) (May, 1979), pp. 311–341.
Kurihara Akira, *Seiji no Shigaku – Me no Shuhō* [Poetics of History – Technique of Eyes] (Tokyo: Shinyōsha, 1983).
Harumi Befu (ed.), *Cultural Nationalism in East Asia: Representation and Identity* (Los Angeles: University of California, 1967).
Karl Binding; Kinsaku Saitō, *Bindingu Keihōron* [Binding's Essay on Criminal Law] (Tōkyō: Waseda Daigaku Hōgakkai, 1936).
Yasumoto Biten, *Sōsaku no Himitsu: Sakka no Seikaku to Shinri* [The Secret of Creativity: Authors' Personality and Psychology] (Tokyo: Seishin Shobō, 1963).
Peter Dale, *The Myth of Japanese Uniqueness* (London: Routledge, 1986).
Norman Farberow (ed.), *Suicide in Different Cultures* (Baltimore, MD: University Park Press, 1965).
H. Fujimori, M. Sakaguchi, T. Wakejima, M. Shintani, and M. Kamei, "Matsuzawa Byōin ni Okeru Kako 30nenkan (1951–1980) no Seishinbunretsubyōsha no Jisatsu Gaisuirei" [Thirty Years of Analysis (1951–1980) of Suicide Committed by Psychiatric Patients at Matsuzawa Hospital], *Seishin Shinkeigaku Zasshi*, 84 (July, 1982), pp. 483–502.
Christopher Harding, Iwata Fumiaki and Yoshinaga Shin'ichi (eds.), *Religion and Psychotherapy in Modern Japan* (New York: Routledge, 2015).
Akimoto Haruo, *Seishin'igaku to Hantai Seishin'igaku* [Psychiatry and Anti-psychiatry] (Tokyo: Kongō Shuppan, 1976).
Nakahara Hiromichi, *Seppuku* [Suicide by Disembowelment] (Tokyo: Kubo Shoten, 1971).
Inamura Hiroshi, "Burando Hakushi no Kōen wo Kiite" [Listening to Brandt's Speech], *Seishin Igaku*, 17(8) (August, 1975), pp. 871–874.
Inamura Hiroshi, "Seinenki to Jisatsu" [Youth and Suicide], *Seishin Igaku*, 19(12) (December, 1977), pp. 1323–1333.
Inamura Hiroshi, *Jisatsu no Genten: hikaku Bunkateki Kōsatsu* [The Origin of Suicide – Comparative Cultural Analysis] (Tokyo: Shinyōsha, 1979).
Minami Hiroshi, *Nihonjinron no Keifu* [The Genealogy of the Nihonjinron] (Tokyo: Kōdansha, 1980).
Inamura Hiroshi and Shimoyama Tokuji, "Seishōnen no Jisatsuron" [An Essay on Suicide among Teens], *Chishiki*, 56 (August, 1986), pp. 142–155.
Naka Hisao, "Shakaigaku ni Okeru Jisatsu no Riron" [Sociological Theories on Suicide], *Ōtani Gakuhō*, 40 (March, 1961), pp. 11–23.
Naka Hisao, "Shakaigaku ni Okeru Jisatsu Riron no Kentō" [Considerations on the Sociological Theories on Suicide], *Shakaigaku Hyōron*, 60(15) (April, 1965), pp. 30–48.
Taisaku Honbu, *Seishōnen no Jisatsu ni Kansuru Kenkyū Chōsa* [Survey on Suicide in Children and Teens] (Tokyo: Sōrifu Seishōnen Taisaku Honbu, 1979).
Agari Ichirō, *Jisatsu Kōdō no Shinri to Shidō* [Psychology and Guidance of Suicidal Tendencies] (Kyōto: Nakanishiya Shuppan, 1980).
Agari Ichirō, *Seishōnen no Jisatsu* [Teenagers' Suicide] (Kyōto: Dōhōsha, 1988).
Susumu Iizuka, "Michizure Jisatsu, Konjaku" [The Double Suicide, Past and Present], *Bulletin of Momoyama Gakuin University*, 15(2) (1982), pp. 207–208.

Ōtani Izumi, *Sonkeishi Gensetsu no Tanjō* [The Genealogy of the Term 'Death with Dignity'] (Tokyo: Ritsumeikan Daigaku Daigakuin Sentan Sōgōgakujuku Kenkyū Hakuronbun, 2006).
Karaki Junzō, *Jisatsu ni Tsuite* [On Suicide] (Tokyo: Kakukawa Shoten, reprinted in 1979).
Nakamura Kazuo, "Tōdai 'Jisatsu Sōdanjo' Hanjōki" [Substantial Records of the Consultations at Tokyo University], *Fujin Kōron*, 8 (August, 1962), pp. 141–146.
Serizawa Kazuya, *Jidai ga Tsukuru 'Kyōki': Seishin Iryō to Shakai* [The Era that Produces 'Fool People:' Psychiatric Treatment and Society] (Tokyo: Asahi Shinbunsha, 2007).
Okonogi Keigo, *Jikoai Ningen: Gendai Narushishizumu Ron* [Human Self-love – Modern Theory of Narcissism] (Tokyo: Kōdansha, 1984).
Hirano Ken, "Sakka no Jisatsu" [Novelists' Suicide], *Shinchō*, 69(7) (June, 1972), pp. 167–171.
Ōhara Kenshirō, *Nihon no Jisatsu* (Tokyo: Seishin Shobō, 1965).
Ōhara Kenshirō, "Jisatsu Bōshi Katsudō no Genjō" [The Contemporary Status of Suicide Prevention], *Seishin Igaku*, 11(2) (February, 1969), pp. 143–144.
Ōhara Kenshirō, *Jisatsu wo Kangaeru* (Tokyo: Keizai Ōraisha, 1971).
Ōhara Kenshirō, *Jisatsugaku – Jisatsu to Bunka* [Suicidology: Suicide and Culture] (Tokyo: Shibundō, 1974–1975).
Ōhara Kenshirō, "Aoi Jisatsu yo Hashiru Nakare" [Stop Youth Suicide], *Ushio*, 227 (April, 1978), pp. 174–183.
Ōhara Kenshirō, "Tōron" [Discussion], *Seishin Shinkeigaku Zasshi*, 82(12) (December, 1980), pp. 802–819.
Ōhara Kenshirō, *Ikiru Koto to Shinu Koto – Hito ha Naze Jisatsu Suru no ka* [To Live and to Die – Why People Kill Themselves] (Tokyo: Asahi Shinbunsha, 1996).
Tatai Kichinosuke and Katō Masaaki (eds.), *Nihon no Jisatsu wo Kangaeru* [Thinking of Suicide in Japan] (Tokyo: Igaku Shoin, 1974).
Moriyama Kimio, *Gendai Seishin Igaku Kaitai no Ronri* [The Theory of Dismantling Modern Psychiatry] (Tokyo: Iwazaki Gakushutsu Shuppansha, 1975).
A. Kitamura, M. Shimizu, K. Wada, E. Kitamura, Y. Inoue, and A. Yamamoto, "Seinenki jisatsu no misuirei to gaisuirei to no hikō" [A Comparison between Committed and Attempted Suicide among Teenagers], *Seishin Shinkeigaku Zasshi*, February 1980, No. 82(2), pp. 121–129.
A. Kitamura, M. Shimizu, K. Wada, E. Kitamura, Y. Inoue, and A. Yamamoto, "Seinenki Jisatsu Kito no Jūdanteki Kenkyū" [A Longitudinal Research on Youth Suicide], *Seishin Shinkeigaku Zasshi*, 83(6) (June, 1981), pp. 372–384.
Satō Kiyohiko, *Nippon Shinjūkō* [Thoughts on *Shinjū* in Japan] (Tokyo: Bunshū Bunkō, 2001).
Isoda Kōichi, "Mokokusekisha no Shiten" [Viewpoints of a Stateless Person], *Bungakkai*, 20(5) (May, 1966), pp. 175–184.
Kamijima Kunitoshi, "Seishin Bunretsu Byōsha no Jisatsu ni Tsuite – Gaisui 96 Rei no Bunreki Kara" [A Study of 96 Successful Suicides in Schizophrenic Patients], *Seishin Igaku*, 23(9) (September, 1981), pp. 893–902.
David Lester (ed.), *Current Concepts of Suicide* (Philadelphia: The Charles Press Publishers, 1990).
Brian McVeigh, *Nationalisms of Japan, Managing and Mystifying Identity* (Lanham, MD: Rowman & Littlefield Publishers, 2004).
Takeda Makoto, *Hito ha Naze Jisatsu Suru no ka* [Why Do People Kill Themselves?] (Tokyo: Genshū Shuppansha, 2005).

Iga Mamoru, "Suicide and Japanese Youth," *Suicide and Life-Threatening Behavior*, 11(1) (Spring, 1981), pp. 17–30.
Iga Mamoru, *The Thorn in the Chrysanthemum: Suicide and Economic Success in Modern Japan* (Los Angeles: University of California Press, 1986).
Iga Mamoru, Joe Yamamoto, Thomas Noguchi, and Koshinaga Jushiro, "Suicide in Japan," *Social Science and Medicine*, 11, 12(6a) (1978), pp. 507–516.
Kōsaku Masaaki and Usui Jishō, *Nihonjin no Jisatsu* [Suicide of Japanese] (Tokyo: Sōbunsha, 1965).
Hirayama Masami, "Bunretsubyō to Jisatsu" [Schizophrenia and Suicide], *Seishin Shinkeigaku Zasshi*, 82(12) (December, 1980), pp. 769–786.
Nakazawa Masao and Utsuno Yuki (eds.), *Seishin Eisei to Hoken Katsudō* [Mental Hygiene and Social Work] (Tokyo: Igaku Shoin, 1985).
Bessho Naoki, *Jisatsu no bigaku* (Tokyo: Nichigei Shuppan, 1972).
Kondō Nobuyuki, "Shōnen no Jisatsu" [Youth Suicide], *Bungei Shunju*, 57(3) (March, 1979), pp. 126–149.
Kenshirō Ōhara, *Shinjūkō – ai to shi no Byōri* [On Shinjū – The Pathology of Love and Death] (Tokyo: Taiyō Shuppan, 1973).
David P. Phillips, "The Influence of Suggestion on Suicide: Substantive and Theoretical Implications of the Werther effect," *American Sociological Review*, 39 (1974), pp. 340–354.
Maurice Pinguet, *Voluntary Death in Japan* (London: Polity Press, 1993).
Katō Shigeru, *Jisatsu no Genshōgaku: Sei no Kiretsu* [The Phenomenology of Suicide – a Crack in One's Life] (Tokyo: Kōbundō Shuppansha, 1980).
Komatsu Shinroku, *Bi wo Mishi Hito wa: Jisatsu Sakka no Keifu* [Connoisseurs of Beauty: The Genealogy of Novelists' Suicide] (Tokyo: Kōdansha, 1981).
Iino Shirō, *Nihonjin no Shinikata* [How Do Japanese Die] (Tokyo: Kanki Book, 1973).
Edwin S. Shneidman, *Suicidology: Contemporary Developments* (New York: Grune & Stratton, 1976).
Edwin S. Shneidman, *Definition of Suicide* (Northvale, NJ: Aronson, 1994).
Saitō Shō, *Jisatsu Oyobi Satsujin no Tetsugaku* [The Philosophy of Suicide and Murder] (Tokyo: Yuzankaku, 1951).
Yamana Shōtarō, *Seikai Jisatsukō* [Considerations on Suicide around the World] (Tokyo: Sekkasha, 1970).
Araki Shun'ichi and Murata Katsuyuki, "Suicide in Japan: Socioeconomic Effects on Its Secular and Seasonal Trends," *Suicide and Life-Threatening Behavior*, 17 (Spring, 1987), pp. 64–71.
Steven Stack, "Suicide: A Comparative Analysis," *Social Forces*, 57(2) (Special Issue, 1978), pp. 644–653.
Kikawa Takehiko, Yano Toru, "Seishin Byōsha no Jisatsu he no Ryokudōteki Sesshin" [A Dynamic Approach to Suicide Patients], *Seishin Igaku*, 10(11) (November, 1968), pp. 876–882.
Doi Takeo, *Amae no Kōzō* [The Anatomy of Dependence] (Tokyo: Kodansha, 1971).
Aoki Tamotsu, *'Nihonbunkaron' no Hen'yō* [Phases of Theories of Japanese Culture in Transition] (Tokyo: Chūō Kōron Shinsha, 1990).
Shibusawa Tatsuhiko, "Gyakusetsutekina 'Jisatsu no Susume'" [Paradoxical Advice on Suicide], *Chūō Kōron*, 1046 (May, 1974), pp. 196–197.
Yagiri Tomeo, *Seppuku Ronkō* [Debates on Seppuku] (Tokyo: Chūō Kōron, 1970).
Fuse Toyomasa, *Suicide, Individual and Society* (Quebec: Canadian Scholars Press, 1997).
Geoffrey M. White and Anthony J. Marsella (eds.), *Cultural Conceptions of Mental Health and Illness* (Holland: Reidel Publishing Company, 1982).

Kataguchi Yasufumi, *Sakka no Shindan: Rōrushahha Tesuto Kara Sōsaku Shinri no Himitsu wo Saguru* [Analysis of Novelists: Searching the Secrets of Literary Creativity through the Rorschach Test] (Tokyo: Shibundō, 1971).
Okada Yasuo, *Nihon Seishinka Iryōshi* [History of Psychiatry in Japan] (Tokyo: Igaku Shoin, 2002).
Nakano Yoshie, *Ningen no Shinikata* [Human Ways of Dying] (Tokyo: Shinchō Sensho, 1969).
Inamura Yoshimasa, "Jisatsu to Kisho" [Suicide and Suicide Notes], *Gengo Seikatsu*, 190(1897) (July, 1967), pp. 50–56.
Kosaku Yoshino, *Cultural Nationalism in Contemporary Japan* (London: Routledge, 1992).
Takeuchi Yoshitomo, "Kodomo no Jisatsu" [Kids' Suicide], *Sekai*, 402 (May, 1979), pp. 18–26.
Takahashi Yoshitomo, *Gunpatsu Jisatsu* [Suicide Clusters] (Tokyo: Chūkō Shinsho, 1998).

Conclusions

> Concepts of health and illness are based on, among other things, value systems and both individual and collective experiences; they are therefore culture-bound and subject to changes according to their historical and social context. As explanations for health and illness change with the mores of the times, actual medical theory and practice change, and these in turn have an effect on the epidemiology of disease.
>
> Margaret M. Lock, *East Asian Medicine in Urban Japan* (Berkeley: University of California Press, 1980), p. 1

Although suicide is a multifactorial phenomenon that can be approached from a range of different perspectives (theological, philosophical, demographic, sociological, psychodynamic, psychological, cognitive, biological, evolutionary, constitutional, biochemical, legal, preventive, global, and political), the media discourse and academic scholarship that have narrated Japanese suicide since the early 1900s both inside and outside of the country has focused on its cultural aspects. The origins of Japan's reputation as a 'Suicide Nation' can be traced to the early 1900s, when a narrative on voluntary death that evoked the past sought to protect the nation from the modernity that was encroaching upon it. This same reputation was produced again by the cultural narrative of the 1930s and the 1970s. Although the medical community was actively involved in medicalizing suicide throughout the twentieth century, a persistent cultural narrative constructed a 'conventional story on suicide' within Japan, a story that seemed to overlook the neurobiological discourse. This story obstinately asserted that Japan had the highest suicide rate in the world, a pronounced disposition to commit voluntary death for altruistic reasons, and distinctive suicide patterns. More importantly, the conventional story ordained the Japanese themselves as the sole interpreters with the competence to decipher the suicide phenomenon – which was assumed to be 'quintessentially cultural.' Rather than overtly contesting the emergent medicalization of suicide, the cultural discourse simply disregarded suicide's biological foundations, instead linking the phenomenon to a melancholic longing for a return to pre-Westernized Japan. This narrative recounted old suicide cases as archetypal examples of romantic and noble acts and propagated a sense of nostalgia for an uncontaminated past.

By interrogating the persistent belief that some forms of suicide are unique to Japan and express positive values of the nation, and by exploring changes in the evolving conceptualization of voluntary death, I have attempted to unveil the way in which the revival of narratives of premodern suicide patterns served to defend autochthonous values from the invasion of Western knowledge and to shape the identity of the nation. My argument is that Japanese suicide as a peculiar feature of the Japanese people is a modern creation, and that the glorification of the values of honor and self-sacrifice in the discourse on suicide in the twentieth century were actually a modern integration of tradition rather than its direct and straightforward expression. I hope to rescue historical studies of suicide from the simple model of the continuity of tradition typically demonstrated in *nihonjinron* studies, and explain that what I call 'the conventional story on suicide in Japan' is in fact a glorification of Japanese 'otherness' – that is, of a special Japanese character defined in contrast to the rest of the world. This story was built on three premises: firstly, nationalism exerted a coercive and mobilizing influence on the medical, academic, and media communities; secondly, and consequently, suicide was viewed as a monolithic and static ethnocentric concept according to the dictates of the nationalistic discourse; and thirdly and finally, suicide was made the stronghold that resolved the implicit tension between two meta-narratives, the traditional and the modern, by reasserting the primacy of the premodern ethos. If, as argued by Marx and Peuchet, "the classification of the different causes of suicide would be the classification of the failures of our society itself," then the 'conventional story on suicide in Japan' served to rationalize, exalt, and legitimate the 'level of sophistication,' 'nobility,' and 'superiority' of a unique society.[1]

Thus I have aimed to shed light on the invention of the tradition of suicide in modern Japan and to present a series of subtle analyses showing how this invention came to be and how people lived or died within its framework. In debunking the ethnocentric conception of voluntary death, I maintain both that framing suicide in this way is a stagnant way of thinking and, more importantly, that there is no scientific support for this view. My argument, however, is that suicide has not been molded solely by the nationalistic discourse but rather forged by the reciprocal contamination among political, environmental, intellectual, and cultural conditions. Whereas the story of suicide as an individual pathology and the story of suicide as a unique feature of the Japanese have followed two separate paths over decades of scholarship, in fact the genealogy of the notion of suicide in Japan can be traced to the alternation between and mutual contamination of these two narratives. The conceptualization of suicide, its diagnosis, its treatment, and its political meaning have been built on multiple factors and influenced by discourses on diverse issues such as nationalism, gender, and tradition. Although biological science defined various symptoms that might plausibly be linked to suicide as a disease, social influences largely determined which symptom clusters would be interpreted as signs of disease. In the critical tension between the highly politicized cultural discourse and the biological assessment of suicide, the frameworks of culture and biology each dominated at particular times. In other words, diverse narratives converged and separated, an iterability that shaped and reshaped their internal logics, progressively generating the notion of suicide in Japan throughout the twentieth century. My main argument is thus that the conceptualization of suicide was never free of cultural constraints: suicide is not only an isolated biological event, but a social and cultural construct that mirrors medicine's intellectual and institutional history. As Rosenberg and Golden claim, "disease does not exist until we have agreed that it does, by perceiving, naming, and responding to it."[2] Exploring the relationship between the biological and the cultural assessments of suicide is thus essential to understanding how the notion of suicide evolved throughout the twentieth century and how images of consensus and resistance arose and became rooted in different social strata.

Whereas the usual story on suicide claims that voluntary death has been an unchanging, atemporal concept, I argue that the conceptualization of suicide has been profoundly shaped by the intermittent historical presence or absence of nationalism. Some scholars have speculated that two different types of 'mobilizations' occurred in the 1930s and in the 1970s. They claim that the first was coercive and intimidating (that is, medical professionals were forced to adhere to national values) and the second entailed a voluntary embrace of the surging cultural nationalism. The social psychologist Minami Hiroshi, one of the foremost theorists of the *nihonjinron* debate, contends that by the late 1970s a nationwide cultural mobilization was evident – what he called a precondition of *nihonjinron*.[3] I take a different position in this regard, however, and argue that the medical community maintained a certain degree of agency even during the peak of national mobilization. When we explore how the psychiatric theoretical apparatus was revolutionized, reconstituted, and 'customized' by medical professionals in the 1930s and in the 1970s, it becomes clear that an ethnocentric conceptualization of suicide was not a coerced and reluctantly accepted outcome, but instead was eagerly welcomed. With the rise of the totalitarian regime in the 1930s and of cultural nationalism in the 1970s, the medical community was certainly solicited to serve the government ideology and the imperative of national sovereignty, and asked to reinforce cultural generalizations that claimed suicide as a typical and traditional index of a static, homogenized society and a feature of 'Japaneseness.' In this context, psychiatrists agreed to relax their biological and medical views: the biological conceptualization of suicide proved to be malleable enough that it could forsake a monolithic and consistent scientific rationalization of the suicide phenomenon. Instead it gradually welcomed the vocabulary of the nationalistic narrative, tending to reconceptualize suicide less as a disease and more as a historical act, to the detriment of psychiatrists' theoretical coherence and standardization of practices. By accepting two different explanations for suicide, one medical (that is, the notion of suicide as an individual pathology that could be biologically explained) and one sociocultural (that is, suicide as a collective, culturally, and socially negotiated construction), these psychiatrists allowed the romanticization of suicide to quietly coexist alongside its pathologization. In fact, the medical community had its own strong motivations not to deconstruct the 'conventional story on suicide in Japan' by challenging its lack of a scientific basis: the cultural conceptualization of suicide demanded by the nationalistic discourse served the medical community's purposes by making suicide and its treatment 'ordinary.' The softening of psychiatrists' scientific apparatus under the influence of the culturally evocative discourse, with its familiarizing and normalizing vocabulary on voluntary death, ultimately amplified their capacity to speak to a larger audience. This in turn enabled the Japanese to become familiar once again with their own 'illness': for many, a romantic portrayal of suicide was surely more compelling than its biological standardization. The incoherent yet firm approach taken by psychiatrists guaranteed that they would maintain their central position in the wards: they continued to diagnose and treat suicide as the disease of a culture, but they also transformed the disease into a potential threat to the culture's very survival. A tension thus lay in the contradictions embodied in the concepts of national identity and culture: Japanese cultural identity was construed both as that which 'cures' and as that which must be cured, as a pathogenic agent and a curative panacea. The integration of the enthusiastic discourses on national pride and romanticized Japanese exceptionalism revealed the pressures felt by the medical community to frame suicide within a logic that made it acceptable, both socially and morally. Doing so meant, to a considerable extent, diluting blame. This rationale may explain the degree to which the cultural discourse on suicide permeated medical interpretations. The dialectic between the medical and the cultural discourse generated a scientifically built and rhetorically attractive conversation that was able to promote suicide's popularization through a language evocative of the past; it concealed the complexity and diversity of the suicidal by creating a static, ahistorical, standardized image of the Japanese. Pushing it a bit further, the medical and the popular discourses on suicide were thus mechanisms of homogenization and standardization that incorporated victims into social subsets by writing their national history, a history imagined in the contest for a 'peculiar and unique' national identity.

The leitmotif shared by both narratives – the medical pathologization of suicide on one hand and the nationalistic discourse that enhanced the historicity of suicide on the other – was the effort to silence the political nature of voluntary death and the authoritative role of the individual in choosing it. In the 1930s and in the 1970s, both narratives led to a lessening of the authority and independence of the individual's self-sovereignty, reducing the act to a symptom of brain abnormalities or rendering it as a conveyance of cultural traditions tied to historical continuity. In other words, suicides were led to kill themselves by forces – whether social, cultural, psychological, or biological – over which they as victims had no control. The suicide was seen to have no agency. Even in the discourse that treated the suicides of novelists as exceptional, culture tended to be evoked in a more determining role than the individual's own will. I thus argue that suicide was de-politicized, with Japanese patients seen as 'victims' of disease and/or 'victims' of culture. While the act of suicide was socialized and reduced to a collective phenomenon, at the same time psychiatrists discriminated against, constrained, or excluded certain individuals determined to be biologically abnormal or defective. This too diminished an individual's responsibility for his or her actions. If the beauty and the nobility of suicide were idealized, this idealization was also put firmly in its place. Those who lived up to ideals of independence were perceived as a menace to society and the nation, threatening the established order they were intended to uphold. On the other hand, suicides committed in the wake of nationalism or of cultural fanaticism were contesting neither medicalization (that is, the way in which a non-medical problem becomes defined and treated as medical), nor the conceptualization of illness (in other words, the way in which a set of symptoms came to be defined as a legitimate illness by the biomedical community), nor the experience of illness (how patients managed their lives, how their illness was viewed by others). I push this argument even further, claiming that the individual disruptive voice emerging from suicide acts was silenced, and individual subjectivity was reduced to the acceptance of cultural conventions. This development eventually annihilated the monological function of suicide as a political statement and progressively re-enhanced the dialogical function of suicide as a cultural artifact or as a response to communally shared conditions. This tendency nostalgically recalled the fact that many proclaimed 'traditional suicides' in Japan fulfilled a dialogical function such as expressing gratitude, bidding farewell, or redeeming a serious offense that had caused shame. The private sphere was pushed further and further into the public one, until the performer's action was perceived as a public, rather than a private, one. I claim that this transformation of the monological private character of death into a dialogical public event acted to turn a potential disturbance into a functional expression of historical continuity. The individual's personal death took on a 'public function' as the society found ways to socialize that death and to limit the potential meaning of suicide by framing it within a pre-made narrative. As a consequence, individual autonomy was suppressed by a sense of collective solidarity, by responsibility for dependent others, and by the duty to respect the customs and the harmony of one's community, further reinforcing the idea of the homogeneity of Japanese society.

I also want to challenge the assumption of the usual story on suicide that sees voluntary death as an unchanging traditional aspect of the Japanese. This book refuses the postulation that an opposition exists between the modern and the traditional meta-narratives: suicide as a biological event on one hand and as the expression of a traditional ethos on the other; suicide as a category of Western science versus suicide as an indigenous practice. I hope to shed light on the fallacy of such suppositions and to highlight that a more fruitful way to understand systems of social relations and practices is based on a hegemonic formation involving a mutual contamination of identity and difference. It would be a mistake to characterize the cultural narrative as merely 'traditionalistic,' implying that the community in question was mired in its own past and was unable to face present imperatives. Rather, the past was used as a resource, in a number of ways. The manner in which 'traditional suicide' was invoked was strongly indicative of the kinds of circumstances that made such a reference to the past salient. We thus encounter the paradox that although the reassertion of suicide as a traditional feature was made necessary by contemporary circumstances, it was often accomplished through precisely those idioms that particular circumstances threatened to make obsolete. The creation of 'suicide' as a traditional aspect of the Japanese was not required to rewrite history but to project a historical past into the present in order to create, or to invent, a tradition that was, and continues to be, uniquely Japanese.

Lastly, whereas the usual story on suicide acknowledges a homogenized group of suicide victims, the narrative here explores a deep rift between the conceptualization of suicide by youth and that of suicide by the working population, as well as between that of suicide committed by men and that of suicide committed by women. Whereas men's suicides, for example, were generally portrayed as caused by overwork and nervous exhaustion or by non-physical reasons such as economic hardships, women were perceived as foolish and fragile and their suicides steered by forces, mainly biological, over which only psychiatrists could have control. In such narratives, women's agency was weakened and removed. Such a biased approach was probably not only the consequence of the reassertion of traditional gender constructions, but also the paradoxical effect of the biological rearticulation of patterns and values (such as the assumption that deviations that led to voluntary death were located most typically in the central nervous system for men and in the reproductive system for women) that repositioned the phenomenon of suicide differently within the notion of normality for different subjects.

In conclusion, I hope to debunk the myth that suicide in Japan is the result of normal responses to standard social expectations, and demystify the ethnocentric idea that suicide in Japan is correlated to unique cultural factors. I unveil instead how the powerful and resilient epithet of 'Japan as a Suicide Nation' is the outcome of a superficially reconciled tension between the cultural and the medical narratives. Whereas the medical discourse sought to maintain its dominance by de-romanticizing and de-politicizing voluntary death, denuding suicide of its cultural layers, the cultural narrative sought to attach suicide to a premodern apparatus of values and beliefs, freeing it from the label of mental illness. Neither of these narratives, however, resolved the conceptualization on the lines of 'either neurobiological abnormality or cultural pride.' Both discourses were rather involved in a dialectic of alternation and/or contamination that operated around the concept of voluntary death in its social, political, cultural, and scientific aspects; ultimately this dialectic did not destabilize the cultural aestheticization of suicide, nor did it ever fully undermine its medical conceptualization. This situation was made possible by the ontological conversation that existed between the cultural and the medical discourses, which left the incongruities between the two discourses unresolved, but ultimately allowed for the idea that voluntary death could be socialized and that a latent process of de-politicization could take place. Acknowledging Japan as the 'Suicide Nation' was the last and most natural step in this dialectic.

In drawing the history of the conceptualization of modern suicide in twentieth-century Japan, questions that might be further pursued in the future have emerged. A thorough exploration of how the medical discourse was mirrored in the media in the early twentieth century, for instance, would provide a more complete picture of the evolution of such a complex debate on the phenomenon. How did fictional works contribute to discursive readings of suicide and how was their narrative reframed within the debate over suicide that occurred in early twentieth-century Japan? An overarching exploration of fictional sources that absorbed and contaminated the cultural narrative on suicide would help to identify the modus operandi that animated this dialectic, and could consequently contribute to more recent research that insists on the complexity of the prewar moment and the temporary nature of any perceived or proclaimed cultural homogeneity. In addition, an investigation of the gendered aspects of the medicalization of suicide as mental illness would help to fill the gap in the literature on the social and political construction of bodies and illnesses. It would be crucial to discover how the gendered aspects of suicide are culturally generated when gendered pathological mechanisms of the disease are unproven or unprovable. A further topic of research is related to the history of suicide from the perspective of the Japanese family. Historically, the family members of suicidal patients have been significantly involved, socially and emotionally, as their guarantors in the decision-making process regarding medical treatment and institutionalization. Despite the fact that most of the researches have focused in particular on the relationship between the institution of the asylum and mentally ill patients, understanding the role played by the guarantors of suicidal patients would shed light on the social norms that contributed to the conceptualization of voluntary death. The conceptualization of suicide is far from being a value-free enterprise, and multiple aspects still warrant serious academic attention.

Notes

1 Karl Marx, Kevin Anderson, and Eric Plaut (eds.), *Karl Marx on Suicide* (Evanston, IL: Northwestern University Press, 1999), p. 64.
2 Charles E. Rosenberg and Janet Golden, *Framing Disease: Studies in Cultural History* (New Brunswick, NJ: Rutgers University Press, 1992), p. xiii.
3 Minami Hiroshi, *Nihonjinron no Keifu* [The Genealogy of the *Nihonjinron*] (Tokyo: Kōdansha, 1980), p. 3.

Bibliography

Minami Hiroshi, *Nihonjinron no Keifu* [The Genealogy of the *Nihonjinron*] (Tokyo: Kōdansha, 1980).
Karl Marx, Kevin Anderson, and Eric Plaut (eds.), *Karl Marx on Suicide* (Evanston, IL: Northwestern University Press, 1999).
Charles E. Rosenberg and Janet Golden, *Framing Disease: Studies in Cultural History* (New Brunswick, NJ: Rutgers University Press, 1992).

Index

www.ingramcontent.com/pod-product-compliance
Ingram Content Group UK Ltd.
Pitfield, Milton Keynes, MK11 3LW, UK
UKHW022128190926
475702UK00013B/1695
* 9 7 8 1 1 3 8 3 5 1 5 0 9 *